Elements of Sociology

BOOKS BY VILHELM AUBERT

EN LOV I SØKELYSET (*with Eckhoff* and *Sveri*)
(*A Law in the Searchlight*)

OM STRAFFENS SOSIALE FUNKSJON
(*On the Social Function of Punishment*)

LIKHET OG RETT
(*Equality and Law*)

THE HIDDEN SOCIETY

RETTSSOSOSIOLOGI
(*Sociology of Law*)
To be published by the University of Oslo Press

ELEMENTS
OF SOCIOLOGY

by

VILHELM AUBERT

University of Oslo, Norway

CHARLES SCRIBNER'S SONS

NEW YORK

Library of Congress Catalog Card Number 67-15485

PREFACE

WHILE SOCIAL thought is very old, sociological thinking, in the sense of the application of a specialized scientific approach to society, is of recent development. The lack of agreement on concepts and terms, the absence of well-founded theory, and the important lacunae in empirical knowledge, make it extraordinarily difficult to produce proper texts for beginning students of sociology. There exists no single definite point of departure for an introductory textbook.

I have a pluralistic view of sociology as a science at this stage of development. There is no one road to Rome, for the scholar no more than for the beginner. An element of arbitrariness exists in any author's choice of design for an introduction to the field of sociology. The present volume is frankly one-sided. It does not pretend to stand alone as guidance to those who want to make their first acquaintance with sociology. It must be supplemented by other texts which take a different point of departure and which include different materials. I see merit in cultivating one single approach in each volume, rather than trying to mix a variety of approaches within the covers of one book.

The approach of the present book has been influenced by the difficulties I experienced when studying sociology. I began reading sociology shortly after I had completed the study of law. My greatest difficulty was to get the "feel" of the approach to the new subject. I understood the research reports and the precepts on methods and techniques, and even grasped the definitions of many of the concepts in books on theory. But it was difficult for me to form a sociological vision of society as a functioning whole. I hope that this book conveys the results of my efforts to surmount this difficulty and that it may aid the reader to form a vision of society.

A sociological vision, however, requires simplification, or even oversimplification. It can be achieved in several distinct ways: first, by construing society from an individual's point of view; second, by

making an inventory of social institutions, like the family, government, and the church, and thereby arriving at a conception of what
society is like; and third, by basing the design upon methods of
study and by illustrating the various methods with chosen pieces
of empirical research. For this book, *Elements of Sociology,* I have
chosen the first approach: I have begun with familiar experiences
of individuals, and from these everyday events I have developed a
conception of larger social structures. The sociological concepts are
here developed on the basis of simple psychological phenomena.

The introductory course in sociology, in my opinion, which
would combine the three points of view that I have mentioned
would yield optimum results and discourage one-sided learning.
Since *Elements of Sociology* is brief, it can be supplemented by
books expressing other points of view even in the short introductory
course.

ACKNOWLEDGMENTS

A TEXTBOOK IS normally influenced by numerous sources. It is impossible to acknowledge even those scholars whose works have most
strongly contributed to form my approach to sociology. But I would
like to thank specifically those who gave me direct assistance in
preparing this volume for publication. The following colleagues
gave advice or aid which was helpful in getting out the Norwegian
edition: Mrs. Anne Margrethe Kaltenborn, Dr. Yngvar Løchen, Dr.
Thomas Mathiesen, Mr. Axel Bull Njå, and Mr. Erik Rinde.

There are several people I should like to thank specifically for
their help in preparing the American edition of this book. The
publisher's College Editorial Department has aided me with great
skill and patience in the difficult task of trying to convey my views
clearly and simply to an audience of American students. Because of
circumstances under which the American edition was prepared, Mr.
Karl Tangen of the Institute of Social Research has carried a heavy
burden in the preparation of the manuscript, for which I am much
indebted to him.

CONTENTS

I

THE PERCEPTION
OF OTHERS

᭐᭐᭐᭐᭐᭐᭐᭐᭐᭐᭐᭐᭐᭐᭐᭐᭐᭐᭐᭐᭐᭐᭐

THE SIMPLEST social situation is one between two actors. We shall start out with an inspection of such relationships. Although simple, they can be viewed from many different angles, each one contributing to an understanding of the total social phenomenon. We shall first consider the passive aspect of the relationship, how one of the individuals is being perceived by the other one. The perceiving individual will be termed *Ego*, the one who is being perceived is called *Alter*. It is not, however, assumed that any asymmetry prevails between the two. But as observers we have to inspect one person at a time in order to grasp the phenomenon which lies at the very heart of sociology as a science: the interaction between human beings.

At the moment when Ego is noticing Alter, an extensive development of the faculty to perceive others has already taken place. As a phenomenon in the physical world, Alter exhibits great complexity. If Ego had arrived from Mars, it would be difficult for him to make sense out of the way in which Alter appears to him. Innumerous movements, nuances of color, shapes and noises would meet Ego in a chaotic and disturbing fashion. Ego might even have difficulties in recognizing Alter as a distinguishable entity if he met him in a bus or train. He would experience problems when trying to discriminate between Alter and animals or other moving objects which make noise. The rationale for this kind of speculation is to emphasize that Ego's perception of Alter as a human being with needs and volition, capable of sociability, receptive to influence and capable of satisfying Ego's needs is not an obvious concomitant of a natural order. The ability of Ego to perceive Altera and to understand them is the outcome of a process of learning which began at the time of the infant's initial contact with its mother.

It lies beyond the framework of this book to trace the general influence of early childhood experiences upon those attitudes which are later activated vis-à-vis Alter. It is known, however, that general traits, such as the degree of trustfulness or suspicion with which Ego tends to meet Altera, are codetermined by the experience of the child in relation to the first, and overwhelmingly significant Altera in its life—the parents. Other basic traits in the perception of Altera are, similarly, determined by early impressions, such as whether Altera tend to appear as manipulable means to achieve Ego's ends or as equals, whether they can be influenced or must be assumed to be immovable. If we were to explain systematic differences between individuals' perceptions of others, the individual life stories would be a central concern. Our task, however, is of a different order, and we must resign ourselves to a mere recognition that each Ego in a concrete situation meets Alter on the basis of a set of personal experiences which often belong to a distant past.

What concerns sociology is that Ego always encounters Alter on the basis of a background which they share and which forms a pattern in which those who belong to the same culture participate. The meaning attributed by Ego to the appearance of others is dominated by schemes for the perception of Alter in particular types of situations, which have been crystallized in a culture. These schemes for attributing meaning to sense impressions could, as a matter of fact, very nearly serve as a definition of the term "culture" as used in a sociological context. Rules exist concerning the proper way of perceiving others, some of them widely known and generally recognized, others more ambiguous or more narrowly limited to certain groups or subcultures. Some of the rules are consciously formulated and explicitly sanctioned, such as the rule that the administration of justice under certain conditions considers that a criminal offender may be sick, and that he should, therefore, be examined by psychiatrists. Other norms are tacitly accepted without being verbally formulated; for example, we are entitled to deal with Alter as if he were in a kindly mood if he smiles. If Alter smiles, and if Ego assumes that he is kindly disposed and acts accordingly, it would be improper for Alter now to take offense. Alter would have no right to be offended. But these "rights" are nowhere to be found enunciated in written form. All we can do is to observe that people, as a matter of fact, tend to act *as if* such rules existed. To describe and analyze such rules, which informally but forcefully dominate intercourse between individuals in their daily life, is an important task of sociology.

The Danish psychologist Franz From has in some detail shown that the perception of Alter consists of a rapid, intuitive synopsis of a large number of discrete sense impressions:

> Let me begin with a quite ordinary situation from everyday life: I watch a man, who has just placed a cigarette between his lips, put his hand in the pocket of his trousers to find his matches. I do not observe—and would not, without a very special attentiveness, be able to observe—that he moves his hand down along his thigh, followed by a slightly upward movement of the hand underneath the edge of the jacket, and then afterwards down into the pocket. What I see is that he puts his hand in his pocket to get hold of the matches.
>
> If we stick to such an ordinary experience of someone else's action, the meaning and the purpose of the action is given, is implicit in the material course of events. We perceive what people intend doing with the action which is being executed. When I see a young lady watch her face in the mirror, then take up her powder compact, I perceive immediately that her intention is to put powder on her face, and when she arrests her movement with the powderpuff half raised, I can see that she is deliberating whether she ought to give her nose another stroke, or whether it has had enough. Were I afterwards to consider the matter, I would perhaps regard some of the things I saw as symptoms of some mental process, but, ordinarily, I do not regard them so while I actually observe them. The sign and that which it signifies are one and do not appear separately in my actual perception of the behavior. The perceived material events, and the goals, intentions, purposes, deliberations, which I attribute to the person are implicitly given in my experience of the other's action.
>
> The goals, intentions and so on, which are implicit in the material events, do not, however, by any means appear clearly and

precisely in my experience of the other's action. I may experience these phenomena distinctly and clearly, but often they are only very diffusely present in my experience of the other. I see that a man is about to light a cigarette, and if I set my mind to it, his intention may emerge quite clearly. I see that the young lady is arranging her make-up, and if I take a further interest in her behavior, her deliberations impress themselves upon my experience of her. If I am uninterested, however, in the man and do no more than indifferently perceive his behavior, his "inner life" will often be present only in a less differentiated form; something mental is present, but it may be very vague and imprecise, the perception is not much elaborated. Only if we set our mind to perceiving his "inner life" will we further elaborate it, so that the other's intentions emerge clearly in our experience of his behavior. . . .

The fact is that we normally describe behavior by referring primarily to the mental processes which form parts of the perceived behavior not by describing the physical events. Furthermore, it turns out that it may be difficult to give a description of this course of events. Only rarely do we at all, in our experience, distinguish the separate movements which occur when we perceive the behavior of someone else. Thus, I have often seen a man put his hand in his pocket to fetch matches, but only a thorough examination made it clear to me that the movements which constitute this little action varies according to whether the man wears a single-buttoned or double-buttoned jacket, or according to whether the jacket is buttoned or open.[1]

Two aspects of From's presentation are of special concern to us. First of all that Ego's attitude, his aim when perceiving, influences decisively the perception of Alter's intentions and ends, even though Alter's behavior will be perceived as goal-directed and as meaningful. Secondly, we notice that it may be difficult for Ego to make sense out of Alter's behavior and describe it unless he is intuitively able to attribute a purpose or a goal to Alter's movements.

These observations have implications for our later analysis, one of them being the need for caution against assuming that Ego's perception of Alter is self-evident, and exclusively determined by how Alter "really is." Ego needs rapid access to a scheme for the perception of Alter, simply to forestall chaos. In order to understand Alter's behavior, to memorize it, learn from it and act ac-

4

cordingly, he needs a scheme of interpretation. Only the scientist, and maybe not even he, can allow himself to meet others without preconceived notions. Ego as actor, however, must understand and react on the spot, must apply prefabricated schemes, whether they can stand up to a scientific test or not.

This insight leads to a dual concern in what follows: Observing the various schemata and rules for how Ego ought to meet Alter, we shall, on the one hand, hypothesize that the schemata are necessary and useful, that they are functional. On the other hand, we shall not immediately assume that the usefulness derives from the objective scientific truth of the schemata. Schemes for the perception of Alter have evolved in order to take care of practical needs which arise in the everyday encounters between Ego and Alter. The schemata are not immediately given by how Alter "really" is or acts. It is always a legitimate question to ask why one schemata was chosen in preference to a different one. The answer can be expected to accrue, not from a more intensive psychological study of Alter, but from increased knowledge about the situational needs which influence Ego, and particularly from knowledge about those types of situations which recur with high frequency and regularity.

Will, cause, and chance

In the passage of From, a specific scheme for the perception of Alter was mentioned, that which organizes sense impressions around a purpose as goal-directed behavior. Perhaps this is the one scheme which most commonly occurs in everyday life. It assumes that Alter's *will* lies behind the movements and noises he makes. The changes which take place in the state of Alter are interpreted by Ego as *actions*. This is not, however, the only schemata for the perception of others.

Consider the following situation: Ego is a cab driver passing by Alter who raises his hand in the direction of the street. Ego interprets the hand movement as a sign that Alter wants something, that he has a purpose, namely, to take a cab. This interpretation is determined by the fact that a cab driver's occupation and his daily tasks encourage him to pay a very special attention to the hand movements made by people in the street. Ambiguous situations may arise, however, when a person at night, somewhat unsure on his feet, waves vaguely with his arms. In this situation Ego may perceive Alter as having no sensible goal with his hand movements. He may, rather, assume that Alter is drunk and that his waving arms are no more than an expression of high spirits. Ego makes sense out of Alter's behavior, and he thinks that he understands him. But this understanding does not derive from an attribution of will to Alter, but from the perception of an emotional condition as the *cause* of movements which Ego can directly observe.

Let us consider another situation: Ego observes Alter while Alter's mouth is contorted and opened and hollow sounds emerge from his chest. Ordinarily Ego will interpret these physical events as an instance of coughing. Alter's coughing is a symptom of or is caused by a common cold, asthma, or some other disease. Normally Ego will attribute no purpose to Alter. When attempting to make sense out of this course of events, he does so by ordering them in a causal scheme. But ordering in a causal scheme will not always follow when someone observes another person coughing. If Ego is a military doctor and Alter a soldier who has come to him in order to obtain a discharge on medical grounds, Ego may possibly apply a scheme based upon goal striving in his perception and interpretation of Alter's behavior. He may arrive at the conclusion that Alter wants something with his coughing: he coughs because he wants to be discharged from further military duty. In this case it is clear that Ego's choice of schemata cannot be understood in terms of Alter's behavior alone. The point is that the social situation, the existing role relationship between Ego and Alter, is of such a kind that an unusual interpretation of Alter's behavior may seem to be an appropriate working hypothesis. The situation is one in which people, who ordinarily resent being sick and treated as patients, now stand to gain by being classified as sick. From this interpretation follows the suspicion that the coughing may be volitional, purposeful, and not the outcome of causes over which Alter had no control.

We are approaching the classical problem of freedom of the will

6

and the validity of laws of causality in human behavior. We are not concerned, however, with the question of whether Alter as a matter of fact possesses a free will or acts under the compulsion of causes. The problem is how Ego interprets Alter's behavior in this regard. Strictly speaking, we are not even concerned with what explicit theory Ego entertains with respect to whether Alter acts according to a free will or to causal laws. Our primary interest is focused upon the schemes of perception which intuitively and spontaneously are applied to Alter's behavior in concrete everyday situations.

The schemata based upon will, purpose or intention, and those based upon causality, do not exhaust the possibilities inherent in Ego's perception of Alter's behavior. From mentions a third alternative: "In other instances meaninglessness may be the most salient feature, and the experience is related to situations where we do not understand the meaning of the other's behavior. The movements are not experienced as expressions, but as a type of behavior characterized precisely by the apparent lack of goal and sense. On the contrary: the lack of meaning is the dominant trait which bestows a particular characteristic upon the perceived behavior. In extreme cases we may be apt to describe the behavior as more or less crazy." [2]

The last paragraph suggests the attribution of some meaning even to this kind of behavior. If Ego perceives the behavior as crazy, he may perhaps believe that Alter is insane or drunk. If so, he has perceived Alter's behavior as linked to underlying traits, to causes. The behavior has acquired meaning in the sense that it has been located in a chain of cause and effect, thus furnishing Ego with guidance about his proper mode of action vis-à-vis Alter. Cases may occur, however, when Ego is neither able to find an explanation in terms of causality nor one in terms of purpose. This is a problematical situation if Ego has to deal with Alter. He does not know what to expect from Alter, and he does not know what is the appropriate response to the observed events.

However, a lack of explanation in terms of goals or causes need not leave Alter's behavior meaningless in the sense that Ego lacks any guidance for the proper reaction. In criminal law there exists a concept, "accidental act," covering such apparently meaningless situations. An accidental shot is meaningless in the sense that the hunter whose bullet hit another person had no intention of killing any human being. It is also meaningless in the sense that we may be unable to discover any causal chain underlying Alter's shot, unlike a situation when insanity is used as a causal explanation of a murder. The accidental shot has no such explanation; it has no meaningful relationship to any event outside the phenomenon itself. It just happened, no one was to blame, nothing lies behind it, and it could have happened to anyone. Although this is no scientific explanation, it moves the event from a state of chaos into a category of events which have been given a name and to which folk traditions have attributed stereotyped meanings. Also this type of classification has ethical connotations, it carries definite moral and legal implications. By and large, it is implied, the proper reaction to Alter is to treat him as if nothing had happened. The meaning bestowed upon the behavior of Alter by the term "accident" or poor luck, is above all negative: it removes other possible explanations as irrelevant in this case. The explanation in terms of chance is far from trivial. This fact is vividly proved by comparing our understanding of chance with primitive law and magic. In primitive societies chance is often interpreted as the voice of the gods.

We shall, consequently, reckon with a third scheme of perception of Alter's behavior, a scheme which refers to a general class of phenomena which is due to chance. If Ego knows that Alter's behavior is to be located in this class of events, it has wide implications for his conduct and demeanor vis-à-vis Alter. Only in situations where Ego is quite unable to choose between the three schemes of interpretation will he be confused concerning what constitutes proper behavior on his own part.

The perception of other people is a very complex phenomenon. Ego perceives Alter in accordance with schemata, but these are far from simple. I have started with a classification of these, according to whether they are dominated by goals, causes, or chance. But no presuppositions have been made about *what* purposes or *what* causes Ego has attended to. The distinctions drawn are very abstract ones, but they correspond to distinctions which have been much stressed in modern social psychology.

Quality and performance

The distinction between a scheme based upon will and another one based upon cause is closely connected with the current sociological distinction between quality and performance.[3] Ego is quality oriented in his perception of Alter when attending to who Alter *is,* and not primarily to what Alter *does,* or, to be more precise, when Ego emphasizes in his perception those among Alter's qualities which are innate and over which Alter has no control. Sex and age are the two most obvious examples. These qualities are caused, not willed. Excepting the very rare transformations of sex, these qualities cannot be achieved through conscious effort. No one can be blamed for them, and they cannot be modified. Ego's reactions to Alter are, however, frequently dominated precisely by Alter's age and sex.

Ego is performance oriented in his perception of Alter when he emphasizes what Alter has been doing or has wilfully contributed. Ego's emphasis upon actions and purposeful achievements links performance orientation to the scheme based upon the perception of will. A clear-cut case of performance orientation is found when an umpire in a sports contest prepares the list of results, or when an examination committee is distributing grades. It is immaterial to the assessment of performance *who* the competing athletes or students are. Within each separate class of competitors, the judgment should rest upon the performance, and upon nothing else, neither upon sex, nor upon age or status.

We have been dealing with the alternatives of performance and quality in terms of choice of a perceptual scheme in everyday interpersonal relations. The great significance of this pair of concepts lies, however, in its sociological usefulness as a means of characterizing total societies, or even whole epochs of social development. It is commonly assumed that primitive societies are dominated by quality orientation. Who Alter *is,* for example what sex and age he belongs to, is decisive for Ego's response. The distribution of tasks, of power and resources depends very largely upon these qual-

9

ities over which the individual has no control. It is commonly assumed that performance bears much greater significance to Ego's reaction to Alter in modern industrial society. Positions are filled according to achievements, in the form of examinations or skills exhibited in the previous stages of a career. Political power does not derive from inherited qualities, as the case was under the absolute monarchy, but depends upon victory in the competition for the favor of an electorate or upon other types of political achievements.

It is not my intention here to take a stand on these theories concerning a typology of societies or of stages in social evolution. The purpose is merely to illustrate how the perceptions of other people on the micro-level may have their counterparts in the macro-analysis of social structures.

In practice it is difficult sometimes to distinguish between quality orientation and performance orientation vis-à-vis Alter. When promotion follows seniority, age is being rewarded, and no one can, by his own effort, make time pass faster. But it is also possible to view promotion according to seniority as a reward of experience, based upon the confidence that experience enhances skills. If so, there is an element of performance orientation implicit in promotions according to seniority. This aspect of promotions would become clearer if the board of a factory faced the choice of appointing either an experienced and gifted manager or the son of the owner as managing director, assuming that the heir was new in the business. Inheritance of property or of position may present examples of the dominance of quality orientation.

The preceding examples suggest how it may be possible to study empirically the development of social norms from quality orientation to performance orientation. Observing that it becomes more and more common for managing directors of business firms to be selected outside the ranks of the heirs, we may conclude that achievement orientation is gaining ground at the expense of quality orientation. The same conclusion may be warranted if it becomes customary for heirs to a business to attend universities or to accumulate experience before taking over leadership in the firm. However, even if surveys ascertain that success in a society is closely correlated with education, grades, and demonstrated ability, we cannot unequivocally say that performance orientations have entirely supplanted quality orientations. Education and perhaps also abilities are closely connected with inherited social characteristics, like the father's occupation and social rank. Performance in school and in occupational life seem to be codetermined by innate qualities. Hence, it is not easy to arrive at any definite conclusion concerning the spread of, respectively, achievement orientations and quality orientations.

This lack of clarity is also inherent in the typically verifiable characteristics, age and sex. Also in our society, age has an important bearing upon Ego's reactions to Alter. Thus, it is impossible for teen-agers to be elected members of most Parliaments. Underlying this restriction is probably a rather clear-cut achievement orientation, based upon the hypothesis that a younger person will be unable to meet the minimal demands. Women are excluded from certain types of positions only in rare instances because of sex. When they are excluded, as they are in the army, the rule is founded partly upon a belief that women lack military skills and partly upon a pure quality orientation associated with sex. In areas where women are formally admitted, but where actual female participation is minimal, as in engineering, the low degree of participation is to some extent due to an evaluation of potential contributions. But it is also based upon quality orientations, opinions about what is "suitable work for women."

As categories of perception, quality and performance cannot be considered as mutually exclusive poles. The two types of schemata occur frequently in a mixture in Ego's perception of Alter. The problem is one of degree, whether the one or the other is dominant in a certain type of social situation, and in what situations and what kinds of societies performance orientation prevails and where quality orientations rule.

Diffuseness and specificity

Another way of classifying Ego's perceptions of Alter is concerned with the number of traits pertaining to Alter which are considered relevant.[4] Situations may occur, in particular when Ego and Alter are far removed from each other, where only a single characteristic of Alter is considered worthy of attention. When a citizen receives a notice from the Bureau of Internal Revenue concerning the payment of taxes, the citizen will hardly pay attention to the characteristics of the official who has signed the letter, other than noticing that he is an employee of this branch of the government. Even if Ego were to meet the official personally, this one characteristic— his official capacity—would probably dominate their interaction. Other aspects may, however, be added to the situation. Some taxpayers believe that they are good at "handling" tax officials. This may, among other things, imply that they are capable of treating the "bureaucrat" as a human being, who is also governed by needs, wishes and emotions of various kinds. The taxpayer may have grasped that it can be economically advantageous to try to understand the bureaucrat in his humanity, and not remain constrained to the perception of Alter as a public official of a certain kind. Regardless of what happens, however, the interaction unfolds itself against a background wherein looms very large that Alter is, after all, an employee of the Bureau of Internal Revenue, and that this fact is decisive.

Let us contrast this situation with the one in which a young man is considering marriage. Let us assume that he is a bit hesitant and feels the need to consider the matter carefully before taking such a fateful step. When thinking about his beloved, a large number of her characteristics probably occur to him: her looks, abilities, family background, her interests, what she feels towards him, whether she is fond of children, whether she fits in with his friends, gets along with his family, and everything which is summed up in the term "personality." If such private deliberations first get started, although they need not, few traits may be excluded as wholly irrelevant to Ego's perception of Alter. The difference between this situation and the one involving the tax problem is the following: In the tax example the framework of Ego's perception was positively determined by the overwhelmingly significant aspect of Alter's status as an employee of the Bureau of Internal Revenue. In the second example, there is no positive delimitation of the perceived characteristics. No single definite trait of Alter commands the attention of Ego to the exclusion of everything else. If any characteristic is to be set aside as irrelevant, it is the setting aside which needs a specific justification. The burden of proof for exclusion of perceptual elements as irrelevant is reversed.

Whether Ego perceives Alter within a perspective which is limited to a few characteristics or with attention to a great many characteristics depends upon several factors. Personality traits in Ego will be operative and may induce more or less openness or constraint in the perception of Alter. Psychic stress induced by certain types of situations may, likewise, determine how diffuse or how specific the perception of Alter is. After many years of marriage a man may no longer have a many-sided perception of his wife, but may have become completely obsessed by one trait, say, that she is untidy. The prevalence of such phenomena is indubitable and of great importance, but they do not properly belong among those which this book attempts to expound and explain. We are concerned with types of situations which recurrently, and with great uniformity, call forth specific or diffuse perceptions of Altera. The problem is, under what social conditions is it appropriate or legitimate to react on the basis of a specific orientation, while in other types of situations such a reaction may be inappropriate, or even morally condemnable.

The modern criminological slogan "treat the criminal, not the crime" summarizes very clearly an evolution from specificity to diffuseness in the perception of a certain class of persons. The traditional notion was that the penalty should fit the crime, the delinquent act being a very specific aspect of the defendant. According to the modern view, treatment ought to take into account a large number of traits pertaining to the defendant, like personality, social background, age, and family situation. A similar tendency can be observed in the reactions to alcoholics and other socially deviant groups. The same evolution from specificity to diffuseness can also be observed within medicine, in the increased significance attributed to psychosomatic causes and to the corresponding types of therapies. These go far beyond the physical complaint and may take into account a number of elements in the life situation of the patient, like family relations and occupational adjustment.

13

Subjectivity and objectivity.
Particularism and universalism[5]

Ego's perception of Alter may be strongly determined by Ego's personality. If it is, the perception tells us more about Ego than it does about Alter. There exist generally distrustful individuals who seem to be revealing themselves more than they reveal Alter when they give vent to their feelings of being irritated, offended, or persecuted by Alter. To some extent every Ego is apt to form the perception of others through a selective process whereby Ego observes what he *wants* to see. In psychoanalytic theory this phenomenon has been dealt with as decisive for the formation of projections. Projection is the tendency to attribute to Alter motives and qualities which Ego has suppressed in himself, like aggression, egoism, authoritarianism, and unconventional sexual desires. But Ego's perception of Alter may also be shaped by his personality through different mechanisms. Individuals who harbor much anxiety will tend to attribute threatening qualities to others, not because Ego himself possesses these traits, but because he is generally and irrationally scared of other people. Subconsciously he is searching for rational explanations of his own, otherwise inexplicable, behavior.

It is implicit in social interaction that Ego's perception of Alter is determined by Ego's emotions, as well as by the objective characteristics of Alter. Our concern is that the degree of subjectivism or objectivism may be dependent upon socially determined rules about the extent to which subjectivism is permitted or objectivism is demanded. To return to the example of the prospective marriage, it is not a priori obvious that an objective analysis of Alter, the beloved, is the most appropriate basis for Ego's perception and for his choice of a mate. In such situations proof that the perception of Alter was strongly influenced by Ego's own needs would not contradict our cultural norms concerning the basis of marriage. However, it would no doubt be deemed inappropriate for a psychiatrist or a psychotherapist to let his diagnosis be influenced by personal needs. "Love is blind" goes a proverb, condoning the state.

14

It refers to the fact that the mutual perceptions of the partners are strongly influenced by what each one of them needs and wants to see in the other one. What an outside observer deems to be the objective situation is largely irrelevant to Ego and Alter. But, of course, if the degree of realism is too low, Ego's distorted perceptions of Alter may have fatal implications for their future relationship.

Family relations are quite generally characterized by a relatively high degree of subjectivism or particularism. "Each one thinks best of his own" holds as a norm for relations between most parents and children, and not only for the most doting fathers or mothers. A great change occurs in the life of the child when it leaves the home where it has a particular relationship to the parents as *their* child, and not only as one specimen of the general class: children. The school is governed by more objectivity and more universalism; all children of the same class level are ideally treated equally. The teacher is not supposed to show differential treatment of the pupils, and the children are discouraged by their classmates from attempting to establish a special relationship to the teacher through apple-polishing, or maybe even by outstanding performance in class. A major function of the school is to train the growing individual in the norms of objectivity and universalism, while the home cultivates and protects subjectivism and the particularistic bonds which make Ego evaluate Alter within the framework of the relationship which prevails between the two.

From situation to situation the perception of others varies, with the tacit approval of society's norms, from particularism to universalism. Objectivity is demanded of the lawyer in the assessment of his client's prospects, but not a maximal objectivity. *His* client can make demands upon him, which no one else can make, for example, the adversaries in the litigation. The attorney is entitled to trust the evidence given by his client under circumstances where it would have been his duty to show distrust and dissect evidence of a similar quality brought forth by the adversary. For the judge, however, the norms of objectivity and universalism carry a maximum of weight. He must never perceive any defendant or any party to a suit as *his* client. If someone attempts to make him perceive one of the parties in a certain fashion by indebting the judge to the party through a gift, such an action would be strongly condemned as bribery.

Other criteria

There exist well-nigh unlimited opportunities for the schematizing of others' behavior. The schemes mentioned above do not, by any means, exhaust the possibilities. The choice of variables and dimensions has been influenced by theories of social relationships in society at large with its various institutions. The presentation of simple interpersonal perceptions anticipates points of view which properly pertain to the concluding chapters of an analysis of social structures. This is, apparently, inevitable. It seems impossible to construct a sociology out of the simplest social elements, completely unbiased by any advance image of the resulting complex structures. We move in circles, or spirals, from simple phenomena to more complex ones, and then back to the simpler ones, illuminated by insights gained on the macro-social level.

Schemes for the perception of others which have not been dealt with above might include the location of Altera as "above" or "below" in terms of social rank, as a particularly important type of classification. Each society has norms about the proper selection of criteria for such hierarchic orderings of individuals. Likewise, society produces rules concerning the classification of individuals as outsiders or deviants. To some of these schemes we shall have occasion to return later.

The preceding analysis of schemes of perception of others is strongly influenced by Talcott Parsons' "pattern variables." It seems natural, then, to bring in a further pattern variable, unmentioned so far, the contrast between *affectivity* and *affective neutrality*.[6] The dilemma consists in whether Ego can give expression to emotions vis-à-vis Alter or whether he should exhibit a factual, unemotional attitude. The choice may often coincide with the choice between universalism and particularism or between a specific or a diffuse orientation. There is a general tendency to clustering of the pattern variables. Affectivity, particularism, diffuseness and quality orientation will occur simultaneously, while affective neutrality, universalism, specificity and performance orientation likewise occur together. The opportunity to uncover such wider patterns in Ego's perception of Alter lends great sociological significance to these variables.

/

II

EXPECTATION
AND NORM

Ego perceives Alter's perception of Ego

ONE ASPECT of the perception of others is of particular significance for human interaction: Ego's perception of how Alter perceives him. Such perceptions can be classified in the same way that we did in the last chapter. The difference is that a mirror has been introduced in the process of perception. Consider a situation where Ego has failed to fulfill an obligation, for example, by not attending to his job, and argues with himself: "The boss will certainly believe that I am ill, and everything is all right." Or he may say to himself: "He will understand that I have been too lazy to show up, so I will be in trouble." Once more a distinction can be drawn between the perceptions of events as causally determined or as volitional, although two steps removed from the object of perception.

The additional feature which enters the situation is that Alter now also appears as perceiving, as a subject. And Ego, who was treated as a perceiving subject, is now also being perceived. We assume now that two persons who interact with each other both have the characteristics of an Ego and an Alter, depending upon how we focus our instruments of observation. This does not, however, apply in all social situations. There are circumstances under which only one of the parties has Ego character, and only the other party possesses Alter character: the surgeon in relation to his anaesthetized patient on the operating table, or the mother in relation to her sleeping child. And there exist situations where there are two Egos, but only one Alter: a spectator observes a person without himself being seen. Both of them are acting and perceiving, but only one of them is being perceived by the other one.

The situation described in Chapter I is in a certain sense static. Ego's perception may have a motivating influence upon himself, but does not necessarily affect Alter. Only when both parties assume Ego characteristics as well as Alter characteristics is a dynamic element introduced into the situation, and we can observe movement and interaction. The key to the interpretation of interaction, and of the relationship between two actors as a movement towards consummation of an end, is the concept of *expectation:* Ego perceives that Alter expects him to do something.

The concept of expectation signifies a relationship between a present and a future state of affairs. True, this relationship may often be simply one of stability; Ego is supposed to carry on as usual. But often there lies implicit in the expectation an assumption of change in the direction of a goal. The expectation is that element in social interaction which ties together actions, events, or intentions which follow upon each other in time. Apart from this, expectations differ widely. An expectation may take the form of a prediction, a hypothesis about what is actually going to happen; or an expectation may have the normative form of a wish, an evaluation or an order directed towards a future state or action. We should perhaps also include a third group of expectations, those which put questions: "I wonder what you (Alter) are going to do. It concerns me."

In philosophical analyses much has been made of the distinction between factual expectations and normative ones, sometimes based upon the implicit assumption that only normative expectations have motivating force and can prompt behavior. Although we use the distinction between descriptive and normative expectations, this distinction does not imply that the former, the expectations about what, as a matter of fact, is going to happen, are incapable of motivating behavior. When a doctor, on the basis of a diagnosis, is voicing the purely factual expectation that a patient of his will be able to get out of bed in three days, this prediction can have a considerable psychological impact upon the patient. It may cause optimism, hope and a will to get out of bed, thereby indirectly influencing the course of the cure. A medical prediction might also have the opposite effect, by depriving the patient of hope and courage if the prospect of getting well seems far off. Occasionally a prognosis may appear overly optimistic and is perceived as an unreasonable demand upon the patient. Expectations concerning a factual state of affairs in the future may create perceived obligations or rights.

Expectations and explanations

The fact that Ego perceives Alter perceiving him does not always mean that future events are being referred to. It may also refer to Ego's past. We are often vividly preoccupied by the question of whether others attribute guilt to us, in other words, how they interpret events which belong to the past. Our reasons for being interested in how others perceive our past may have to do with the future implications of a settlement of a question of guilt. Not infrequently, however, the interest in Alter's "historical" interpretations is motivated by their implications for Ego's self-perceptions and identity. Ego is concerned with how Alter explains his behavior and interprets his past because it may support or refute the image Ego has formed of himself.

Expectation is a central concept in modern sociological theory, while explanations have been accorded less attention. In social anthropology, however, in the scientific analysis of primitive cultures, native systems of explanation are accorded much more scope. It may have something to do with the fact that sociology is "modern," oriented to the present and the future, while social anthropology has been much concerned with origins and archaic social traits. Anthropological literature abounds with records of supernatural explanations of general phenomena, like human life and society and reports of how the primitives explain everyday phenomena, like illness, death, natural catastrophes and other accidents. After observing primitive societies it is apparent that social determinants are operating in such explanations. But also in modern industrial societies a theory which explains certain events may gain currency because it satisfies the needs of important social groups and not merely because of its scientific merits. The writing of history, for example, is often influenced by the national interests at the time of writing.

Ego's perception of Alter's expectations

Let us first consider the realism of Ego's perceptions of Alter's emotions and perceptions. Psychological investigations show, as one might assume, that actors are equipped with a certain capacity to sense whether others have sympathy with them or not. However, the ability to recognize sympathy and antipathy in others is far from perfect. Misinterpretations do occur, and they occur more frequently with respect to antipathy than with respect to sympathy. Ego's realistic assessment of the extent to which others feel antipathy against him may sometimes be quite deficient.[1]

Generally speaking, if we like other people, we tend also to believe that they reciprocate our feelings, and vice versa, if we dislike somebody. In order to predict how Ego perceives Alter's feelings, knowledge about Ego's feelings vis-à-vis Alter is more important than information about whether Alter actually likes or dislikes Ego.

It is not always so simple for Ego to form a realistic picture of Alter's attitudes, and consequently not of his expectations either. Ego may base his perception upon a variety of cues from Alter. An unequivocal situation may be established when Alter explicitly states that he wants Ego to act in a certain way. This desire may be expressed as a demand, as it does when a father tells his son that he must pull himself together and do his homework for school. Or it may take the form of a prohibition when the mother tells her daughter not to be out after midnight. Often it makes little difference whether an expectation is expressed as a demand or as a prohibition. Certain types of expectations are, however, difficult to formulate as positive demands, like, for example, the expectation that people should under no conditions steal from others.

When Alter's expectation has the form of a prohibition or a demand, Ego may feel that he is under an obligation to Alter.

Whether he accepts the obligation as binding upon him depends upon the qualities of Alter and upon the nature of the relationship between Ego and Alter. Let us, however, first discuss whether Ego can experience expectations from Alter's side which do not restrict him and obligate him, but which bestow rights upon him, and which enhance his situation.

It is quite common to describe the environmental expectations as restraining, limiting, and burdening for the individual. This is, however, a one-sided description. Alter's expectations need not exclusively create duties for Ego, they may also establish *permissions*. Others may accord us permissions by letting us know that they have no objections to our doing this or that, that we may do as we please, that we should behave "as if we were at home." In a certain sense this is a negative element in the definition of the situation, a denial of the presence of any expectations to us. The relationship to the normative system is, however, linguistically hinted at in the term to be "allowed." In many instances there may be only slight social significance to a permission, as when a passing stranger observes that we have his permission to frequent the streets of the city. However, if we are permitted by a policeman to pass through a street which is closed off to traffic because of a fire, the permission has more social implications. The policeman has accepted our passing through the street, and has decided that no social sanctions are to accrue from this otherwise prohibited type of behavior. It may be a matter of taste whether the term "expectation" suits these types of situations or not.

The expectant relationships between Ego and Alter can be reduced to two basic types: *duty,* which may be expressed either as a demand or as a prohibition, and *permission*. It should be emphasized that a permission is not identical with a *right*. No right may obtain without the implication of a permission, as for example, the permission accorded Ego to use his property and dispose freely of it within certain limits. But this permission is not sufficient to establish a right, which is a more complex phenomenon. That Ego possesses a right means that he himself has a permission and that others have duties towards him, obligations to perform or to abstain from doing certain things. Duty and permission express the simplest relations between Ego and Alter, while the concept of a right is constituted by a combination of these simplest relationships.[2]

It is impossible to define the implications of Ego's rights vis-à-vis Alter through a description restricted to those two actors. If Alter chooses to ignore his obligation and steals Ego's car, or fails to pay his debt, Ego's right might be of little avail to him in practical terms. What makes Ego's permission and Alter's duty enforceable is that there exist sources of sanctioning and decision-making outside the two. It is the relationship to a third party which defines the presence of a right between Ego and Alter. That Ego has a right means that he can meet Alter's failure to perform a duty with a demand upon a third party, who is supposed to help Ego achieve the fulfillment he is entitled to. In its most abstract and diffuse form this third instance may be society with its normative structure. Ego appeals to a shared set of norms which is binding upon Ego as well as upon Alter by referring to a tradition, to public opinion, or the judgment of others, and may thereby convince Alter that he ought to fulfill his obligations. In its most concrete and efficient form, the third instance is a court of law. The court sees to it that the apparatus of force monopolized by the state would be mobilized against Alter to enforce the right if he fails to perform voluntarily.

Demands and prohibitions, as well as permissions, may be voiced by Alter through varying means. They may be expressed as Alter's will, wish, or hope. Alter's expectations also appear in his *sanctions* of Ego, that is, through subsequent expressions of disappointment or of satisfaction. There may be different psychological consequences whether Ego states his expectations through general advance announcements, or whether he does so through the application of sanctions afterwards.

In his analysis of the perception of other people's expectations, Rommetveit lists four different types of signs from Alter from which Ego may draw his conclusions: 1. The factual predictions Alter makes with respect to Ego's future behavior, what he believes Ego will do. 2. Alter's expression of wishes and hopes concerning Ego's future behavior. 3. Expressions of satisfaction or dissatisfaction with what Ego has actually done. 4. The use of overt sanctions, reward or punishment, as a reaction upon Ego's conduct. The first two categories refer to advance announcement of an expectation, while the last two are *ex post facto* notification of expectations. The borderlines between, respectively, 1 and 2, and 3 and 4, may be significant, but are often hard to draw with precision. The use of overt sanctions will frequently be interpreted as symptoms of satisfaction or dissatisfaction, and their impact may depend precisely upon this aspect of the sanctions.[3]

Expectation and norm

From the expectations we proceed to the norms. Social norms are made up of expectations. If certain expectations are regularly released in certain types of situations, this is evidence of the operation of a norm. It means that the expectation is something more than the expression of a whim or an incidental aspect of a particular idiosyncratic situation. For a norm to be present, expectations must be enduring and have a certain stability. They must appear with regularity each time a certain type of situation arises. Rommetveit has defined the concept of norm with reference to an enduring social pressure between two or more actors. By social pressure he refers to what we have termed expectations. The actor who exerts pressure is the one who holds the expectation and is termed a sender of norms, while the actor who perceives the expectations as directed to him is termed a receiver of norms.[4]

As a consequence we must reckon with two types of norms: sent norms and received norms. An Alter may entertain expectations and even exert enduring social pressures which go unnoticed by Ego. If so, the norm which is present is nothing but a sent norm. Usually, however, Ego will sense the presence of a social pressure and will perceive the expectations which are directed towards him. In that case, the norm is also a received norm. On occasion norms may be received without having been sent. Ego imagines that other people have expectations of him which, as a matter of fact, they do not have and which they did not express. Rommetveit has termed this phenomenon fictitious social pressure, and he found clear evidence of it in a study of religious belief among youth.[5]

The point of departure for Rommetveit's investigation was the hypothesis that youth in strongly religious communities are under conflicting social pressures. They perceive their parents expecting one type of attitude to religion, based upon the Christian faith, while their peers appear to expect a different, less orthodox, attitude in these matters. Rommetveit did not ask directly what each respondent thought his friends expected of him. He made the assumption that each one entertained a desire for others to share his convictions, and that he, consequently, assumed everyone else to expect *him* to conform. Through questioning the respondent about the religious attitudes of his friends, it should be possible to deduce what expectations the friends experienced from their peer group's side. It turned out that each one of the twenty-six boys asked believed "the others" to be less religious than he was himself. Each one perceived an expectation from the peer group to be a little bit less of a Christian than he actually was. This expectation must spring from the operation of a fictitious social pressure since, obviously, not every one of the twenty-six respondents could have been the most Christian one, or could even belong in the most orthodox half of the group. Expectations are perceived and norms are received which have not, as a matter of fact, been sent out.

The concept of norm as defined by reference to sent and/or received expectations is not the only one currently in use. To avoid misunderstandings we shall briefly consider its relationship to some other concepts of norm. In moral and legal philosophy the concept of norm or rule is central. The normal starting point for such analyses are written formulations of a certain kind, normative statements which express orders, admonitions, demands, or evaluations. A widespread conception has been that norms can have no logical meaning, that they cannot be checked against experience, and that they are non-scientific. For certain purposes it may be important to distinguish between norms and verifiable propositions. For our sociological purposes it is not vital to make the distinction. Norms can be present as a part of the social reality of interplay between actors, even if the norm sender has made no explicit statement on what he expects from the norm receiver. A description of Ego's conduct and a prediction of his behavior may be experienced as expectations as much as given orders.

Do all verbally formulated norms, for example, all legal rules, give evidence of sent norms, received norms, social pressure, or expectations? There are statutes which, without having been formally abandoned, can no longer be considered valid law because of non-enforcement. No real sanctions and no social pressure correspond to the legal rule. Similarly there exist some religious norms which few would want to disavow, but which equally few experience as obligatory in practical terms. They stand as symbols of distant ideal states which no one tries with conviction to make real. However, this does not imply that they are completely without impact upon the motivation of actors, although no social pressure operates to enforce the precepts of the norm. We find a parallel in political life where many fundamental principles, in socialist as well as in liberalistic ideologies, are permitted to live their lives in slogans and pronouncements without any attempt at literal enforcement. Often, formulated systems of norms and ideologies possess a diffuse symbolic significance which may be generally stimulating, but which fail to afford concrete guidance for action. Although the Soviet Union has never abandoned the ultimate goal that the state should wither away, this norm does not seem to function as guidance for practical policy. On the other side, many governments profess general support of Christian norms of brotherly love which they find impossible to adhere to when dealing with their political enemies. It is advisable to distinguish clearly between concepts of norm based upon verbal rules, and the sociological concept of norm as defined by the operation of social pressure. There exist interesting relationships between the two, but the relationships do not follow from definition; they are matters of empirical observation.

Occasionally "norm" may be used in still other variants. One method for the determination of the norms of a society would be to map the existing uniformity of attitude and conduct.[6] According to our definition of social norm, uniform behavior or attitude may be caused by the sending and/or receiving of norms of a certain content. But uniformity of conduct and attitude may also have been caused by other factors. The concept of social norm as we use it must always be referred to relations between Ego and Alter. Neither formal, written rules nor uniform conduct are by definition evidence of the presence of social norms. Observations suggest, however, that there frequently exist empirical relationships between these phenomena.

The source of the norms

The expectations and the norms received by Ego may come from individuals or from groups. The first norm senders with whom the child is faced are individuals. He will begin to experience expectations from the parents early in life. The parents become the most important source of norms because they control the satisfaction of the child's primary needs. Control is exerted over those needs which can be satisfied through the child's access to material objects: food and drink, clothing, shelter; and it applies likewise to those social needs which can only be satisfied in trustful contact with other human beings.

The parents do not fulfill their functions as a source of norms for the children through a fully conscious and consistent use of rewards and punishments in accordance with a deliberately developed scheme of indoctrination. They may to some extent conform to conscious principles in their upbringing if they have made a choice between permissive and strict child-training. But to a large extent the parents dispense penalties and rewards on the basis of a motivation which originates spontaneously in the concrete situation, as a response to the immediate situation or in self-defense against the demands of the child.

The emission of norms from these initial sources in Ego's environment are characterized by a mixture of wishes, impulses, and actions which are both deliberate and haphazard, conscious and unconscious, rational and irrational. Since norms are emitted in this way, we can understand why there are vast differences in the norms governing human interaction which are learned by children from different families, although certain minimal standards of non-criminal conduct are learned gradually by most children. Variations not only

27

occur between families; they may also occur within families, between the parents. One and the same parent may even be inconsistent and vary the sending of norms from one point of time to another. The expectations experienced by the child are thus not entirely consistent. We shall not attempt here to describe how such inconsistency, in extreme cases, may constitute a threat to the personality development of the child and to his future mental health.

The possible lack of consistency in norm sending serves as a reminder that important social norms may from the very beginning acquire the tinge of relativism and ambivalence. The child is supposed to be modest and wait until it is served, but it is also supposed—especially if it is a boy—to be forward and participate in the struggle for life. To some extent such conflicts of norms are solved by metanorms which specify under what conditions one of the norms should take precedence, and under what conditions the other one ought to prevail. But the areas of valid application of each norm are rarely so clearly delineated that all contradictions are eliminated. The norm systems acquired by most actors encourage a certain oscillation between different standards of conduct in the same situation. It may even be argued that such a wavering has positive functions in a world which presents the growing individual with new and often unexpected problems to solve.

What does it mean to say that Ego acquires or learns norms? It does not simply mean that Ego perceives Alter's expectations when Alter expresses them. Learning of norms must at least imply that Ego remembers some of the expectations he has met, and that he has made some generalizations towards the establishment of rules, based upon concrete sanctions, expressed dissatisfactions, and other forms of reaction. Often, however, something is intended over and above this when it is claimed that someone has learned a norm. The environmental demands upon Ego have acquired independent motivational power and have been converted into demands he makes upon himself; they have become part of his personal norm system, of his own morality. When that has happened, the norm has been internalized.

Individual norm senders do not occur simply as the sources of children's norms. All throughout his life Ego is exposed to the expectations of other persons. These need not necessarily occupy a position of power or authority in relation to him. It is not only the employer who emits norms to the employee. Norms pass also in the opposite direction, although with less chance of being complied with. This does not simply mean that the employees may use their collective power through the unions. A general proposition can be advanced that both parties to an interaction usually possess at least some minimal means of sanctioning the other's behavior. The sanctions need not refer to economic resources or to the distribution of power, but can have a more subtle psychological make-up. A secretary may to some extent, if she is knowledgeable of the rules of the game, convey to her boss pleasant or unpleasant sensations of conforming to, or deviating from, the standards of proper boss conduct. His behavior may be modified, however slightly and without his awareness, by nuances in encounters with others, more in accordance with the norm emitted from the subordinate. No claim is made, of course, that power is equally distributed in society. But it is an important sociological notion that the normative influences in society, the process of norm sending and transmission, may take channels and flow in directions which are unmapped by the formal blueprints for the relations of power in society.

Individuals are not, from Ego's point of view, the only source of norms. Expectations and norms may also emanate from groups. By *group* is meant a number of individuals who directly or more distantly interact with each other. It is not sufficient for the establishment of a group that we can construct it on the basis of some shared characteristics like red hair or brown eyes. A group presupposes a certain amount of contact between the members. The actor must experience his own membership, and that of the others, in a definable collective unit. We shall in the following discussion distinguish between three kinds of groups: primary groups, secondary groups (organizations), and reference groups.

Primary groups, secondary groups, and reference groups as sources of norms

A family, a work group, and a village are among the most important primary groups in a society. Since each group has a small number of actors, each person in the group knows everybody else personally. A certain enduring character is also required of this constellation of individuals before we term it a primary group.[7] No hard and fast line can be drawn between this kind of social grouping and the secondary groups or the transitory assemblies of individuals. It is, however, quite clear that a modern industrial society, a national labor union, or the audience in a movie house do not fulfill the requirements of a primary group. In addition to the foregoing criteria, it is sometimes claimed that a primary group must be joined in some common task or in the fulfillment of shared goals. This requirement would make it dubious whether the smallest territorial units of hamlets and neighborhoods in rural societies ought to be included, and seems therefore a too stringent demand.

Ego receives expectations and norms from those primary groups to which he belongs. The industrial worker will, under certain conditions, experience expectations and social pressure to avoid fraternization with management, to be cool with the foreman, or to stick to production ceilings. Such norms are not, however, perceived as the demands of individual colleagues. Individual colleagues may voice the norm, but Ego would sense that he was nothing but the mouthpiece of the group, acting on behalf of the workers' collectivity. As long as the actor perceives a demand from one of his fellow workers as an expression of the group ethos, it is not so much the qualities of the individual norm sender, as the qualities of the group itself, which determine his reaction to the pressure to conform.

Compared to other types of groupings, the primary group possesses characteristics which make its norms particularly influential among its members. The close personal contact, so characteristic of many types of primary groups, satisfies important emotional needs.

Personal contact facilitates a continuous process of give and take, making the normative demands more elastic and adaptable to the requirements of the situation. The legal sociologist Ehrlich put the case for primary groups in an extreme form when he claimed that they were the source of all social norms and of all legal rules:

> Nothing could be psychologically more erroneous than the widespread notion that people abstain from interfering with each other's property because they fear the criminal law, or pay their debts simply because of the threat of foreclosing a mortgage. . . . Every normative compulsion does, however, depend upon the fact that no individual is really ever a single individual. He is so incorporated, absorbed, intertwined with, and enmeshed in a number of groups, that existence outside them would be intolerable, nay, often impossible . . . Every deviant must be prepared for the contingency that his conduct will dissolve the connections with those who are his own. The one who stubbornly resists the social pressure has unloosened the bonds which tied him to his mates. He will gradually be deserted, avoided and excluded. Here in the social groups is the basis of the compulsory force inherent in social norms. . . .[8]

Next to the primary groups, Ego will encounter the demands of secondary groups or of organizations. Consider for a moment the modern state or the industrial enterprise as transmitters of norms to their members. Since large organizations often comprise smaller primary groups, the efficiency of norm sending within the organization depends a good deal upon these groups. It is too early at this stage to deal with the problems of the large-scale organizations. Let it suffice here to emphasize that the norm senders with which Ego is faced may be distant and abstract phenomena to which he is tied, if at all, by bonds that hardly resemble his personal attachments to family and friends.

Secondary groups or organizations are founded with a specific purpose, and a formal structure has emerged with respect to the division of labor and leadership which aims to further the goal of the organization. Members are included in the organization on the basis of specified characteristics derived from its purpose. It is typical of organizations that members participate only with parts of themselves, with their working capacities, with their religious beliefs, with their leisure-time interests, or with their political convictions, but not as complete persons. Such a limitation distinguishes the organization clearly from the small territorially determined membership groups, like the neighborhood, which may be all inclusive. Membership in the organization is based upon principles of functional specificity. Recruitment takes place with reference to universalistic and objective criteria, while relationships between members are based more upon achievement than upon ascription. Interaction must, in large measure, be supported by specialized means of communication, and cannot simply take place face to face. Through lines of command, written instructions, newsletters, and other means of communication, interaction in the organization is maintained. The organizations exert enormous influence as norm senders due to the resources over which they dispose, and which they distribute among the members as wages, influence, or other privileges.

The reference group is a rather watered-down version of a group; it should perhaps be termed a quasi-group. Its members need not be tied together by anything more than Ego's experience of them as, in some respect, belonging or being uniform. Reference groups consist of categories of actors with whom we compare ourselves.[9] These comparisons may have a decisive influence upon our perception of the demands made upon us and of the rights which accrue to us. Implicit in the comparison is the perceived expectation that Ego ought to behave like others in similar situations and should be permitted to. Social strata, such as other white-collar workers, other managers, or "other children of my age," may constitute such categories of actors from which Ego borrows his norms of conduct, his outlook, and his style of life. For the one who makes the comparison and wants "to be like everybody else," this may be enough to perceive an expectation and a norm of conduct.

The strength of the norm sender

A norm may be received by Ego without necessarily achieving much influence upon his behavior or his attitudes. If it does achieve great significance and contributes to important modifications of

Ego's beliefs or conduct, it implies that the norm sender is strong. The strength or power of the norm sender depends upon a number of attributes.[10] The first concerns Ego's emotional relationship to Alter, assuming that Alter may be an actor as well as a group. The question is how strongly Ego is attached to Alter, if he likes Alter and is emotionally dependent upon his support, or, in short, what attraction Alter has for Ego. In this respect there are obviously enormous variations among the norm senders encountered by Ego. The child's emotional dependency upon its mother provides a strong basis for her power as a norm sender. In many relationships between employer and employee, however, such a basis of power may be completely lacking.

When attraction forms the basis for the strength of a norm sender, it is because Ego wants to comply; he wants to be as Alter wishes him to be, as a means to preserving the relationship to Alter. In intimate personal relationships the situation may be considerably more complex. Two people may be strongly attracted to each other, but feel no strong need to comply in all respects, provided that they feel security and trust in the relationship. Maximal conditions for norm sending will perhaps obtain when the relationship is characterized by some uncertainty, as for example, when a child has some fear of losing the emotional rapport with his parents. However, compliance may then be associated with anxiety or aggression which may, in the long run, weaken or corrode the power of the norm sender. For the present purposes we may assume as a general rule (with exceptions) that the power of the norm sender increases with the attraction he exerts upon Ego.

The opportunity to control the satisfaction of material needs is another determinant of Alter's power as a norm sender vis-à-vis Ego. The more intense the rewards or penalties at Alter's disposal, the greater the power of penetration of the norms he emits. The principles of seniority from this point of view bestow less power upon the decision makers in relation to their subordinates than do principles of promotion based on performance or loyalty. In the latter case the upper echelons control the access to an important privilege, which in the former case flows more or less automatically from the passage of time, independent of superordinate control.

The power of a norm sender is dependent upon his association with the area of application of the norm, whether it concerns health, politics, music, or whatnot. A competent Alter has more power than one who is incompetent. Competency is in this context a term with wide referents and is not restricted to professional specialties. It also includes the case of a man who attributes great weight to his wife's emotional expectations, because this is a relevant area in a marriage, and one in which his wife is competent to form opinions and make demands. We are, on the other hand, normally not much swayed by the norms concerning health matters emitted by an engineer, or by those from a politician about music, unless they have other means of coercion at their disposal.

Ego's opportunities to find substitutes and alternatives to his relationship with Alter may influence Alter's power as a sender of norms. If Ego is able to find another group to substitute for the group which threatens him with expulsion because of disobedience, the probability of compliance is less than it would have been if he were completely deprived of access to alternate groups or milieus. A general trend in social development may be traced in this respect. In the old rural society the individuals were less socially mobile than they are in present-day urban societies. If an actor wanted to find a substitute for his relationship to the neighborhood or the local community, he would have to migrate physically. In modern urban society, it is possible to change group belongingness in primary groups, as well as in secondary and reference groups, without much concomitant geographical mobility. New places of work are normally available in case Ego wants to quit his present job or is forced to. If one feels estranged from one political party, one may join another one. And if one begins to feel alienated in a Pentecostal sect, one may join the Methodists or the Catholic Church. Group membership has more and more become a matter of individual choice, although many of the choices are made with limited awareness of the consequences or concern for them, and are often motivated by tradition or by the group belongingness of the parents.

The increased freedom of choice has wide ramifications. It enables the individual to withdraw from complete commitment to any one significant group or milieu. He may regard society as a vast social cafeteria where a menu can be construed according to taste, permitting an individualistic and idiosyncratic style of life. Such an attitude may enhance opportunities for self-realization by favoring a life in accordance with a deep-felt and personally elaborated life pattern. But it may also favor the avoidance of all controls and permit the relinquishing of duties without immediate and catastrophic consequence to the actor himself. It is possible to float without sense or direction in a modern city. Many have claimed that an important cause of modern urban criminality lies precisely in the increased opportunity to avoid the social controls of the primary group, assumed to have been so characteristic of rural communities.

A concomitant consequence of the decline of social control by means of primary groups is the increased need for policing and for guidance exerted by the agents of the national society. Society, represented by politicians, educators, the press, radio, and TV, has gained ascendancy as norm sender, parallel to the declining power of the local community to achieve conformity to its norms. The change is not merely one of the forms of social control, but also one of substance, since the inclusive society will tend to send norms somewhat different from those of the small community.

The communication of expectations and norms

From the first page of this book we have presumed that two or more actors may communicate with each other, that it is possible to convey messages. The interest has turned more upon the content of the messages and upon the attributes of the senders and receivers than upon the "technical" problems of communication. The point of departure was a situation where Ego and Alter found themselves in each other's presence and communicating face to face. As we have proceeded to social relations where the contact is largely indirect, as it is in the nation and its large-scale organizations, the question of *how* communication functions becomes more pressing. That the means of communication should attract sociological interest was foreshadowed by the development of social institutions like the press, the radio, and TV. These means of communication are termed mass media, emphasizing the distinction from the more personal type of communication, conversation, and letter writing.

35

The theory of communication is today characterized by attempts to apply the same kinds of principles and techniques to communication between humans, with language as the major vehicle, as to the information process taking place in computers. Characteristic of the latter is the *feedback* process. When the computer emits information from its "brain," the message is received in some other place; from this place a new message is fed back, thereby influencing the subsequent emission of information from the brain. The parallel with conversation between humans is apparent. Ego conveys something to Alter, who responds in a way which informs Ego of the success of his first attempt at conveying his message, thereby influencing his further emission of messages. The ability to learn hinges precisely upon a person's chances of having his "state" corrected through a give-and-take in a feedback process. The founder of cybernetics, Norbert Wiener, attempted to apply the theory of communication systems to such an old institution as law. He assumes the legal system to be a network for the emission and transmission of messages in which the legislators and the enforcement agencies serve as relay stations controlling the flow and feedback of information.[11]

Attempts have been made increasingly to study new social phenomena from the general point of view that they are instances of communication. Some psychiatrists have defined schizophrenia as a particularly grave disturbance of communication. The schizophrenic lacks the ability to understand certain messages from other humans, especially messages which intend to convey the nature of other messages. One instance would be Ego's attempt to inform Alter through his facial expressions that what he is now about to say is a joke, a trial balloon, a question, but no serious or final attempt at stating the truth. The ability to grasp such nuances in the intentions behind communication is crucial to the adjustment between individuals. In this respect something fails in the mental make-up of the schizophrenic, who may well understand the words and the language which is being used. Schizophrenics lack, to some extent, the ability to have their messages corrected by the feedback they obtain. The "communication psychiatrists" claim that the origin of such mental illness lies in problems of communication and are above all caused by fundamental ambiguities in the mother's communication with the child.[12]

The most important types of communication

Communication implies that symbols are transmitted from Ego to Alter. If the physical distance between them is great, communication can occur either by the symbols moving spatially, for example, conveyed by a letter, or by physical mobility of the actors through means of transportation like cars or airplanes. From a sociological point of view it is significant that both of these technical processes are termed communication.

The most important distinction among the means of communication is the one which can be drawn between situations where Ego and Alter interact in each other's presence, and those where they interact at a distance. One reason why this distinction carries significance is implicit in what was said about the feedback processes. In face-to-face interaction immediate corrections of misunderstanding or non-compliance with the message's intention may be made instantly, while this kind of communication is impossible or cumbersome when letters or mass media are used. Another reason for underlining the distinction has to do with the specific psychological processes which are stimulated by Alter's personal presence. Concealment and subterfuge become more difficult on both sides, and disagreements are experienced more painfully than they are at a distance. The course of a process of communication may, therefore, develop rather differently under the two types of conditions. It is known to everyone who wants "to win friends and influence people" that personal contact is in some ways much superior to letter writing.

The distinction between communication face to face and communication at a distance furnishes one important basis for the classification of societies and of their sub-groups. Primitive societies are often defined as illiterate societies, societies without a written language, imposing severe restrictions upon the scope of communications. Industrial society is, on the contrary, characterized by the extent to which important messages are conveyed independently of personal contact between sender and receiver. The distinction between primary and secondary sub-groups within a society is related to the type of communication which prevails. A necessary criterion of the existence of a primary group is the opportunity to communicate face to face with the other members of the group. In secondary groups, like a labor union and a political party, such personal communication between *all* members of the group is unattainable, and written communications are inevitable.

One important type of communication occurs when a sender and receiver interact without having met, and when the message has been conveyed through a line of personal links. Military commands are issued by the commander in chief and transmitted downward through a chain of command until they finally reach the privates. Notes made in a ministry may pass through a similar line of command from a clerk upwards until it is finally, in more or less modified form, received by the minister who is the addressee. In this type of communication there is a higher likelihood of transmission of the sender's intention when the message passes downwards through the line of command than when it passes upwards. The major reason is that the means of sanctions and the resources are accumulated in the hands of the superiors.

Another peculiarity of such chains of communication, and this applies especially to downward messages, is that the senders in the lines of command are not personally responsible for the content of the message. Therefore, the reaction of the immediate recipient (the feedback) can only within narrow limits correct the message and the subsequent flow of communication. Each sender is bound to send the message as he received it, and efficient transmission of the message is decisive for his future status in the hierarchy. Thus, his own interests favor the use of sanctions to make the receiver accept the message in case he should appear recalcitrant. The personal aspect of each link of transmission puts into effect those psychological forces which make it unpleasant to be non-compliant face to face. Lines of communication of this kind appear to be necessary in all organizations which act to further a specific goal such as factories, military formations, departments of state, and other administrative units.

More than any other type of communication, the mass media have put their stamp upon modern societies through the press, books, radio, and TV. But there are other types of message transmission over distances which lack the mass character: letters, telegrams, and telephone conversations. In the mass media we usually find a small organized group of senders and a large, but unorganized, category of receivers, an audience, readers, listeners, viewers or spectators. Few phenomena have been more subject to sociological scrutiny than the mass media. The research falls into three broad categories: 1, the studies of an organization, an "industry," which produces mass media, such as the moving picture industry; 2, studies of the messages contained in the mass media through the numerous content analyses of the press, and treatment of various issues; and 3, studies concerned with the recipients, the audience, and with the extent to which the messages reach their addressees, and how the various audience groups react.

The last type of investigation is the one which has attracted most popular interest, probably because a study of recipients offers an opportunity to gauge the efficiency of the mass media, and also because sociological studies have contributed greatly to knowledge of the impact of the mass media. Some sociological research has tended to belittle the assumed dominance of the mass media as sources of influence in modern life. Lazarsfeld and others have shown that people have more trust in an intimate personal source of communication than they have in the mass media. Personal influence, the transmission of messages from man to man, may be more significant than what is being conveyed through radio and the press. Or rather, unless the messages transmitted by the mass media receive support through personal influence, their impact may be negligible.[13] Frequently quoted examples are the presidential elections when Roosevelt and Truman were elected in spite of the fact that the press was overwhelmingly on the side of the rival candidate.

III

SOCIAL
ROLES

A MAN walks downtown in the morning. He enters the courthouse. After putting his coat on a hanger and perhaps attending to a few matters at his desk, he dresses in a black coat and walks into a room where some people are assembled. They rise to their feet as he enters the room. He commences to say something which he has said many times before in the same situation, announcing that the court is convened and that the proceedings may begin. A process unfolds itself, various actors taking the floor in a patterned sequence which has been repeated over and over again in this very room. The man in the black coat who presides over the proceedings bears a demeanor strikingly different from his behavior during breakfast before he left his home. He had been engaged in a lively discussion with his wife and his daughter concerning various problems related to a party which his daughter had planned to give for her friends. He had talked voraciously, without heeding the comments of his family, and had been rather temperamental. His anger subsided, however, when his wife made him laugh. Finally, he broke away from the table with an exclamation that he was late for the office, he kissed his wife and ran down the staircase. Presently, in the courtroom, no irritation can be sensed in his demeanor, although there is much to be annoyed about in the case on trial before him. There is no indication that he might yield to fits of temper or that he might laugh hilariously if anybody made an amusing remark. An olympic tranquility and factual, staid comments in a strange and somewhat old-fashioned dialect of the vernacular characterize his appearance. His authority seems unshakable in a way which it did not during the breakfast scene. If we assumed that he "was being himself" at the breakfast table, we would be inclined to think that he is participating in a play in the courtroom. He plays a role, the role of the judge.

What is sketched here is the actor's conduct, his role behavior. When speaking about roles in sociology, the concept is usually defined by the expectations and norms to which the behavior is a response. *A role is the sum of the norms which are linked to a certain task or position.* The role surrounds Ego with a ring of expectations, and the expectations may be expressed in laws, regulations, instructions, administrative blueprints and the like or the role may be informal, made up of the social pressures created by the wishes and demands of friends or acquaintances. The judge's role is largely made up of formal laws, above all the rules of the law on courts and the various procedural enactments. But these formal rules do not exhaust the content of his role. Other less formalized norms may influence his demeanor, like common consent concerning the amount of gravity and dignity befitting a man in this kind of office. There also exist informal norms concerning the style of his approach to the litigating parties or to the defendant in a criminal case, and these may vary from period to period and between different legal cultures, nay, even from one judiciary to the next.

The task or the position affords the key to the role. A social role is made up of those norms which are associated with a certain task and with the corresponding position. There are no great problems inherent in this definition in the case of the judge. Formal decisions make it clear who are appointed as officers of a court. Ego's incumbency of a position on the bench, an easily observable social fact, releases all the norms of which the role of the judge is composed. What makes the concept of role useful is that information concerning a person's position enables us to make a number of inferences concerning the expectations directed towards him, in the form of duties as well as of permissions. If we know an actor's title, we know immediately a great deal about the expectations he is being met with by his environment, and we are often able to infer a good deal about the kind of response he will make to these expectations. Essentially, the concept of role serves much the same function of thought economy and predictability in everyday life as it does in sociology. Sociology makes explicit and systematic what common sense more intuitively and less systematically accomplishes in dealing with social relationships.

From the preceding it will appear that there are three phenomena which have to be distinguished: The position, the role, and the role behavior. The position is the external, often formal, announcement that an actor "is" this or that: woman, man, prime minister, bus conductor, and so on. The announcement of the actor's position may take place in various ways—by birth, contract, document of appointment, census registration, uniform, door placard, and advertisement. Some, like the anthropologist Ralph Linton, have used the term "status" instead of position.[1] This terminology will not be followed here, partly because we want the term "position" to be defined somewhat more narrowly than "status," and partly because the term "status" too strongly directs attention towards the place of the actor within a system of social stratification, towards those characteristics which determine his place on a scale of rank and prestige. This is one aspect of the position, but not the only one, and not always the most significant one.

From the position we arrive at the role. It is made up of all the expectations which are released by announcement of Ego's incumbency of a position, including Alter's expectations of Ego as well as Ego's expectations of himself. When an actor appears in the uniform of an air stewardess we expect her to aid us, feed us, and advise us to get out at the right airport. We have also bestowed upon her the right to make certain demands upon us, like fastening seat belts, extinguishing cigarettes and, quite generally, keeping order in the cabin. We have made ourselves amenable to such demands and have acquired corresponding rights by assuming the position of passenger announced by our tickets and boarding pass. We encounter here a very general aspect of role phenomena, namely, that roles are complementary. If a certain social role has developed, it has usually emerged through interplay with an "opposite number" of some kind. What pertains to one of the roles as duties, pertains to the opposite one as permissions or rights. Some of the many examples of such role-pairs are those of husband and wife, and of parent and child.

The exact line of demarcation between position and role is not always easily drawn. Some people have an influence in politics which transcends the formal positions they hold. Their real position can only be determined through a detailed examination of the role they are playing. An individual may, likewise, enjoy much influence and esteem within a circle of friends although there exist no external symbols of his position. As a general rule, however, there is a point in making the distinction between those simple, external criteria which announce Ego's incumbency of a position, and the very diverse, often subtle and manifold norms concerning how an actor in this position is entitled to, and ought to, behave.

Norms are an aspect of the relationship between Ego and Alter which is established by the announcement of the incumbency of a position. A social pressure exists which is due to expectations and norms sent by Alter and received by Ego. The pressure may also arise, however, from internalized norms in Ego, telling him what his duties and rights are as an incumbent of the position, independent of the demands and wishes expressed by his environment.

From the fact that Ego finds himself in a specific role, we can draw no certain conclusions with respect to his actual conduct. By and large we tend to assume that Ego will conform to the norms of the role when he enters a position. To assume a position is interpreted as a promise to play the role according to the rules of the game. Nevertheless, it is necessary to distinguish between role and role behavior, because the behavior does not follow by logical necessity from the prescriptions of the role. It is not difficult to find examples to show that incumbents of positions often deviate from the legitimate expectations of others. In particular this is apt to happen before the actor has grown into his position. Following an appointment or a promotion a certain amount of time may elapse before the new incumbent learns to behave in conformity with the new role. We shall not, by way of a definition, presume a perfect harmony between the expectations of the social environment and Ego's conduct. Conflict and deviance are ubiquitous phenomena which a sociologist's conceptual apparatus must be as capable of describing as it is of describing conformity and equilibrium.

In the preceding presentation we have taken individual actors as our point of departure and then constructed the role by providing Ego with a position. One might also look upon society as a network of roles which is filled with personnel. The sociologist's construct of society will then resemble a system of shelves or niches with mutually defined interrelationships.

Recruitment

It makes little difference which one of the two points of departure we choose for the understanding of specific role phenomena in a society, the one which equips actors with roles, or the one which fills roles with personnel. The latter point of view, which assumes an originally empty network of roles to be filled, poses more clearly the problem of recruitment: How are the roles filled and by what mechanisms is an available pool of manpower distributed upon the shelves and niches of society? In other words, how does an individual come to enter a position to which a certain role is attached?

One quite general answer is that Ego enters a position, and the corresponding role, by exhibiting traits or displaying conduct which qualifies him for entrance according to the expectations of the social environment. This answer implies that to each role are linked two sets of norms, those stipulating the conditions for assuming the role, and those which are released by incumbency of the position. These two sets of norms may coincide, for example, when entrance criteria make demands upon the ability of the recruit and the demands continue to serve as guidance for performance of the role. But there may also be a gap between the norms applied prior to occupancy of the role and the rules pertaining to behavior *in* the role. Positions of political authority are frequently acquired as a consequence of propagandistic skills, and these skills may be less highly valued, nay, even deprecated as contrary to popular expectations, once the political ambitions have been fulfilled and the agitator or party worker has become minister, president, or has assumed some other high office. It is a quite common phenomenon that a person must qualify for entrance to a role by exhibiting traits or conduct

44

different from the behavior expected in the role. One particularly striking example is the significance once attributed to a classic education in England as a prerequisite to assuming high political or administrative office.

Two main alternative principles may govern the allocation of personnel to a society's positions and roles. In part the recruitment takes place on the basis of individual traits and personal qualities over which Ego has no control and exerts no choice. In this case the status or the role is ascribed. In part, however, the recruitment takes place on the basis of choice and actions on Ego's part. If this is the case, we deal with an achieved status, one which is based upon performance.[2] The roles of woman and man and of old and young are occupied as a consequence of ascribed criteria. Occupational roles are, however, to a very large extent achieved roles, dependent upon the choice of the actor and of his exertions, abilities, and other requirements such as examination grades. It has not always and everywhere been so. There have existed, and still exist, societies where individuals are born into their occupations. In many modern societies student statistics suggest that recruitment to the academic professions is not wholly independent of birth and social inheritance. The ideology of modern, industrial culture, however, stresses the free choice of an occupational career and the equality of access to the means of qualification, as well as the application of criteria of achievement when appointments and promotions are made. We see this tendency, and also the strong counterforces, very clearly in the struggle for the equality of women within the occupational life.

The relative weight attributed to ascription or achievement as the basis for recruitment to social roles has afforded an important point of departure for the comparison of primitive and modern societies. This factor has also been used to summarize essential aspects of the evolution of modern societies subsequent to the industrial revolution. The trend is still moving in the direction of open competition for all roles, with an opportunity of participation for all those who can perform in accordance with the demands of the role, irrespective of what ascribed characteristics they possess. An extreme example of the trend is found when a person decides to change sex through an operation in order to assume a new social role. In the political field universal voting rights and the corrosion or abolition of monarchy is a less extreme, but more significant, example of the tendency to substitute achievement and choice for ascription and quality as a basis for power and authority. In the economic field large inheritance taxes serve to abolish or weaken birth as a criterion for the incumbency of positions of wealth and economic power. In all fields of social life the trend is discernible, although not always as strongly as democratic ideology would make one believe.

Role conflict

The actor is not always faced by clear and consistent expectations from others and will not always find it easy to determine what is socially accepted conduct. Role conflict has come to be of vital concern to sociology. Role conflict may signify that Ego as the incumbent of one and the same position is met by contradictory expectations with respect to what constitutes proper role behavior, or that Ego simultaneously occupies two (or more) positions to which are linked mutually exclusive sets of norms. In the former case the conflict is inherent in the nature of the role itself. In the second case the conflict is caused by the simultaneous incumbency of two roles by one actor; the distribution of personnel upon roles results in some actors experiencing conflict although each single role is free from contradictions.

Let us choose an example to illustrate the first kind of role conflict. In studies of legal agencies in Greenland, Goldschmidt found considerable uncertainty regarding the judgment of various criminal offenses. The uncertainty seemed to be caused by the fact that the judge in Greenland was exposed to the influence of two very different legal cultures, one from the Danish which had provided for the formal rules, and one from old Eskimoan customs which still persisted in the expectations of the population. An actor in the role of criminal judge in Greenland would thus be in a conflict concerning what constitutes proper behavior for a person in his position: "It must be assumed that the legal officers, when faced with a variety of actions, whether it be rape, sexual relations with minors, assault on animals, abortion, or the violation of rules of wild life preservation, to a considerable extent perceived social norms which "pressed" in opposite directions. These conflicts of perceived norms seem to have caused some uncertainty in the attitudes and evaluations of the officers of the law, while in other cases one of the two sets of norms had gained ascendancy and decisively influenced their decisions. The influence of the perceived norms varied not only according to the group relations of the legal authorities at any one time, but also exhibited changes from one period to another. The latter is the case with respect to norms concerning forced sexual relations. The extremes are represented by a precolonial time when such behavior was common, and the present situation where such conduct is termed rape and the perpetrator sentenced as a rapist." [3] Which one of the contradictory norms gains ascendancy in the decision-making process depends, according to Goldschmidt, upon those factors which were enumerated in our previous treatment of the "strength of the norm-sender."

The other type of role conflict is the one which may arise for a woman if she simultaneously has a family and a job outside of the home. The conflict does not arise from internal inconsistencies in the norms applicable to each position. However, to play two such roles does create conflict because each one makes demands which interfere with the fulfillment of the other. The conflict may, for example, be due to competing demands upon the expenditure of the scarce resource of time. Many other role conflicts originate to a large extent from the competing demands upon the use of time. But this is not the only difficulty. In the case of the professional woman with a family, other problems may arise if her husband's expectations are strongly influenced by traditional sex role patterns, with the implication that the wife ought to be around the house, have inferior skills outside the domestic fields, and enjoy less authority. She might, as a career woman, bring into the home and into the circle of the family's friends, a social position which makes it impossible for the husband to play the role in his relationship to her for which he has been prepared by existing traditions. A role conflict may arise on a normative basis, even if the problem of time allocation is soluble.[4]

47

As a consequence of such conflicts the two conflicting roles may be transformed to facilitate their simultaneous incumbency by one and the same actor. With respect to the woman's role in modern society, the modifications have taken place primarily as changes in her role as wife and housekeeper. In part the change has been practical, through the emergence of kindergartens and the technical development of home equipment such as the electrification of the kitchen. In part, also, the change has been furthered by a slow transformation of constituent norms of the woman's roles and, more generally, of society's sex role patterns. Expectations which were prevalent fifty years ago have to a considerable extent become outmoded and have been replaced by new norms. The extent to which role conflicts of this kind may be solved, and the contradictions wiped out, depends upon whether it is inevitable that one pool of personnel must fill more than one role. Since it has seemed inevitable that the man should have a role in his family concomitant with his occupation, his two roles have been synchronized at an earlier stage. However, there is a potential for conflict in his situation with respect to the allocation of time and in regard to style of conduct and normative patterns.

The role set

The examples above suggest that one and the same actor may be exposed to different groups of norm senders who entertain discrepant expectations about Ego's conduct and thus cause conflict. Let us have another look at the role conflict exemplified by law enforcement in Greenland, where the discrepant expectations were directed towards Ego as the incumbent of one and the same position. It is a common property of many social positions that they turn one side to certain categories of Altera, while showing another face to a different class of Altera. Consider the role of the attorney at law. It has one aspect which affects the clients, one which concerns other attorneys, and still a third which is brought out in relation to the judiciary. From these groups emerge expectations to the attorney which are rather different, and even in some respects, contradictory. In his relations with the clients, the attorney encounters expectations which may be independent of legal considerations. The layman expects the attorney to help; the expectations are formed by what the client finds just and reasonable from his own moral point of view, which is strongly clouded by personal involvement and often but little influenced by the prescriptions of the law. The judge and other attorneys, however, expect the attorney to conduct his litigation on a firm legal basis, or at least upon one which is not obviously untenable juridically. This latter demand has also normally been internalized by the attorney in the course of his training and during his previous practice.

The attorney is, consequently, in a situation where he is supposed simultaneously to meet the expectations from highly divergent groups of Altera. His role does not consist simply of the sum of expectations entertained by the clients, nor exclusively of those expectations which colleagues and judges direct towards him. The role is made up of the sum of the norms sent by all the affected groups to the incumbent of the position. We may term this the "role set." [5] Inherent in the role set lie problems which must be solved or ameliorated unless serious role conflicts are to arise.

One solution is afforded through separation and creation of barriers between the various groups which make demands upon the incumbent of a position. In the example of law enforcement in Greenland, the judge was in a position where he could keep one façade vis-à-vis the authorities in Denmark, while showing a slightly different face to the local population. There was not much risk that these inconsistencies would be revealed by a confrontation of the two types of conduct. Many positions permit a certain double play due to physical or social distance between the various groups to whom the role set refers.

Another example of this emerged during an interview with the chief officer on board a tanker. He reported that the captain, a somewhat withdrawn and authoritarian individual, used the formal term of address, "De" (they), third person plural, to everyone aboard his ship, and was himself addressed in the same way by crew and officers. Since, however, the chief officer and the captain had previously served together as mates on the same ship, they used the familiar form of address, "Du" (thou), second person singular, when

49

they were by themselves. If someone from the crew approached them, however, they would in his presence switch to De. We may interpret this conduct as indicating the captain's exposure to different norms vis-à-vis the crew and vis-à-vis his chief officer. The problem was partly solved by the device of assuming one kind of posture when the two of them were alone, and another one when they were in the presence of others. The opportunity for physical separation of audiences afforded a partial answer to the problem. However, if the physical barrier broke down and they were in the presence of a third person, a norm of priority settled the latent conflict: The De-norm, indicating formal address, assumed ascendancy. In many situations one may distinguish behavior which takes place in privacy "off-stage," or "in the smoke-filled rooms," from conduct aimed at putting on a show or keeping up a façade vis-à-vis an audience.[6]

Sometimes Ego plays his role differently vis-à-vis different groups without the aid of physical barriers between the separate audiences. The position of the attorney as a go-between in the layman's encounter with the judiciary is to some extent facilitated by the fact that he moves within two sets of "languages," and the clients do not fully understand the terminology used by the professional lawyers. In the interest of the client the attorney is compelled to use a technical language, but he thereby debars the client from exerting full control concerning the extent to which the attorney actually fulfills his expectations. We might also refer to physicians discussing the patient's condition in Latin terminology across the hospital bed. Conflicts may, however, arise because the attorney, like other service professionals, has duties to perform in various directions. A highly debatable point is the relationship between the defense counsel's duty to protect the interests of his clients and his obligations towards "law," as represented by the judge, to present all factual matters in accordance with the truth.

A third way of solving or staving off incipient conflict due to the role set is for the incumbent to play out the various groups against each other, thereby achieving for himself the position of a mediator. Interviews with ships' officers and subalterns furnish evidence of a tendency to emphasize this in-between character of their roles, with a concomitant legitimation to mediate. They feel, as it were "between the devil and the deep blue sea." This problem is a serious one for the bosun who is expected to deal with the crew as a *primus inter pares,* at the same time that he must uphold the authority needed to get the work done to satisfy the wishes of the chief officer and the captain. As other foremen, he attempts to deal with these conflicting demands by emphasizing to both groups, the crew and the commanding officers, that he is also under some pressure from the other party. By having both groups accept his argument, the most serious sources of role conflict may be eliminated. This type of solution of incipient role conflict is particularly suited to the situation of the politician, who invariably represents groups with partly competing interests. His success as a politician will in no small measure depend upon his ability to convince each group that it is mandatory for him to also pay some attention to the interests of others if he is going to have any chance of furthering their own specific interests.

The problems of the role set may, finally, be solved through specialization. A role is often divided into several new roles, each one catering to one of the specific groups upon which the role set is established. Naturally, such specialization is often called forth by the insufficiency of any one actor to be expert in the solution of all the tasks of one position. A contributory cause, however, is the presence of conflicts which originate in the role set. Such conflicts are apparent, for instance, in the emergence of new welfare functions within industry and in other institutions. The welfare officers are appointed to positions which enable them to contribute to the welfare of the employees and to take care of human problems in the organization, without interfering with the authoritarian and occupationally specific types of relationships which are considered necessary within the line of command proper. Thus, the new roles save the foremen, the engineers, and other managerial personnel from being entangled in conflicts between the demands of the firm and the humanely understandable expectations of the employees to obtain support, amelioration, and the occasional release from obligations. The medical doctor in a military camp, in a prison, or in an industrial plant may, likewise, fill a specialized function over and above the purely medical one, a function which would cause conflicts if the task were taken on by other managerial personnel.

Complementary roles

From the discussion of the role set it has emerged that little can be concluded concerning the way in which an actor will play his roles without some knowledge of his "opposite numbers." It is often more realistic to discuss *role pairs* than to discuss single roles. To each role corresponds one or more opposite roles. To mother corresponds child; to husband, wife; to doctor, patient; and to shopkeeper, customer. Social life is, from an important point of view, a network of role pairs and of the mutual expectations which govern these relationships.

This approach has some consequences which deviate from the way in which common sense would describe social interaction. The postulate that the tasks of the medical doctor have been organized into a role represents no fresh departure, but the claim that being a patient can be interpreted as the incumbency of a role is alien to everyday reasoning. Assuming tentatively, however, that the concept of role is applicable to this situation, specific social conditions have to be fulfilled before an actor may become accepted as a patient. Here, also, a question of recruitment arises, of what mechanisms admit some to occupancy of the role, while others are kept out as hypochondriacs, simulants, truants, or deserters. Once admitted to the role, a number of rights and duties result: the right to abstain from work and social intercourse, the right to receive care, comfort, and cure, and the permission to give vent to pain and helplessness. On the other side arise the obligations to be careful, to seek medical aid and listen to the doctor's advice to use medicine, to abstain from pleasures and amusements, and to try to get well.[7] Through hospitalization the entrance to the role is publicly announced; in other cases the announcement may be less explicit and possibly less convincing.

A similarly complementary approach may be taken to the role of the customer. To be a "good customer" has a certain socially recognized significance, bestowing some special rights upon the customer. But, quite generally, to be a customer is to assume a social role. It is, however, one so tenuously circumscribed that we would be unable to observe it were we not to consider it as but one element in a role pair, the sales clerk representing the other element. When does one enter the role of the customer? By walking into a shop? This is not always a sufficient condition for obtaining the full rights of the role, including time-consuming aid from the sales personnel in selecting potential commodities to buy. An actor may walk around in a shop, having been shown a certain amount of what it has for sale, while it becomes gradually more clear that he entertains no serious plans to purchase anything. One aspect of the training of the sales personnel is to learn the cues which make it possible to distinguish a prospective buyer from a mere browser, and especially from shoplifters. If the sales clerk has reached the conclusion that someone is not going to buy anything, he may gradually reciprocate by failing to grant the visitor to the shop the full service normally accorded to a customer. The cues, or announcements, involved in this process of disillusion and disengagement may be of a very subtle kind; they, nevertheless, represent a type of phenomenon which is ubiquitous in social life.

Inside the role pair there is a reciprocity in rights and obligations; from this follows a certain opportunity for variations of the role behavior. The norms of the roles are constituted by "if-then" expectations. If Alter strives hard and successfully to fill the demands of his role, it is incumbent upon Ego to reciprocate and do his best to conform. If Alter relaxes in his efforts to fill the role, Ego may also become less serious about compliance and reduce his performance correspondingly. This change is not, however, true of all role pairs. The degree of reciprocity, "the freedom of contract" as it were, may vary from one pair of roles to another. A mother cannot with impunity refrain from fulfilling her maternal duties just because the child does not play its role according to normal standards for children of its age. The parents find themselves in the situation of having to teach the children the very moral principle of reciprocity which later in life will influence all the role pairs in which they participate.

Through the role pair and the concept of reciprocity a formal similarity emerges between social life and games. This similarity has long been noted in a variety of contexts, with the implication that social norms have been likened to rules of the game. These are of two kinds: the *constituent* rules and the *strategic* rules. In chess there are two sets of norms which jointly determine each move. One set of norms is the one which Ego cannot violate without having Alter ask whether it is his intention, or not, to play chess. To the constituent norms belongs the rule that the bishops can only move along the diagonals, while the castles can only move along the parallels. The strategic norms are rules laid down about how to move in order to win the game within the framework of the constituent norms.[8]

In a rough way the distinction between constituent and strategic norms corresponds to the distinction between moral and "technical" norms. It is morally wrong, and it would injure his relationship with Alter, if Ego attempted to play a role for which he does not fulfill the minimum demands, as for example, by falsely pretending to be a doctor or attorney without having the proper training and license to practice. If he merely fails, however, within the framework of the accepted constituent norms to perform at the top level, and offers his client service inferior to that offered by the best people in his profession, such a failure may be ascribed to his lesser gifts, for which he is not to be blamed. Moral censure need not be incurred if the reduced performance on a professional's part can be reciprocated by a reduced fee, although a reduction of the fee may be perceived as a social sanction. The actor need not necessarily fear expulsion from his position, but he may feel under a social pressure to perform his role better according to the strategic norms of how success can be achieved in the game he is playing.

The role and the personality

The encounter between the role and the personality of the role-player is the common ground of sociology and psychology. It is often claimed that a certain position "suits" one person but not another one. Sometimes it is even claimed that someone is "born" for a certain position. Obviously, common sense assumes that it is possible to speak respectively about harmony or conflict between a role and a personality. Generally it may be hypothesized that a role suits a specific person if the fulfillment of the demands of the role and the reaping of its benefits satisfy him more fully than it would other actors with different personalities. Certain roles are, however, quite generally more gratifying than others, almost regardless of the personality of any particular incumbent. To be a well-paid business manager facilitates the satisfaction of basic human needs for housing, clothing, food, amusements, travel and education for the children more readily than does the role of hired hand on the railroads or the role of streetcleaner, almost regardless of the personality type of the incumbents. Obversely, it may be possible to single out certain personality types who encounter difficulties in attempts to fill roles almost regardless of the roles involved. It is common practice today to keep certain personality types out of certain roles, for example, in the military. The whole field of aptitude testing and vocational guidance aims in a certain sense at determining the relationship between personality traits and roles.

Conformity between personality and role might in part arise because certain personality types are attracted to, or selected for, roles which fit them. The conformity is here due to the recruitment. But the congruence between role and personality may also be due to the shaping and modifying of the personality by the role incumbency to make the actor better adjusted to the demands of the role. Studies of occupants of certain social positions, like those of creative scientists or artists, suggest that these roles attract recruits with special characteristics, not only in terms of aptitudes and intelligence, but also with respect to emotional character.[9] On the other hand, claims have been made that bureaucratic roles in the long run move the individual incumbents towards a "bureaucratic personality."[10]

The available knowledge concerning the relationship between personalities and roles is still tenuous and preliminary. Regarding the recruitment of selected personality types for certain roles, we should bear in mind that occupational choice rarely is based upon exact knowledge of, or acquaintance with, how the role looks as seen from the inside. The wide discrepancy between the appearance of a role to the outsider and the realities of life for those who are in it is nowhere more apparent than in the role of the seaman. A discrepancy of this sort may account for the very large turnover in this occupation.[11] If the adjustment between roles and personalities were to be facilitated through the mechanisms of recruitment, it would have to take place as a consequence of trial periods in different occupations, enabling Ego to experience in practice the demands made by a set of alternative work roles. However, the extensive periods of education or apprenticeship which now are a prerequisite to entering many occupations reduce the opportunities for such experimentation.

It is doubtful to what extent a personality is being shaped by roles. As many psychologists use the term "personality," it covers precisely those profound and stable traits which have been formed in early childhood and which may even to some extent inhere in the biological equipment of the actor. If we have reason to deduce that a role shapes a personality, it must be due to some evidence that the incumbent *generally* displays the traits required by his position when he acts outside of the role also. Thus, an employee of the railroads, a stationmaster, may as a consequence of his occupational duties become such a slave to time and the watch that his pedantry permeates his whole life, encompassing also his relationship with his wife. Or it may be a teacher who can never stop treating others, family, friends and casual acquaintances as pupils, or the physician who treats everybody as a potential or actual patient. Not infrequently it may be observed that the personality of someone who has been appointed to a responsible position develops in step with the increasing demands of the new role.

We have dealt with the relationship between the role and the personality as if the personality, excepting the mechanisms of recruitment, is merely passive and adaptable to the demands of the role. It may seem that conflicts between the role and the personality must lead to the compliance of the personality or to the personality paying the price if harmony is not achieved. But this is not always, maybe not even generally, an accurate description of what takes place. The personality may actively contribute to form the role, especially if the role is new, or if the social system which

56

embodies the role is a small one like the family. Roles which are surrounded by much formality and publicity may also take shape according to the personality of the incumbent, to a smaller or larger extent. We may consider the very different flavor of the American presidency under three consecutive presidents like Eisenhower, Kennedy, and Johnson. This observation brings us to the question of whether the "same" role in different societies may exhibit variations because they are filled with actors who tend to have somewhat different personality types. Such an inference is derived from "national character" which distinguishes members of different societies from each other.[12]

The self and the social identity

George Herbert Mead, more than anyone else, has pioneered a theory of the social self. Mead depicts the self as something clearly distinguishable from the physiological organism; the self is an entity with a development. It was not there at birth, but has grown on the basis of social experiences. A body may function intelligently, like many animals, without reasonably imputing a self to it. "The self has the characteristic that it is an object to itself, and that characteristic distinguishes it from other objects and from the body." [13] It follows from the reflexive nature of the term "self" that it points to something which is simultaneously an object and a subject. The term implies that Ego may experience Ego. The self is something being perceived, just as material objects in the environment or other actors may be perceived.

Situations may occur in which Ego is unaware of Ego because he is wholly absorbed by a demanding external situation, like one where he spontaneously flees under the threat of an imminent danger. All conscious attention seems to be caught by the threatening situation and by choosing the proper means to escape from it. However, even from situations of grave threat to the actor's life, we get reports that the previous life of the actor passed like a cavalcade through his memory and inner vision. Under such extreme circumstances a self-perception also seems to lie in readiness, a conception of who one is, not immediately connected with the external situation. In many situations it is, of course, blatantly obvious that the actor is consciously preoccupied with his self and concerned about how it appears to others.

Mead raised the issue of how the subject, Ego, gains the perspective which enables him to perceive Ego as an object. His answer is that we learn through the eyes of others.

> The individual experiences himself as such, not directly, but only indirectly, from the particular standpoints of other individual members of the same social group, or from the generalized standpoint of the social group as a whole to which he belongs. For he enters his own experience as a self or individual, not directly or immediately, not by becoming a subject to himself, but only in so far as he first becomes an object to himself just as other individuals are objects to him or in his experience; and he becomes an object to himself only by taking the attitudes of other individuals toward himself within a social environment or context of experience and behavior in which both he and they are involved.[14]

Without a social environment no self can arise. Even if a mature individual has developed definite conceptions of the self, extended isolation may threaten to disturb or destroy the perceptions of the self because they find no confirmation in the environment. A famous refugee from the Germans during World War II tells of his lying in a snow-covered igloo on the Arctic plateau near the border between Sweden and Norway: "I am Jan Baalsrud. I have a father and a sister. I . . . ." etc.[15] The episode presents an example of how the self, the sense of identity, may be so weakened through isolation and the absence of external stimuli that extraordinary efforts are required in order to retain and protect the conception of self.

Through experiments with individuals submerged in water of body temperature, from which all noise and light has been kept out, the physiologist Lilly has created a state of extreme sensory deprivation, of poverty of stimuli. Ego receives no "messages" from the environment. Under such conditions grave psychic disturbances may arise after a relatively short lapse of time, disturbances which must properly be described as a partial and temporary dissolution of the Ego and of the perception of the self.[16]

From the point of view of Ego, the self can be construed as a *personal role*. It is the sum total of the expectations Ego has of himself, not because he is an office clerk, a grandfather, or a member of the golf club, but because he possesses all these characteristics and many more. The personal role is made up of all the expectations Ego entertains of himself because he happens to be the unique person he is. He may, of course, come to anchor this perception of the self very heavily in a single, and commonly applicable, criterion, like sex and occupation. Other qualities will, however, always contribute with a coloring of the self-perception because Ego has a need to experience himself as something unique, something which is not wholly replaceable by anybody else.

The *social identity* may be defined as the self seen from the environment, as the actor's personal role expressed through the expectations of others to him. From this point of view the expectations may be more or less firmly tied to simple, universal criteria such as age and sex. However, the environment also has a need, occasionally, at least, to distinguish Ego from everybody else and to treat him as unique.

It is a widespread belief that the self, as well as the social identity, has become problematical in modern times in a way which cannot be compared to similar phenomena in the old rural and agrarian society. This must somehow be related to the characteristics of those social mirrors by which we see ourselves, and which thereby influence the perception of self. Diverse and changing reference groups blur the image in the mirror and make it contradictory. A gap may arise between the subjective self and the outwardly defined social identity. Society may look upon the actor as a clerk in the office of internal revenue, while he, on his part, comes more and more to define himself as an amateur musician or as a bird watcher with membership in a club of ornithologists. In these roles he finds an opportunity, subjectively, to express his own perception of who he "really" is. His real self may even be defined precisely by the contrast to the external social identity. Behind the mask he lives his own secret life.[17]

Mead claimed that the perceptions others have of us form the basis of the perceptions of self. Ego's perception of self is determined by Alter's perceptions of him, but which one of the many available

Altera? Those norm senders who possess the greatest strength will in the long run most decisively influence the individual's perception of himself. However, the development of the self is a very complex process. Mead emphasized the great significance of what he termed "the generalized Other." [18] Based upon experiences with specific Altera, Ego builds up a general picture of a more abstract Alter, "the others." The generalized Other is the mirror in which Ego views himself. The generalized Other may be anchored in one person, for example, one of the parents, in a primary group, an organization, or in a reference group.

The phenomena dealt with by Mead are closely parallel, possibly identical to, those which we have discussed under the heading "internalization of norms." Norms which originally appear as external pressures and expectations from others become a part of—are being internalized in—Ego's personality. The external demands are gradually transformed into demands which Ego makes upon himself. Ego develops expectations, notions of what he is actually like, notions of what he ought to do, or of whom he ought to be. In order to understand the functions of social norms it is important to know whether they have been internalized or whether they exert their influence solely through external sanctions. This distinction has, for example, played a great part in the analysis of the social functions of legal rules and punishment. Some legal rules and some penalties may exert an influence merely by making it credible that crime doesn't pay, while other rules and other penalties may activate internalized norms in the audience, and thus have an effect which transcends pure deterrence.[19]

Sanctions against the perception of self

Sanctions can be of many different kinds. In debates on the use of penalties in the family and in school, and on imprisonment, the focus is usually how Alter may use his control of Ego's access to resources to influence his conduct. In this context, however, we will deal with a different type of sanction which is of great importance but not always so easily understood. Through his actions and demeanor Alter may to a larger or smaller extent, depending upon the relationship between Alter and Ego, influence Ego's self-perception, support it, weaken it, or at times possibly even destroy it. This opportunity of sanction follows from our general assumptions concerning the origin of the self and the mechanisms of preserving it.

Just as Ego may exhibit a certain type of conduct in order to convince himself and others that he is the kind of person he would like to be, so Alter may act in a way which signifies a certain image of Ego. If Ego's perception of self is threatened, as may be the case if he is accosted by the police, he may retort to this challenge with actions designed to show that his own perception of self is, after all, the correct one. Conversely, if Ego receives the strong support of his self-perception, he may afford to discard some of those actions which he would otherwise use to bolster the self. But, of course, the sanctions from the environment are not solely met by counter-moves and attempts to protect and preserve the self. Under some conditions the self-perceptions are changed by the pressure of the environment, as they were once formed by the influence of others.

Sanctions which aim consciously and systematically at the perception of self can be found in religious and political ceremonies of conversion where confessions of guilt and subsequent redemption are key events. By seeing himself as he really is, weak and sinful, and through the admission of his offenses, Ego is reshaped in the desired direction. Modern psychotherapy has, likewise, an element directed at the reconstruction of self which may imply the partial destruction of the old self. Considering the vital significance of self-perceptions to the actor, it is obvious that the possibility of disturbing an established self or a social identity may constitute one of the most forceful mechanisms of social control.

Two points ought to be stressed in the present context. The first one is that sanctions, in order to have motivating force, must be adjusted to the existing self-perceptions. Assuming that Sutherland has accurately summarized the self-perception of the professional thief in the United States, his self is not likely to be vulnerable to imprisonment unless the incarceration is due to the stupidity or clumsiness of the inmate. The professional thief conceives of himself as a criminal, and his self-perception is merely confirmed by the verdict and by the imprisonment.[20] The efficiency of the threat of penalties will in this case depend upon what other satisfactions the criminal is being deprived of if caught and punished. The situation is probably different if an ordinary citizen is brought before the courts on a charge of drunken driving and is being sentenced to a fine or a brief prison term. This verdict may effect his self-perception, because the person customarily regards himself as a good, law-abiding citizen. The ensuing wound to his self-perception is probably a more decisive consequence of the penalty than are the frustrations of material needs which may result from a brief term in prison. However, the reactions to the challenge against previous self-perceptions may be various, ranging from a stubborn conviction of having been unjustly sentenced to a humble admission of having been surprisingly irresponsible and an eagerness to atone for the offense.

This leads to the second point which needs stressing in this context: According to some psychological findings an irrational and frustration-instigated response is most likely to occur when the sanctions are being perceived by Ego as a threat to his self.[21] Instead of motivating Ego to avoid the kind of behavior which released the sanction, such penalties release a response aimed at restoring or protecting the vulnerable self. A boy may have committed an aggressive and daring offense in order to show off and to demonstrate his independence of any authority. A threat of sanction, or the actual enforcement of a penalty, may constitute a threat against his belief in his own courage and independence, while also offering an occasion to demonstrate anew that he possesses precisely these precious qualities. He may want to comply with the rules in order not to lose privileges of a practical kind, but he can afford even less to suffer a blemish upon his self-image than to miss certain material privileges. The boy must persist in the delinquent behavior pattern in order to protect and preserve his self rather than behave to avoid the penalty or to minimize its consequences. He has to ignore the dangers, and may even be under some compulsion to provoke sanctions, in order to establish a test case where his self-image, even more than he, is on trial, and where he has the chance to show that he is indeed indomitable and fearless.

On acting and being

Self-perceptions are among those factors which form the basis of social action. When acting, Ego is prompted by a motive to demonstrate who he is and to show that he is living up to the expectations which others have of him. Put in its extreme form, this motive would imply that social life is a theatrical play on the great stage of social reality. Some sociologists have chosen to cultivate precisely this aspect of social interaction. Goffman introduces his analysis of the presentation of self by announcing that he is going to treat social life from a dramaturgical point of view.

> The perspective employed in this report is that of the theatrical performance; the principles derived are dramaturgical ones. I shall consider the way in which the individual in ordinary work situations presents himself and his activity to others, the ways in which he guides and controls the impression they form of him, and the kinds of things he may and may not do while sustaining his performance before them. In using this model I will attempt not to make light of its obvious inadequacies. The stage presents things that are make-believe; presumably life presents things that are real and sometimes not well rehearsed. More important, perhaps, on the stage one player presents himself in the guise of a character to characters projected by other players; the audience constitutes a third party to the interaction—one that is essential and yet, if the stage performance were real, one that would not be there. In real life, the three parties are compressed into two; the part one individual plays is tailored to the parts played by the others present, and yet these others also constitute the audience.[22]

Goffman's point of departure is that interacting individuals must possess some guidance for mutual predictability. They need information on *who* Alter is. Many of those traits in others which affect us most decisively, like their reliability, responsibility, ability, and their real feelings towards us, are not immediately observable. We have to make inferences about these qualities from the more obviously available criteria. The meanings which are attributed to external forms and modes of conduct constitute an important key to the understanding of social interaction. Through the established relationships of meaning between signs and underlying states Ego may, consciously or unconsciously, present himself as the one he wants to be taken to be. Thus, by dressing in a certain way, he may convey the impression of being wealthy, sporty, bohemian, conservative, or eccentric. Through choice of language, demeanor, ways of moving, the actor may create an impression of the underlying "real self" which is of such vital concern to those Altera with whom Ego deals in important matters.

> Society is organized on the principle that any individual who possesses certain social characteristics has a moral right to expect that others will value and treat him in an appropriate way. Connected with this principle is a second, namely, that an individual who implicitly or explicitly signifies that he has certain social characteristics ought in fact to be what he claims he is. In consequence, when an individual projects a definition of the situation and thereby makes an implicit or explicit claim to be a person of a particular kind, he automatically exerts a moral demand upon the others, obliging them to value and treat him in the manner that persons of his kind have a right to expect. He also implicitly forgoes all the claims to be things he does not appear to be and hence forgoes the treatment that would be appropriate for such individuals. The others find, then, that the individual has informed them as to what is and as to what they *ought* to see as the "is." [23]

Goffman's approach yields important insights into one significant aspect of social situations. But it is a stylized and simplified view of human behavior which can make no claim to be universally applicable or to encompass all aspects of social interaction, as the author himself is well aware. When Ego interacts with Alter, he may be simultaneously prompted by many motives, of which one is to show Alter who Ego is and wants to be taken for. The guest in a restaurant may wish to show the waiter and the other guests that he is a certain kind of person, a person who expects to receive prompt and good service as his due right. But he may also be in a hurry or terribly hungry and thirsty and, as a consequence of this, particularly impatient with any delay in the kitchen or on the waiter's part. If the guest presents himself as a certain kind of person, he may conceivably speed up the serving of the meal, but it is difficult to disentangle the need for food and drink from the purely social needs which are exhibited, and possibly satisfied, in the encounter between guests and waiter.

It is not easy to distinguish between those situations where Ego plays a role in the dramaturgical sense, and those where he is being himself, either oblivious to the way he presents himself to others or unconcerned with manipulating the impressions others have gained of him. The term role-playing is used by sociologists in both types of situations as long as there are norms associated with the position in which Ego finds himself. The determination of the borderline between "being" and "acting" would probably in general be considered a philosophical problem, falling outside the proper confines of sociology. However, it may well be that sociology, precisely through systematic investigations of this aspect of human interaction, may offer a new contribution to an understanding of what man is.

IV

THE

SOCIAL SYSTEM

LET US assume that we are visiting on board an empty ship in a harbor. Looking around we observe a number of cabins, each one of them furnished with a title, but no name above the door. There seems to be some order or system in the way the cabins are located and equipped. The titles of officers are only found above doors amidship, while the crew titles are assembled aft. The cabins are graded with respect to size and furniture, closely connected with the ranks and functions associated with the titles. The captain has the largest and best-furnished cabin, followed by the chief officer's and the chief engineer's quarters. Low-grade junior personnel are assigned the smallest and most simply furnished cabins, located in those quarters where there is most noise and movement.

Such observations on board a ship give us an impression of having viewed the physical model of a social structure. It would have become even clearer had we simultaneously studied the organizational blueprint of the ship, the contracts with the crew, and the payroll. This study would reveal how closely the location of the officers and the crew conform to the pattern of distribution of other privileges, tasks, and responsibilities on board. It is feasible to form a relatively clear conception of the social system of the ship even on board an empty vessel. The social system is not a network of persons; it is primarily a *set of roles between which reciprocally defined relationships obtain.* We may describe the social system of a ship without describing any one crew aboard any one vessel. Moving from one empty ship to another in a harbor, we should have been struck by the similarity of structure.

In the preceding chapters a simple relationship between Ego and Alter provided a model which was elaborated. However, the relationship between Ego and Alter, the role pair, is nothing but a special case of a more general phenomenon: the social system. The social system is built up on the basis of role pairs and of social roles quite generally. In the discussion of the social self, it was suggested that there are limits to how far we may treat social life as role-playing. It does not seem feasible to analyze all aspects of social life simply by a description of the network of roles within a social system. Although the role structure on board ships of the same class is fairly uniform, considerable differences between individual ships are recognized by the seamen, as well as by company representatives. There exist dissimilarities in style with respect to atmosphere on board and the degree of satisfaction experienced by the crew. The style on board may be heavily influenced by a single person, by the skipper, the mate, the bosun, or even by an outstanding character among the crew. It may also be determined by examining the ship's environmental and physical factors: is the ship trafficking in tropical waters, is it a tanker which almost never is in harbor, or is it a passenger ship paying regular visits to the home country?

It may be useful to return for a moment to the distinction previously made between constituent and strategic norms. Suppose that two ships have an identical role structure and that the personnel on board both ships fill the minimum demands required, that is, that they play their roles in conformity with the constituent norms. Everybody on board each of the two ships behaves like seamen in the positions to which they have been allocated. Nevertheless, as it turns out, the atmosphere on board one ship has become quite different from that on the other. The difference might be due to the fact that some role incumbent on one of them pursues different strategies from those of a colleague of the same rank on the other ship. It is possible that the bosun on board the first ship followed strategic norms derived from a strong orientation towards the crew and tried to satisfy the able-bodied seamen with whom he is in daily association. His colleague, on the other ship, may have followed a strategy which aimed more at satisfying the demands of his superiors and the company, even at the cost of friction with his men. These discrepant strategies might have wider consequences affecting social relations on board the two ships and causing appreciable differences in atmosphere, although the bosun in both cases played his role within the broad confines of the constituent norms for bosuns.[1]

Roles make room for variations in behavior. Within their framework differing approaches may be developed, determined by variations in goals and motivations, as well as by differing skills. An analysis of social systems cannot omit the occurrence of systematic choice behavior within the framework of the role, even though this may preclude a rigorous application of the concept of a social system as a network of social roles and nothing more. The social system is also a system of action and a network of interaction, in part determined by the demands and permissions of established roles, in part determined by strategic choice.

Contributions and sanctions

Social interaction in a role pair is governed by a principle of *reciprocity*. According to the norms of social life Ego is entitled, as well as obliged, to adjust his behavior to Alter's conduct. If the employee, without due cause, discontinues to play his role as employee by staying away from the job without permission, for example, the employer may then disengage himself from his duties as employer. Conversely, if the employer has deviated from his role by discontinuing payments to the employees, the employees may disengage themselves from their role and quit the job. This interaction implies that we consider social behavior as an *exchange* of *contributions* and *sanctions*. Ego contributes with an action, to which a certain type of reaction on Alter's behalf corresponds.

In economics a similar interaction occurs. To a certain commodity, service, or amount of work corresponds a certain price or wage. In some cases the terms of exchange are set by a superordinate authority, like the setting of prices of train tickets within a state-operated railway system, or generally in periods of price controls.

In other instances the price may be a matter of unrestricted bargaining, permitting wide variations for accommodating the needs of the buyer and seller, such as a prospective buyer negotiating with a contractor for a new home.

Sociology also applies this approach to contributions which have no price or remuneration in a market and to sanctions which cannot be meted out in dollars and cents. Certain forms of courtesy illustrate this. For example, Ego's polite manner of greeting Alter should be reciprocated by Alter's polite response. If Alter fails to respond in kind, something is wrong.

From a sociological point of view all social interaction may be regarded as transactions involving contributions and sanctions. All relationships between an Ego and an Alter may be considered as instances of an exchange.[2] In its primordial form the relationship of exchange may consist in no more than Ego's obtaining Alter's company in return for offering Alter his own. For both of them, to be in someone's company may have value per se, and especially if the two are forced to pass in darkness through unsafe territory. Conversation and the interchange of opinions may likewise be regarded as exchanges. Messages sent by Ego correspond to certain returning messages from Alter and vice versa. Conversations lose their meaning and become absurd when the demands to a correspondence between contributions and sanctions fail to be met: for example, if Alter does not respond to Ego's question, but responds as if another question were asked; or if Ego changes the subject abruptly, or fails to complete sentences, or laughs in the wrong places, or reacts strangely.

The distinction between contributions and sanctions is a purely relative one, depending upon their location in a sequence of exchange. Social exchange is a feedback process. Ego's contribution is converted into a response from Alter, which returns to, and impinges upon, Ego. Therefore, social interaction is to some extent self-correcting. If Ego has asked a "silly" question, Alter may, more or less subtly, make him aware of the fact, thereby enabling Ego to ask a more intelligent question.

Let us suppose that a certain employer has issued an order which causes much dissatisfaction among his employees. When he learns of the reaction to this order, he may be dissuaded from enforcing his order in its original form, he may withdraw the order, or, contrarily, he may increase the threat of sanctions if his order is not obeyed. The dynamic element in social life consists of such sequences of interchange which are often composed of long series of consecutive contributions and sanctions and which may be difficult to describe.

Social control

By sanctions in the narrow sense, we refer to Ego's actions which are apt to influence Alter's future conduct because of their capacity to satisfy or deter him. It may be natural, however, to widen the concept somewhat and also define as sanctions Ego's reactions which aim towards influencing Alter's behavior, even if they fail to achieve the desired conformity. We may, actually, distinguish between three types of sanctions: those which aim successfully at influencing Alter's behavior; those which unsuccessfully aim at the same result; and, finally, those actions which, without specifically aiming towards influencing Alter, nevertheless have his conformity as a consequence. The process which is being instigated when sanctions are applied may be termed "social control."

A sanction, whether it be a term in prison or a mere shift of facial expression, appears subsequent to the sanctioned behavior. Sanctions, however, also make their impact prior to the choice of conduct in the form of threats and promises. Threats and promises of sanctions may be perceived due to a generalization from many single instances of previous sanctions. These have prompted Ego to expect sanctions when he is doing something which has previously been met with a sanction. However, social control may also be exerted because Alter has sent a general norm containing a threat or a promise to apply sanctions under certain specified circumstances. Normally, our expectations with respect to sanctions derive from an interplay between the perception of general norms and the observation of concrete instances of norm enforcement.

One may speak about positive and negative sanctions, about *rewards* and *penalties*. These are, however, relative concepts. What Ego in a specific situation perceives as a threatening penalty depends upon what alternative courses of development he might expect. In a report on young recidivist offenders, a psychiatrist quotes an inmate who claimed that he liked his stay in prison because there was more work and better food than he was used to.[3] He did not experience the imprisonment as a penalty in the full sense of the term—that is, if we are to take his words at their face value. It was frequently claimed in England during the nineteenth century that deportation, at the time a common penalty, constituted no great threat to the criminals. To many of them deportation to Australia would imply a change for the better, not for the worse. We must, consequently, distinguish clearly between a psychological concept of punishment, implying a sanction which is experienced as a deprivation and a threat, and the more formal concept of penalty as defined by society. This is not to deny that the two, as a general rule, tend to coincide rather nicely.[4] Similar reasoning may be applied to the rewards, distinguishing between what is felt as satisfying and rewarding, and what is outwardly defined as a privilege or an honor.

In principle the implications of sanctions for interaction between Ego and Alter are simple enough. In real social situations, however, their functioning may be difficult to disentangle. We do not deal with a clearly circumscribed class of reactions from the environment which, by virtue of a definite set of characteristics, either necessarily encourage or deter Ego. Ego's background influences decisively how he perceives the sanctions and the motivating impact they will have. The importance of background influences offer one reason why promise of reward or threat of punishment so often remains ineffectual, or even exerts an influence contrary to Alter's intentions. Some important limitations exist to the general validity of the pleasure principle which are of crucial relevance to the sociological problem of sanctions.

Conformity and deviance

When presenting Ego's action as a response to Alter's expectations and sanctions, we use the terms "conformity" and "deviance." Conformity implies that Ego's action fulfills Alter's expectation, while deviance implies that Ego's action fails to fulfill Alter's expectation. In a contractual relationship we may speak about conformity if Ego fulfills his obligations, if he pays his incurred debt, or delivers the goods as stipulated by the terms of the sales contract. In a contractual relationship non-delivery is an example of deviance. In criminal law normal law-abiding behavior constitutes conformity, while the criminal offense is an instance of deviance.

Conformity is a certain type of logical relationship between expectations and the response to expectations. It is parallel to the relationship which must obtain between a scientific proposition and certain specified factual conditions in order for the proposition to be true. Alter's expectations contain references to facts, namely, to some aspect of Ego's future behavior. The wife, expecting her husband home for dinner, makes daily predictions concerning his future behavior. The husband, on his side, is aware that she makes these assumptions. Conformity characterizes his conduct if his behavior makes the assumptions and predictions come true. One difference between these expectations and a scientific hypothesis is that the wife probably feels that her husband *ought* to be home in time for dinner, not simply that he is likely to turn up. Social expectations may be predictions, imperatives, or both.

There is another important difference between social expectations and most scientific predictions. While the truth of scientific predictions are rarely influenced by the presence of the hypothesis as such, conformity with social expectations is normally caused precisely by the presence of these expectations as psychological facts. Social expectations can often be described as self-fulfilling prophecies,[5] supported by sanctions. This means that there exist two types of relationship between Alter's expectations and Ego's compliance: a logical conformity of behavior to norms and a causal relationship between the expression of the norm and the compliant action. It is worth noting that the two need not always accompany each other. Many people behave in abeyance of laws without having been influenced by the expectations of the legislators or by the sanctions meted out by the law-enforcing agencies. Conversely, some people show non-compliance as a consequence of the influence from the threat of sanctions. They want to demonstrate their independence or they want to obstruct or sabotage laws they don't like.

Deviance takes place whenever Alter's expectations remain unfulfilled in Ego's behavior. Here also it is possible to discern a parallel to the testing of scientific hypotheses. However, the relationship between norms and deviant acts must be compared to scientific propositions which are not corroborated by the facts. One is less apt to seek for a causal influence between Alter's expectations and Ego's deviation. The causal explanations of deviance are usually sought in entirely different factors, which operate in spite of, not because of, the presence of norms and sanctions. However, normative demands and the threat of sanctions may at times provoke deviance.

Deviance is not always detected, and this is one reason why many deviations are free of sanctions. Detection is particularly difficult when Ego and Alter interact at some distance as in the relationship between the citizen and some agencies of law enforcement. A very large proportion of all criminal offenses remain undetected, and only a small percentage of actual crimes are met with a formal legal sanction.[6] The Kinsey report showed that infractions of sexual laws occur very frequently, while only a small minority of these deviant acts come to the attention of the police and the courts. Figures on shoplifting and tax evasion, likewise, show great discrepancies between the actual occurrence of illegal acts and the number of prosecuted crimes. Since few are prosecuted for behavior in which many are engaged, there arises a question of selectivity in the enforcement of norms. Probably, the respectable citizen with a good job and a fair income stands a good chance of avoiding prosecution for some offenses which would be quickly detected and prosecuted if committed by an old acquaintance of the police. Embezzlement trials often reveal that the respectable status of the offender for long periods may have served as a shield against suspicion, detection, or prosecution.

The problems of conformity and deviance take different forms, depending upon the type of social norms through which Alter's expectations are expressed. We have previously used a distinction between permissions, prohibitions, and demands (see p. 22). Since

73

permissions may be viewed as the absence of prohibitions as well as of demands, it is the distinction between the latter two concepts which is of concern in this context. The claim that Ego's conduct conforms to Alter's expectation makes most sense when Alter has voiced a demand, such as the economic fulfillment of a contractual obligation. To conform is to positively do what is required, like paying a debt on time. We encounter some difficulties with regard to the prohibitions because they do not always specify to what situations and to which actors they apply. This subject will be dealt with in Chapter VI.

System borders

In the preceding section certain elements of social systems have been discussed. But how can we go about determining that an entity is a social system and no mere part of a larger social system or a composite of many smaller systems? Where is the borderline between a social system and its environment? One general answer to this kind of query would be that a borderline is recognized by the fact that the frequency and/or intensity of social interaction is reduced or disappears as we move from the central parts of the system and approach the borders. The border of the ship's social system is fairly clear as long as it is at sea. Interaction is dense and often intensive between the personnel on board. Between the crew and the rest of the world there is no other daily interaction than the trickle of messages passing to and from the radio officer's keyboard. The density of social interaction is drastically reduced when the border of the ship has to be crossed, the border being physically represented by the rail and the ship's side.

More doubts may arise in the attempt to demarcate territorially determined social systems, that is, units of settlement. Is a municipality or a county a social system? There is often more interaction within the municipality than across the municipal borders. For example, most marriages and most movements may take place inside the municipality. However, some parts of the municipality may be so located as to make interaction with the population of the neighboring municipality more facile, and consequently more frequent. This points to the relativity of any delineation of social systems. The density of interaction may decrease near the border, but not sharply and not uniformly. True, some types of interaction will be clearly and formally limited to the municipality. Taxes are paid to one's own municipality and not to the neighboring one, and voting rights are likewise restricted to the home community. Consequently we may say that the municipality constitutes a clear-cut social system with respect to some functionally specific activities. But it does not normally constitute a social system in the more general sense of setting up barriers to any kind of interaction, as the ship at sea tends to do.

A ship, as well as a municipality, is part of larger social units, of more inclusive social systems. The ship is a part of the shipping company, of the national merchant marine, and of the country where it is registered, although the latter kind of membership may be of a highly specific and limited kind. The municipality is a part of a county and of a nation, which also constitute social systems. It is, on the whole, characteristic of social life that it seems to be located inside a set of Chinese drawers, composed of systems within systems.[7] The actor's conduct is alternatingly to be interpreted with respect to his membership in the nearest system and to his simultaneous membership in more inclusive social systems. The ordering of systems within systems provides an eternal basis of role conflicts. Is a man to behave merely as a good provider of his family when making his yearly tax declaration, or is he also to be a good and thoroughly law-abiding citizen and member of the national system when doing so?

The borders of a system are determined by a variety of factors. At times they are created by the exigencies of geography, as is the case in remote districts of a modern industrialized nation where daily interaction is restricted to a tiny hamlet. Nevertheless, the behavior of the population would be incomprehensible without taking into account the ties to the more inclusive national society. There is more that binds people to the inclusive system than divides them from it. The isolated hamlets are far from self-sufficient, economically or culturally. They receive the basic necessities to a very large extent from the outside, and they often sell their products on an international market. Radio and the printed word bring a world-wide culture into their homes, and their children are educated by teachers who grew up and were trained outside the small social system. Patterns of interaction across the old system border would rapidly increase if a road connected such a hamlet to the outside world. In these cases the *geographical distance* between the systems is considerable, while the *structural distance* which will be discussed below, sometimes may be negligible. The actual frequency of interaction with the outside environment is very low, but the readiness for such interaction is high.

The situation is quite different if we observe small hamlets or villages of Maya Indians in southern Mexico. Some of these Indians live at a great distance, geographically, from the cities representing the centers of the inclusive social system. Studies have shown, however, that the very noticeable social distance between these small systems and the Mexican society with its urban population depends upon factors other than the dispersal of the settlements and the physical obstacles to interaction. Instances are recorded of Indian tribes living for centuries in villages a few miles from a Mexican city, and tribesmen regularly selling their products on the city market, without much ensuing influence upon the tribal culture and internal role structure.[8]

The structural distance cannot be measured by geographic factors, nor can it be gauged from density of interaction alone. The structural distance can be revealed only by a study of the mutual attitudes between the two population segments and by determining the significance which the norms entertained by one of the groups has had for the development of the role structure in the other one. Such studies reveal that the structure of roles and the recruitment of positions within each one of the two sets of systems have been surprisingly autonomous. The borders have been physically permeable to a much larger extent than they have been permeated by the social norms of the neighboring group.

Hamlets and villages are spontaneously created social systems, having developed through a gradual process, usually without a definite date of foundation and without a specific purpose. The hamlets and villages *are* there, and the young are born into them as members. The ship, which is also characterized by territorial borders is, on the other hand, built and manned with a definite purpose, and the crew has consciously chosen to become members of the system. The borders of the system are determined by a patterned network of roles so designed as to make the incumbents jointly participate in a productive task. The lack of interaction between crew and environment is physically determined and need not imply any great structural distance. If the opportunities for contact were better, more interaction would result.

In observing many types of social systems the geographical or ecological points of view would not lead us very far towards a map of the borders of the systems. The ship is an extreme case, similar to a prison, a cloister, a psychiatric hospital, or a boarding school; all of them occupy a relatively well-defined territory. In many cases where the system is established as a role structure designed to fill a specified task, the physical borders are more blurred. They are still fairly clear if we consider a factory or a school. However, a trade union, a political party, or a legal system has no clear territorial localization, although some influential members of these systems are located at certain office addresses. They constitute, nevertheless, social systems in so far as they have a role structure established to fill a task. Interaction between members is more frequent and/or has a more important character in relation to the system's purpose than does interaction with non-members. But the presence of a formal structure does not always imply that it represents a system in a socially meaningful sense. A determination of the borderlines of a social system is often the end product of a study rather than a foregone conclusion.

Fusion and fission

Flying over great plains and watching settlements from above, one is reminded of patterns of iron filings exposed to the forces of a magnetic field. One may observe dense and diluted zones. In some places it is as if a social magnet had pulled the population together in a mass. Other areas show large empty stretches, as if negative forces had pushed the population away from invisible borders. Were we able to visualize a "social landscape" independent of physical geography, but following definitions of what is up and down in society, and what is inside and outside groups, we should also recognize this tendency to clustering and dispersal. It is as if everywhere there were simultaneously forces of cohesion and of dissolution in operation. Fusion and fission are ubiquitous phenomena.[9]

A great deal of that influence for order which is due to fusion and fission may be traced to the interplay between three factors: *proximity, equality,* and *complementarity.* Proximity is a geographical concept, one which pertains to spatial arrangements. It implies quite simply the physical opportunity of interaction between Ego and Alter. Equality means that Ego and Alter share likes or dislikes and/or that they have roughly the same chances of obtaining something which they both value, like money or independence. Complementarity does not necessarily imply that Ego and Alter share value assumptions or that they have equal access to values. But it means that there is a communality of interests between them;[10] they need each other, often because they are unequal, as the case may be with the employer and his employee. Based on the state in which these three factors are found, hypotheses may be developed concerning fusion and fission in social life, and predictions may be made concerning the emergence of social systems, the coalescence of systems, and their dissolution.

Let us take as a point of departure that the proximity of the neighbors in a local rural community may induce certain kinds of equality. A shared world of symbols emerges as a consequence of mutual identification and communication, as well as of similar economic opportunities. Parallel to this process of fusion, however, a differentiation of roles may take place. There is a need for a division of labor among those who live close to each other. A certain amount of specialization and complementarity is a consequence of this need, as, for example, in the person of the local schoolteacher, the storekeeper or agronomist; consequently specialization and complementarity may introduce a source of inequality and fission in the local community.

Let us now take an existing state of equality as our starting point, as, for example, a number of individuals with roughly similar incomes, power, prestige, style of life and attitudes on many issues, but who are territorially dispersed. As time passes we may observe that these people are brought geographically together in a highly priced residential district. Equality has induced proximity. New interaction patterns may emerge within the residential district. For most of the residents, however, the chances are that the complementary relationships to other actors outside the district, to their employees, their customers or business associates, will remain more important than the newly established neighborly relations. It is unlikely that the proximity will induce further differentiation and specialization within the neighborhood. The residents can satisfy their highly diversified needs through their exchange with the larger society outside the residential district.

Let us finally assume an initial complementarity of needs and personnel. This can most visibly be observed where a pioneer community grows up around one single new industry, like a power plant or a mine. The first projected plans tend to attract manpower with diversified skills. Without the prior existence of a specialized society which furnished a basis for the growth of a profession of engineering and of skilled workers, the project could not have been launched; the growing community, with its concomitant new patterns of proximity, could not have arisen. Before the work starts, shopkeepers and various types of service personnel will be attracted to the emergent community to become the neighbors of the workers and the engineers. They are attracted to the place, not because they are like the engineers or the workers, but precisely because they are different in one vital respect which creates an opportunity for mutual need-satisfaction. The workers are interested in consuming what the shopkeepers have to sell.

The preceding examples were not intended to outline any lawful trend in the development of social systems, or to explain when and where fission and fusion arise in social life. The purpose has merely been to suggest that the concepts of fusion and fission, in conjunction with the three factors of proximity, equality, and complementarity, furnish some good and solid building bricks for the creation of models of the structure and functioning of a social system.

Whether a set of social relations is to be dominated by fusion or by fission depends upon an interplay between *interests* and *values*. This interplay has characteristics which counteract a rigorously concentric construction of society, if we mean by a concentric design one where the interaction of Ego with Alter decreases proportionally to the increase in the distance between the two in space as well as in terms of values. There is a force in operation which tends to induce such a social design, but there is also a force in operation which counteracts this pattern. Empirical evidence of the latter can be found in the numerous situations where Ego seeks an alliance with Alter 2, based upon a presumed communality of interests against Alter 1, who is closer in other respects to Ego. The most serious conflicts, of values as well as of interests, seem to arise between actors who are relatively intimate with each other.

There has frequently been a close relationship between murderers and their victims.[11] Popular conceptions often make the assumption that civil wars are the cruelest, and a feud between brothers is worse than any other relationship. The conception of marriage in Strindberg or Albee is another example.

All close social bonds furnish a basis for solidarity, but they may also initiate betrayal and treason. Ego may meet with some of the gravest problems of distribution in his relations to those who are closest to him. The sources of conflict may be exceedingly strong in a group of children who are to divide an inheritance. Those who are closest to Ego also constitute the gravest challenge and provocation to his independence and freedom of action by the demands they make on him. It is in relationship to these Altera, often in contrast to them, that Ego defines his Self and maintains his social identity. Practical and rational reasons, as well as more profound personality needs, such as the urge to enhance one's sense of identity, may engender fission in the closest and most intimate relationships.

There is, of course, the makings of tragedy in this sociological phenomenon: spouses who become the bitterest enemies, neighbors who persecute each other relentlessly, colleagues who compete fiercely, and countrymen who eventually betray each other. On all levels of social interaction a "betrayal" may be kept in readiness, because the forces prompting fission often increase with the strength of the social bond.

From the point of view of the inclusive society the tendencies towards fission look differently and take on a brighter aspect. What takes the form of fission from the perspective of the small system is regularly an instance of fusion from the point of view of the inclusive system. Conflicts in the primary groups may lead to alliances between a member, or a faction, of the group and some more distant and more comprehensive social system. If one of the parties to a dispute takes the case to the courts, hoping thereby to gain an advantage, such an action may represent a "betrayal" of the adversary and the previous social bond between them. However, it does simultaneously reaffirm the ties to the inclusive system of which the court is an agent. If two competing local communities both send their representatives to the ministry of education to argue the case for a schoolhouse in their own district and to reduce the claims of the rivaling community, the solidarity of the municipality may be betrayed, but both neighborhoods by appealing to a higher authority show that they belong to a more inclusive social system.

If the members of each system acted consistently as members of the system, and always accorded first priority to the interests of those who were nearest and closest to them, society itself could hardly ever constitute a social system. A rigorously concentric design of social life, whether based upon geographical proximity, or upon equality or complementarity, would isolate the systems from each other and might impede the development of social cohesion. What ties the sub-systems together is that the members of one system in other contexts act as members of a second or a third social system. This is known as overlapping or multiple group membership. But, of course, there exist other ties between the sub-systems. They need each other within a larger design based upon a division of labor, and they may also be united by some shared value assumptions. However, in the absence of the overlapping or multiple group membership, it would be difficult for a society to find the means of expressing shared values and to act on the assumption of a communality of interests.

In this respect we find some of the most significant differences between so-called developed and so-called underdeveloped societies. In the new African nations the group memberships of the individual are still very largely ordered in accordance with a concentric design. The majority of the citizens of these new states are

81

still born, brought up, get married, exert political influence, and worship God as a member of one and the same village. Except for a minority, this citizenry does not have membership in groups comprising other tribes, or other languages and sub-cultures. They are all members of an inclusive society, the new nation-state, but that is about the only bond which cuts across the concentric circles formed by the more narrow and more vital social systems.[12]

In modern societies a vast undergrowth of voluntary associations, of clubs, parties, firms, and interest groups tie together actors in a criss-cross social pattern. The overlapping or multiple group membership may in some cases already appear in the name of the association, like The Christian Workers' Association or The Women Teetotallers. One worldwide association, the Rotarians, has elevated overlapping group membership to be the rationale for the association; the condition is stipulated that each local chapter of the Rotarians should have one, but only one, representative of each occupational group. If we want to comprehend the finely established balance in a society between fusion and fission, a mapping of the overlapping group memberships becomes a major empirical task of sociology.

Equilibrium

Social systems emerge and disappear. A system may decay, dissolve or vanish in different ways. The system may cease to exist because the borders of the system have been obliterated as a consequence of interpenetration from the outside, from a more inclusive system or from neighboring small systems. Although the members of the old system still interact with each other, the frequency and intensity of interaction inside the system is no longer visibly higher than it is across the previous system boundary. An example would be an old rural community which is being swallowed by a sprawling city in expansion. The dissolution may, however, also take place as a consequence of corrosive influences which operate inside the system. The interaction inside the system decreases in frequency and significance and may disappear completely. An example is a voluntary organization, a branch of a political party or a chapter of a welfare organization, which is being dissolved because of the loss of interest and involvement on the part of its members.

The dissolution from within can take different forms, according to whether the disruption involves the role-player, the role, or the role model upon which the system is founded. A ship's crew is continuously being dissolved in the sense that members of the old personnel disappear while new recruits take their places. However, the system continues to function and is not dissolved. The situation may be different if the members of a more intimate social system are dispersed, like the family.

A family is a social system established by marriage, and regularly dissolved as a system when the members are being dispersed as, for example, when the children move out or when the spouses die. It cannot be claimed that the vacant roles in the system are being filled anew by other actors. The parents do not get new children when their offspring move away from home, as a skipper may get a new mate if he loses the old one. The eventual dissolution of the family is inherent in its biological and social function, and this perspective upon the future is built into its very role structure. It is an obligation of the parents to prepare the children for independence, to teach them eventually "to stand on their own feet." It is impossible to grasp the structure of the family without a consideration of the time perspective. The role structure is continuously undergoing change, and the reciprocal relationships of social exchange are modified as time lapses. The family has a natural history, and undergoes a cyclical development. What may be true concerning a household at one stage in the development cycle may be patently untrue at another stage.

Neither turnover in a ship's crew nor the dissolution of a family through dispersal of its members necessarily constitute any symptom of social pathology or a state of disequilibrium in the inclusive social system. On the contrary, a prolongation of social interaction in a family beyond what is normal might signify a problem. Generally, social problems and social disorders are evident when the dissolution of a system makes the validity of the underlying role models questionable. Frequent divorce has tended to raise questions concerning the validity of established normative patterns of family life. Similarly, an increasing tendency for the members of the family to invest their time and interests outside the confines of the family has been interpreted as a symptom of incipient social disorganization, the family losing its functions. Whether this interpretation is tenable or not depends to a large extent upon whether or not new normative and institutional arrangements emerge, in order to establish a new foundation for the family. If such a change takes place, it may be more reasonable to speak about social innovation than to speak about disintegration or pathology. While the change is occurring, and especially in its earlier stages, it may be well-nigh impossible to draw a distinction between incipient social pathology and the stirring of social innovation. Decay and creation are complementary phenomena, not only biologically, but also in social life.

The dissolution of social systems has a wide variety of causes. The external environment may undergo change, making it impossible for the system to achieve its goals without being divided into smaller systems, or without being submerged in a more inclusive social system. The notion that the preservation or dissolution may be related to the kind of equilibrium or balance which may be found in the system is of particular interest.[13] Behind this idea lurks the analogy with physiological organisms. It is assumed that the separate parts of the system fill a function upon which the other parts depend. If a change occurs in one part of the system, it must be met by modifications in other parts of the system, unless the equilibrium is to be disturbed. A thermostat regulating the heat in a house furnishes a simplified model of the postulated social process of equilibrium maintenance.

It may be tempting to link the state of equilibrium by definition to the persistence of the social system, to the mere fact of non-dissolution. The system is assumed to be in a state of equilibrium as long as it shows no sign of approaching cessation. The claim that a particular system is in equilibrium implies, then, no more than that the system will continue in existence. But this is a much less interesting observation than a proposition about the forces which causally preserve a system or which precipitate its decay or disappearance. An attempt should be made to define the concept of equilibrium in order to permit its use in the presentation of causal hypotheses.

In this context equilibrium will be defined as a characteristic of the exchange relationship between the role incumbents of the system; it is a feature of the content of norms which determines relations between contributions and sanctions within the social system. What matters most for the maintenance of equilibrium is whether the content of the norms corresponds to the conceptions of *justice* prevalent among the members of a system. The equilibrium of an exchange relationship is regularly accompanied by a consensus that the relations obtaining between contributions and sanctions are just. The conceptions of justice refer to two different types of phenomena. They may refer directly to the relationship between Ego's contributions and Alter's sanctions. A child who exerts himself and strives to do well in school or to aid in the home, without receiving any recognition or reward from the parents, may feel that he is being treated unjustly. Conceptions of justice may, however, also refer to a comparison between two actors who do not mutually interact, but who are both involved in an exchange with a third actor. The third actor may be a public agency or an employer who, as such, is concerned with the distribution of duties and favors between the two subordinates. The principles on which the distribution is carried out may be felt to be more or less just by the subordinates and by others.[14]

The problems of distributive justice arise regularly in connection with the determination of wage scales. Available studies suggest that the attitudes of employees of industrial firms are focused upon the amount of authority and independence accorded to a position as the proper basis of wage determination. Remuneration ought to be graded according to the degree of autonomy and independence enjoyed by the incumbent of the position. In a review of a well-known report on these problems, Homans has made this claim: "I have come to believe that the degree of solution of the problem of distributive justice, or the equitable distribution of the rewards available in a society, is the most important determinant of individual satisfaction and effectiveness and of social peace." [15]

It is quite likely that Homans' view is the correct one, although it remains an empirical question which has as yet not been investigated much through sociological research. It seems also that some social systems persist, or even grow, although their members are convinced that relationships of exchange within the system are far from just. The equilibrium hypothesis, if taken to express claims of universality, assumes a freedom of choice in social action which is far from always present. An extreme example is the prison, which is held together as a system and which avoids dissolution notwithstanding the vivid sense of injustice which may be rampant among the inmates. Social coercion, as well as the inevitable restrictions of natural conditions, may keep social systems in one piece even under conditions of marked inequalities in the distribution of burdens and privileges among the members of the system. The opportunities of compulsion depend upon circumstances which may induce further inequalities. Coercive force is a consequence of a concentration of the command over resources and of sanctions in the hands of the powerful. Such a concentration of power will under many conditions be experienced as an unjust favor accorded the few at the cost of the many.

It seems realistic to reckon with two types of foundations of social systems and of their preservation: *equilibrium in the terms of social exchange* and *coercion.*[16] An hypothesis may be ventured to the effect that there is a tendency towards polarization in this respect in social systems. They will tend either to develop in the direction of greater concentration of power, once a move in this direction has started, or they will tend towards more equilibrium in exchange, once an initial move in this direction has taken place. A crucial task of sociology is to determine under what conditions systems emerge and are consolidated on the basis of power concentration and social coercion, and under what conditions a system develops ever more refined mechanisms of social equilibrium in the relationship between contributions and sanctions as a way of achieving cohesion and growth.

The prerequisites of social systems

In order for a social system to be maintained, the roles of the system must, somehow or other, be filled with personnel. Therefore, *recruitment* is a functional prerequisite of social systems. Without a supply of recruits ready to play the roles, the system must, after a while, cease to exist. To enable the new recruits to take their place in the system a period is required during which the recruits learn how to play their roles. The general social process through which recruits grow into new roles and learn to reap their benefits and meet their obligations is termed *socialization*. Like recruitment, socialization is a prerequisite to the functioning of social systems. A third functional prerequisite of social systems is *production*. The system must produce what it needs for consumption, or it must provide for a contribution based upon the members' work, enabling an exchange of goods or services in return for the necessities of life.[17] Since these three requirements of social systems concern necessary relationships of the system to its natural and social environment, they are uniquely important and demand a somewhat more detailed examination.

RECRUITMENT

A tribe in the rain forests of Brazil cannot, or could not until recently, count upon any inflow of manpower, spouses, doctors, priests, or political leaders from the outside environment. When important role incumbents died, the tribe on its own had to master the problem of recruitment; if not, the tribe would dissolve and eventually perish as a social unit, or even as a pool of biological inheritance. Self-recruitment was the only available method, and this self-recruitment had to take place through biological reproduction. Reproduction is also a phenomenon which involves the transgression of a system border. The newborn infant is delivered from a physiological system to a social one. However, for the physiological process of mating to occur, certain social relationships will normally have been established between the parents on the basis of a structural design, that is, the family, wherein the child has a role waiting for him. Socially unregulated mating and reproduction represent deviant cases of limited scope.[18]

Using the concepts of recruitment and reproduction as the point of departure, we may suggest one type of definition of that particular type of social system which is termed "society": society is a social system which depends upon reproduction for its recruitment. True, a society like the United States or Australia may have been founded by immigrants and may develop under the inflow of new immigrants, but reproduction will soon become the dominant mode of recruitment. All societies have to rely upon reproduction, but not all systems which depend much upon reproduction and self-recruitment constitute societies. Reproduction is a necessary, but not a sufficient, criterion of a society. There is, and especially was, a great deal of self-recruitment to the working class, to business, to the academic professions and, of course, among farmers. However, other modes of recruitment to these occupational groups have turned out to be entirely feasible and are becoming more and more normal.

Reproduction is, sociologically speaking, an important special case of recruitment, one amongst a great many ways in which new members may be included in a system. Other types of recruitment are expressed as employment, appointment, election, incarceration, admittance, joining, and drafting. What all these various modes of recruitment have in common is the flow of personnel from one system to another or from one role to another. Through his first employment in a job the recruit moves out of his school, often also out of his home and home community, in order to join a factory, an office, or some other place of work where he assumes an occupational role. It is a characteristic of employment as a mode of inclusion in a new system that it permits much freedom of choice on the part of the recruit as well as on the part of the receiving social system. The recruit decides on his own whether he wants to be a member of the system, and representatives of the system are normally free to accept or reject his candidacy for the job. Freedom of choice is also possible in many of those types of recruitment covered by the term "joining." New members join associations voluntarily, from which the term "voluntary associations" is de-

88

rived. The associations on their part may, or may not, be at liberty to pick and choose among prospective members. Political parties are freely joined by new members, but may themselves have little freedom to reject anyone who seeks membership. Very often fixed rules stipulate who may become members of a voluntary association and leave little room for discretionary decisions.

An actor may, however, be involuntarily included in a system, as the case is with incarceration in a prison or the drafting of soldiers. Recruitment to compulsory schools and admittance to psychiatric hospitals may likewise deny the recruit any voice in the process of becoming a member of the system. The freedom to choose on the part of the system may vary. In order for a primary school to reject a pupil, disqualifying characteristics must be clearly established and the system will be relieved of the duty to include the new member only in exceptional cases. Prisons and military units have little freedom to reject a new member once the proper authority has decided that the new recruit is to be included. These authorities are, however, strictly circumscribed in their power to decide upon inclusion or non-inclusion. Admittance to a hospital is, in principle, a matter of the recruit's free decision, but is often a necessity. The hospital operates under definite restrictions concerning the choice of patients unless it operates under a system of private clinics with very high fees.

Systematic relationships obtain between the types of recruitment, the character of the system, and the way in which membership is discontinued. A citizen is usually, although not always, born into his system, the nation-state, and is normally not released from the obligations and rights of membership before he dies. The employee is employed as a worker or a functionary, as a subordinate or as a manager, and membership is terminated according to a notice of dismissal. The person who is admitted to a hospital becomes a patient and is normally declared well when he does not need further treatment. He is then discharged. Those admitted to a school become pupils or students and leave it after having been graduated or occasionally as a consequence of expulsion. The person who is incarcerated becomes an inmate or a prisoner and is reprieved when his term is served. The draftee becomes a soldier and is dismissed when the armistice occurs or when his service is completed.

These varying modes of recruitment are related to sociologically significant differences between the structures of social systems. They will be more closely examined in Chapter VII. These social systems presuppose the opportunity for sustained social interaction over considerable periods of time. However, society also makes room for social systems which are more ephemeral and tenuous but nevertheless of considerable significance. They often encompass the relationship between the performer of a service occupation, and a client. An extreme example is the relationship between the cabdriver and his passenger. It stands as a prototype of certain kinds of fleeting relations which have left their indelible stamp upon some of the pace-setting centers of the modern world like New York.[19] Even such fleeting social systems require recruitment. For example, the shopkeepers need customers; the attorneys need clients; the doctors need patients; the architects need prospective homeowners; the theatres need audiences; the concerts need listeners; and the restaurants need guests. There is usually marked freedom of choice regarding one's wish to enter such a social system and with whom. However, the sick may be more strongly obliged to seek medical aid than the unlucky partner to a contract is to seek legal advice. And the attorney has more freedom to turn down a prospective client than the doctor has to turn away a suffering patient or the shop to decline the customer service. While "the customer is always right" in the shop, this is not always so in the relationship between lawyer and client, and even less so in the hospital where doctors may be irritated with patients who believe they have medical knowledge. In these fleeting social systems there are systematic relations between the principle of recruitment and features of the internal role structure. Such fleeting systems illustrate that a role structure exists independently of any particular set of incumbents, that it is an empty system of niches held in abeyance, waiting for personnel.

Reproduction is the *sine qua non* for a society. Society must rely upon self-recruitment. But the specific type of sub-system in society where reproduction takes place must not be self-reproducing. The *nuclear family* seems to be recognized in all known societies, although it displays considerable variation in form as well as function. We mentioned in a preceding section that the offspring are not supposed to enter into the roles of their parents to replace them in their *family of orientation,* that is, the family into which Ego is born. They are supposed to find spouses from other families of orientation with whom they form a new *family of reproduction.*

The universal, or near universal, incest taboo prevents sexual relations and self-recruitment within the family. The husband and father cannot marry his daughter when his wife dies, and a brother and sister may not together perpetuate the family which their parents founded. The existing families continuously engender new social relations and new small systems, thereby tying together a number of nuclear families in a more inclusive kinship structure. The form of this kinship structure exhibits an incredible amount of variation, but the basic social ingredients are very simple and are ultimately rooted in the inability of the family to base its existence as an institution upon self-recruitment. We see here also the simplest and most original basis for the development of the structure of societies and for differentiation between them.

SOCIALIZATION

Socialization is the process through which the individual grows into a role. One kind of socialization we may term *upbringing.* Upbringing prepares the individual for general adjustment to social roles, for the introduction to the role of an adult member of his sex in society, and perhaps for belonging to a definite social class or stratum. To a large extent this general socializing task is in the hands of the family: parents and elder siblings. However, more distant kin as well as friends (the peer group) may play their part in child training and in the preparation for adult participation in society. In societies where schools are well developed, formalized educational institutions and professional teachers fill an important socializing function. The school is in this respect a functional alternative to the family, as well as an adjunct to the home by its capacity to provide training for roles that are unknown to the family. The socialization which takes place in the family aims to prepare for membership in the small social systems, for example, in a new family, within a network of kinship in the home community. The school lays the foundation of identification with society

91

and affords training for the assumption of roles in the inclusive social system, as, for example, becoming a citizen. The school educates for membership in the nation through the curricula in history and the native language, in civics, and in many other ways such as saluting the flag and singing the national anthem in elementary school. The significance of this training is manifest if we compare the stage of development of primary schools of a hundred years ago in many European countries, or in the United States, with the present state of primary education in many underdeveloped countries, where only a small percentage of the children are in attendance. In many of the new nations identification with the smallest social systems, family, kin, and village dominate at the expense of the assumption of full membership in the nation. Military conscription has in some respects served a function similar to that of the primary schools, emphasizing the crucial significance of the actor's role as a citizen and member of the nation. It is, from this point of view, hardly an accident that teachers and military officers have played an important part in the political transition from an underdeveloped agricultural society to a modern industrialized nation.[20]

The school facilitates growth into an inclusive society quite generally. But the fact that it is also an agent of more specialized socialization for participation in occupational life becomes gradually more apparent as we move from the primary schools up the educational ladder, reaching the professional schools of the universities. There has been much debate and tension about the relationship between general education in the sense of the old classical curricula and vocational training. In sociological terms this debate concerns the choice between a socialization which emphasizes the growth into society as such versus one which emphasizes the preparation for specific roles and sub-systems of the inclusive society. The technology and differentiation of modern societies has in any event created a very strongly felt need for schools as a means of socialization to take over tasks which previously rested upon the family.

The problem of socializing the young may, in principle, be solved in three basic ways. The family itself may socialize the children and the young for the occupational roles awaiting them. This is feasible as long as the occupational structure is relatively undifferentiated and the division of labor rather undeveloped, as the case was in the old agricultural communities out of which the modern industrialized societies grew. The children learn by observing their elders carrying out the daily tasks, by participating as members of the family in the work, and by receiving guidance from parents and elder siblings. The precondition of this educational pattern is self-recruitment to occupational roles and the maintenance of the family as the basic unit of production.

The extent to which these preconditions vanish will determine what other methods will force their way into the socialization process. The second alternative is that the occupations socialize their new recruits. The prototype of this type of socialization is found in the institution of apprenticeship or trainee. When the son of the craftsman learned the craft from his father, this was in accordance with the principles of socialization in the agricultural communities. However, if the master employed other boys as apprentices, the recruit passed from one social system, his family of orientation, to a new one, represented by the productive unit where he was being socialized for continued and more highly skilled participation. He was, in significant respects, considered to be a member of the master's household, setting up a quasi-family type of socialization as the model.

A modern example of socialization to an occupational role, which takes place within the system of production, is found in the relationship between the novice in the Norwegian merchant marine and the ship. The new recruit is socialized by participating as a junior seaman in the merchant marine, receiving virtually no instruction or guidance but that of the ordinary supervision carried out by the officers. He becomes a seaman by sailing and there are no apprentice positions aboard the ships. This is, however, different in the English merchant marine, where apprenticeship is institutionalized for those who want to prepare for the career of ship's officer. Another example is that of Italian recruits to the officer jobs in the merchant marine who are trained in schools which are completely separated from the ship's communities. In Norway an aspiring ship's officer is supposed to grow into the role of a seaman before he is ready to enter a maritime school. School ships exist, but mean little in terms of socialization for the sea.[21]

The school is becoming the prevalent type of institution designed to solve the problem of socialization. It is a separate social system. One major function of a school is the contribution of well-qualified recruits to fill the roles of those systems assigned to the task of economic production. In terms of normative structure the school occupies an intermediary position between the family and the occupations. The role pair teacher-pupil has much in common with the role pair parent-child. Full reciprocity is not to be expected since the teacher is supposed to contribute more than he will receive and is assumed to possess a surplus of the value around which the role structure is organized: the transmission of knowledge. In the early stages of the educational system, not only achievement but also quality is emphasized. The relationships in school are more diffuse and less specialized than they are in the occupational structures, and they leave more room for the legitimate expression of affect. We expect the good modern teacher to deal with the children as "small personalities" and not merely as members of a certain age-determined class of pupils.

From the point of view of the child, however, his encounter with the school will simultaneously signify his first encounter with some of those normative orientations which govern occupational roles. The children are introduced to systematic work and to the coordination of activities according to a rather rigorous temporal scheme, dominated by the clock. They learn rules of justice and an orientation towards measurable, specific criteria of performance. They learn to take the role of subordinate in a larger social system demanding obedience to figures of authority other than their parents. The internal structure of the school as a social system is as important to the growth of the young into later occupational roles as the specific skills and information which the children acquire, at least in the primary school. It seems probable that the training of the children to find their role within the social structure of the school during the period of industrialization contributed to facilitate an adjustment to the new role of being subordinates in large social systems, in factories, and in other work teams.

At the higher educational stages this point of view becomes somewhat less applicable. The social structure of the university does not share many characteristics with the manifold occupational

94

structures awaiting the graduates. At this stage the absorption of specialized knowledge and the acquirement of specific skills are more important. However, the relative freedom of the course-plans and, in some countries, the measure of self-determination accorded student bodies may serve to ease the transition from the subordinate position of the student to the managerial or independent positions which many academically trained people enter after graduation from the university. The training of recruits for superordinate roles entails a paradox because the student or pupil is always in some sense a subordinate of the teacher before he moves upwards. This may explain why positions of trainees or of apprentices have developed as an appendage to schools in many areas. Management courses, subsequent to some practical experience, may supplement the schools where the basic design of the school as a social system makes a mirroring of the awaiting roles well-nigh impossible.

Although it is an independent vehicle of socialization, the school may be more or less closely affiliated with the family or the units of economic production respectively. Some types of schools, like the American college or the European gymnasium, have a relatively autonomous structure, and are little influenced by the family or by the occupational sectors of society. However, the private tutor, the governess, or the kindergarten represent adjuncts to the family, adjusted to the structure and needs of the household. At the other end of the spectrum we find company schools, factory courses, training on the job, schools of the railways and of the postal service, representing appendages to the units of economic production and being closely shaped to suit their needs. The structure of a society's school system is, no doubt, one of the most sensitive indicators of the structural problems of the inclusive social system.

PRODUCTION

If a social system is to persist and avoid dissolution, it must produce something. It must produce goods which may be consumed by its members, or which they can use as means of exchange in return for consumer goods flowing in from the outside. Reproduction, and even more socialization, can be viewed as special cases of production. The personnel of the schools exchange their contributions to the process of socialization for a salary, enabling the teachers to buy life's necessities. It is characteristic of the product delivered by the schools that it has not, generally, been in sufficient demand by private individuals to provide an adequate basis for the operation of the educational system. If public authorities did not subsidize the schools, the socializing functions of a modern society would not be fulfilled. Mating and reproduction assume the visible characteristics of production when the families receive pensions in return for their contribution to the recruitment of personnel to society, a phenomenon most clearly observed through the operation of the well-known French child pension system. In this context, however, we shall not subsume reproduction or socialization under the concept of production.

Like socialization, production may take place in conjunction with the family or independent of it. The old farm family constituted a social system which had provided for reproduction, socialization, and production at the same time. When the farm family began losing its functions, the tasks related to socialization were transferred to the school. When such families moved to the cities, or when the husband sought employment in a nearby factory, they lost their productive function also. They were transformed into urban-type families, whether they were actually located in the countryside or in a city. Specialization of farming has even reduced the remaining farm families' significance as units of production. This condition is particularly apparent in the tasks of the country women, since they have been shifted, according to the urban pattern, from productive duties to primarily the administration of the family's consumption.

The economic life of modern societies is by and large characterized by the fact that the reproductive system, the family, no longer functions as a system of production or constitutes a sub-system under larger systems of production. The systems of economic production fall into two major classes: the open and the closed systems. In the closed systems the cooperating producers interact with each other, while the maintenance of relations with other systems is left in the hands of a few representatives of the system, located in the management group. A factory, a ship, a mine, a team of construction workers are examples of closed systems. The open systems are generally found within the service sector. The office of a physician may be analyzed in terms of the internal relationships between doctor, nurse, and secretary. The features of the role pair, doctor-patient, are more significant however. The system comprises, then, the producer and the consumer or buyer of the product. Such is also the case with the lawyer, although the American legal system has brought forth attorneys' offices which are of such scope they have been termed "law-factories." The term is justified, not merely because the firm may comprise as many as one hundred lawyers, but because the majority of the employees or partners have little outside contact, either with clients or with the courts. Thus, the systems in the service professions may, contrary to their basic and original design, become closed systems like industrial plants.

All kinds of gradations exist between the open and the closed systems of production. When the physician works in a hospital, the system acquires a more closed character. "The buyer," the patient, must stay in the "factory" and "consume" the service on the spot, which makes him temporarily a subordinate in the system. In large shops there is continuous interaction between sales personnel and customers. Since these relationships are intermittent and fleeting, however, the internal relationships between personnel may assume greater significance in many respects. In the means of public transportation still different types of group relations emerge. Relationships may arise between the passengers, while the employed personnel, like a train conductor, interact alone with the passengers, and contacts with colleagues are restricted to occasional encounters in spare time.

The differences in patterns of interaction between producer and consumer have important consequences. Those who interact predominantly with colleagues may experience their most significant enemies, as well as allies, within the firm. In the absence of outside contact as a representative of his factory, the worker is unlikely to perceive himself as a member of the factory or to experience the factory as "his." The factory belongs, as a matter of fact, to someone

97

else and he perceives himself as a worker, thus set apart from, possibly in opposition to, management and white-collar workers of the same factory. The salesgirl or the train conductor, however, are daily obliged to interact with customers and passengers respectively, and are bound to represent their productive system, speak on behalf of it, counter criticism or complaints, and defend themselves as representatives of the system. The customer is often unable, or unwilling, to distinguish between the employee and the system; the employee is praised or blamed for what the system produces or fails to produce. This situation may contribute to link the self-perception and identity of the sales person or the railroader to the business firm or to the railroads, in spite of the fact that they have important special interests to maintain precisely vis-à-vis the management of the system. The well-known differences between blue-collar and white-collar workers with respect to social ideology and political affiliation are no doubt related also to these structural differences between open (i.e. the railroad) and closed (i.e. the steel mill) systems of work and production.

All systems of economic production have something in common. Achievement or performance is a dominant orientation governing the interaction. It is not important to the customer *who* the shoe producer or salesman is, as long as good and/or cheap shoes are sold. Promotion inside hierarchically designed productive systems depends a great deal upon the application of measurable criteria of performance. This aspect of productive systems has sometimes been overstressed, however. It is clear that the orientations are more directed towards achievement than they are in the family, but they are not unequivocally so directed.

Relations in productive units are to a large extent based upon universalism (see p. 15). What relationship Ego has to Alter means relatively little for their occupational transactions. A businessman cannot, normally, prevent an enemy from buying in his shop. And a foreman ought not to bestow too many favors upon a close personal friend who happens to be in his team of workers. The relationships are specific, restricted to buying and selling, or to a type of collegial attitude with no implication of personal friendship or sharing of social life in leisure time. It has been shown, however, that the workers' collectivity in these respects often tends to circumvent the norms which demand strict specificity, achievement orientation, and universalism. The employees defend with vigor their right to be human beings also at their place of work.[22]

V

SOCIAL
STRATIFICATION

THE LANGUAGE of sociology, as well as the vernacular, makes ample use of spatial concepts to provide for order in social life. Terms like "inside," "outside," "above," "below," "high," and "low" abound in discussions about society. Conceivably, such a transfer of concepts from the physical to the social world may cause bias in the interpretation of social relations. Sociology may in the future come to develop a new terminology where these spatial analogies are accorded a more modest role. For the time being, however, we need these terms. The actors' perceptions of the social system are organized according to such schemes of interpretation, and we cannot easily find adequate scientific substitutes for them.

In the previous description of the social system, the concepts of "inside" and "outside" loomed large. The possibility of drawing borderlines between what is inside and what falls outside a social system is a prerequisite to the analysis of society as a network of systems. Such analyses lead to an *horizontal* ordering of social phenomena. Social stratification, however, refers to an ordering of society according to *vertical* principles. The task consists in locating individuals or roles above and below each other.

Stratification as systematic distribution

Let us begin by looking upon stratification as a distribution of contributions and sanctions between individuals and roles. By "contribution" is meant those qualities or performances of actors which qualify for sanctions. "Sanctions" refer to both rewards and penalties. The distribution may conform to one of three principles, or to a combination of these. Contributions and sanctions may be *equally* distributed. Everybody gives and receives the same, regardless of who he is and of the amount of access that he has to other values. Contributions and sanctions may be *randomly* distributed: there are differences among actors, for example, in intelligence or income, but the differences are not systematically related to other social criteria. Finally, contributions and sanctions may be systematically and *unequally* distributed, that is, related to the distribution of other values. We shall speak about social stratification only in this latter case.

An approximation to the principle of equal distribution can be found in certain types of team sports, such as rowing. It is difficult to distinguish between the achievements of the individual members of the rowing team. An attempt to do so is often even frowned upon. The reward for the individual's contribution is the same for all. The second model of distribution is to be found in social situations, represented by certain types of games, where gains and losses are decided upon by the drawing of lots or some other kind of chance mechanism. The rewards are often very unequally distributed amongst the participants, but the distribution lacks a systematic relationship to other characteristics of the participants.

In both of these cases we are witnessing the functioning of *egalitarian* systems. The scarce goods are distributed equally, or the actors have been accorded an equal chance to obtain the goods. However, these egalitarian principles of social ordering hold their greatest interest to us as forces or as ideals which operate also in stratified social systems. In their pure forms the two principles are put into actual practice only in relatively insignificant social systems, like the betting pools, or in some team sports.

Social stratification implies that contributions or sanctions are unequally distributed amongst the members of a social system in a way which is systematically related to the distribution of other contributions and sanctions. If we have information on no more than one set of values and its distribution, it is not feasible to decide whether the distribution is random or systematic.

Nature exhibits a certain tendency towards random distributions. Men are born with a certain dispersal of qualities or abilities, and natural conditions do not always encounter the same human achievements with uniform sanctions. Nature may be benevolent or miserly in its response to the efforts of men to extract their means of livelihood from it. Implicit in what has just been said is that differences are bound to arise between actors. However, the equal distribution and the systematically unequal distribution are very largely the consequence of the operation of social forces. We may observe tendencies to gather actors whose capacities to contribute are similar within social systems based upon equality of sanctions. Employees of a specific skill category are recruited to the same unions or associations which then attempt to obtain equal rewards for their skills. However, the principle of complementarity works the other way around in so far as any economic enterprise has to be manned by actors of widely differing skills who are also unequally rewarded in terms of wages and other benefits.

We may conceive of two great social forces modifying the initial, socially random, distribution of contributions and sanctions. One of these eliminates differences by bringing actors together in social systems, educational or occupational, where they receive relatively equal rewards. The very selection of members may also have tended to assemble those who are "naturally" rather equally endowed, further preserving the initial similarities. The second, opposite tendency obtains when actors are assembled in the social system precisely on the basis of complementary inequalities, as, for example, age and sex, because the purpose of the system demands such differentiation. The system itself may also engender differences between initially similar actors because a division of labor and of leadership is required.

Wealth, esteem, and power

Not every kind of distribution of contributions and sanctions falls along the vertical axis. The division of labor, specialization, may imply a cultivation of differences which tends to order actors above and below each other, but may also locate them on the same level next to each other. This possibility brings us to a pivotal point in any theory of social stratification: What are the appropriate criteria that place an actor or a role "higher" than another? The distribution of three criteria comes to mind as particularly important: Esteem (prestige), power, and wealth.

Wealth implies that a certain opportunity to use and control the general means of economic exchange, money, is associated with an actor or a role. A skewed distribution of wealth within a social system implies normally a skewed distribution of goods that can be bought, like housing, clothing, food, entertainment, and education. The access to certain types of goods can be singled out as more significant than the access to others. The opportunity of some rich actors to control large means of production establishes also a basis for employing subordinates. Thus, wealth is converted into a source of power over other actors, while this position of economic power in its turn enables the owner to use manpower to increase his own wealth. The control of means of production—a farm, a ship, a shop, and a factory—affords the owner an opportunity to transfer to his offspring or to other heirs not only his wealth, but also to some extent his prestige and power. Today, however, the opportunity to transfer social rank to descendants is also associated with the parents' ability to secure a good education for their children.

It is feasible to rank the members of a social system in terms of wealth on the basis of readily accessible criteria available in the tax returns, although such rankings will not be free of errors. A ranking of the members of the system in terms of esteem or prestige raises greater problems. In the first place it is not immediately obvious what kinds of subjective appreciations of other actors ought to be interpreted as the expression of a prestige ranking. Operationally speaking, what kinds of questions ought to be put to obtain answers which are relevant to how individuals estimate each other? If this question can be settled, there remain the tasks of carrying out sufficiently comprehensive and representative surveys to reveal the distribution of the subjective social evaluations in terms of esteem.[1]

Respect, veneration, esteem, and prestige are some of the positively colored terms associated with the reciprocal subjective evaluations according to which members of a social system are ranked. Difficulties arise, however, when searching for the appropriate labels for a negative subjective evaluation of rank. Contempt, pity, overbearingness, and disdain are possible components of these downward attitudes in a social system, but they have in addition to the aspect of rank, emotional associations along different dimensions. If we had included envy among our positive terms we should also have become aware of the complex structure of attitudes relating to social rank.

Simple and measurable, almost distilled, criteria of social rank may be found in rules of diplomatic precedence or in military and other strictly formalized bureaucracies. However, in order to describe the phenomenon in terms of social interaction, as the actual exchange of contributions and sanctions in terms of rank, such readily observable criteria do not suffice. It is necessary to carry out systematic empirical research on the way in which actors and roles are accorded rank in a social system, by sample surveys based upon formalized questionnaires as well as field observations of behavior.

The power which pertains to an actor or a role is also a more elusive attribute than wealth. However, the reliance upon subjective criteria is less marked than in the case of esteem. According to Weber, power may be defined as "the probability that one actor within a social relationship will be in a position to carry out his own will despite resistance, regardless of the basis on which this probability rests." [2] The bases of power relationships were treated in general terms in the discussion of the strength of the norm sender. Frequently, the very role structure defines the relationship between the incumbents, making it clear that Ego has more power over Alter than Alter has over Ego. The relations between superordinates and subordinates in a civil service exemplify this difference, as do the relationships between employers and employees in an industrial plant or in an office organization. No extensive study of the probabilities of compliance with the norms sent from one or the other of the members of these role pairs is necessary in order to undertake a simple power ranking. However, if a more precise description of these power relations is needed, or if comparisons are to be made between roles that are not formally ordered within the same hierarchy, empirical research is called for. Empirical studies of power meet with difficulties because power is a far from simple phenomenon when we leave the model situation of master and servant. Formal and real power need not coincide as the term "grey eminency" suggests.

Wealth, esteem, and power do not provide us with an all-encompassing catalogue of the criteria in terms of which a vertical ordering of actors or roles may be established in a social system. Intelligence, physical prowess, looks, and personality, as well as pedigree, and much besides these, draw distinctions among actors and offer opportunities for vertical orderings. These additional criteria will, in the present context, only receive attention in so far as they are correlated with the three criteria dealt with in this section. This limitation rests on the assumption that the latter inequalities have major significance for social stratification only in so far as they impinge upon, or are influenced by, these three variables.

Social rank

There are two procedures we may follow when determining the general *rank* of a member of a social system. The rank may be defined in terms of the reciprocal subjective appreciations, of the relationships of esteem and prestige within the system. If this procedure is followed esteem is made the very pivot of social stratification.[3] Naturally, esteem is itself determined by several objective factors such as wealth, power, intelligence, and pedigree. These criteria are, however, merely accorded weight in so far as they have actually been converted into esteem and prestige. The approach is "subjectivistic," and a fruitful application depends upon the availability of reliable and valid empirical measurements of esteem and prestige. The second procedure is applied when the sociologist himself, as an observer, combines the various criteria of rank, each of them separately measured: wealth, power, prestige, and possibly also education, intelligence, pedigree, and others. Apart from the important theoretical implications which flow from the choice of procedure, the latter one has methodological advantages by making the ranking less dependent upon subjective evaluations.

The mutual attitudes of esteem or lack of esteem have important implications for the functioning of social systems. But these evaluations are often hard to get at. One reason for these difficulties is that social systems, and especially society, entertain ideologies about how the questions of social rank *ought to* be settled. The relations which prevail in actual social intercourse may often be at odds with "native theory," the theory which the members of the system entertain concerning its stratification. Therefore, analyses of the factual correlations between the various distributions of contributions and sanctions are necessary and important supplements to surveys about who is respected, why, and by whom. Such analyses may, for example, deal with the relationships between intelligence, education and income, or between family background and occupation.

Wealth, esteem, and power are defined independently of each other. Empirically, however, these three criteria of distribution are related, which provide a justification for speaking about a general social rank.[4] The rich are often also prestigious and may have considerable power. The correlation is, however, far from perfect. Some actors have great power without receiving great incomes, and there exist rich people who neither enjoy much power nor much prestige. The patterns discernible in these statistical relationships provide for an opportunity to make comparisons between social systems and between societies. The sociological problem is not merely what relationships actually obtain, but how the relationships can be explained. It is important to locate the strategic elements in the stratification: Is wealth an effective means to gain more power, or is political power a more efficient means to acquire wealth and win esteem?

Consensus

For an analysis of social stratification to have scientific validity, it must be based upon something over and above the sociologist's own personal evaluation of the contributions and sanctions which occur within a social system. Sociology is committed to strive to keep the researchers' subjective attitudes concerning "high" and "low" outside their professional work. A consequence of this striving for an impersonal estimate is that the very evaluations of the scarce goods which are unequally distributed within a system must be obtained from the social system itself. A prerequisite to using the concept of stratification is that the members of a system exhibit a certain amount of *consensus* in their evaluations. To some extent, at least, there must be agreement on what is desirable and attractive, and what are the marks of superiority and success. There is widespread accord that money, esteem, and power (or at least independence) are to be classified as positive values or sanctions. Likewise, a majority would probably concede that ability, intelligence, trustworthiness, and strength are terms which refer to superior contributions. If every role incumbent thought most highly of what he himself possessed and of his own station in society, no sociological procedure could lead us to any vertical principles of social ordering.

No doubt the consensus has its limits. Not everybody strives towards the same goals or appreciates the same things. The least privileged have oftentimes shown a proclivity to establish a separate scale of values, a "counterproposal" to that of the privileged groups, more adjusted to their own fate and station in society. Proverbs and biblical passages exhibit many examples of a revaluation of basic social assumptions. The reference to "sour grapes" is one way in which people of many countries express a certain reserve vis-à-vis social rank and worldly success. And the Bible has declared that "It is easier for a camel to go through the eye of a needle than for a rich man to enter the kingdom of God."

The members of social systems seem to be in search of a theory which may re-establish a balance in what is actually an unequal distribution of contributions and sanctions. The balance may be sought on a level of pure ideology or imagination, but it may also be sought in a striving towards actual equalization of privileges. Certain types of social systems, like the Indian caste system, seem to have been more impervious to such attempts to balance social inequalities.

A social system is not likely to become stabilized in a situation where equal weight is given to the evaluations of the underprivileged as to those of the privileged. High social rank implies also the opportunity to exert an influence above the average, thereby bestowing upon the higher social strata the ability to formulate the very basis on which esteem and rank are accorded to the system's members. The governmental offices of a modern state, as well as the large industries, unions, and other national associations, have an opportunity to establish norms of social ranking which peasants, fishermen, and unorganized workmen do not have. The relatively low rank of the latter groups, as well as their geographic dispersal, prevent them from effectively propagating the values which they hold and which may deviate from those prevalent in the more privileged groups and in central urban society.

Empirical studies have demonstrated that a widespread consensus prevails in modern societies concerning the priorities of social values, and more specifically with respect to the criteria determining social esteem.[5] Occupational titles are most frequently used as the basis for attribution of social rank. Even across national boundaries extensive similarities are found in the ranking of occupational labels.[6] Such similarities do not necessarily imply, however, that the overlap of individual evaluations is equally extensive when, for example, we are faced with a concrete person rather than an abstract label. It is also somewhat misleading to attribute equal weight to the subjective appreciation by an Ego of any Alter. The rankings of the more powerful actors have, obviously, more far-reaching consequences than those originating among the underdogs. And those evaluations which are undertaken within a tightly knit social system have more significant repercussions than those undertaken in a crowd of passengers on a train or bus. There may likewise be considerable discrepancy between national evaluations of occupational labels and the estimation of a concrete incumbent in the local community. Thus, in nationwide surveys the occupation of the primary-school teacher comes out with a rather low social rank. He has, however, in practice often been a local leader, enjoying higher social rank within his community than does a distant ambassador or president of a large enterprise. Such complexities of the ranking problem make it unrealistic to hope that it would be feasible to rank all the members of a society within a single unidimensional system of social stratification. It seems necessary to specify rank by explicit reference to the particular social system which sets the framework for the ranking.

The functions of social stratification

A central and controversial issue in sociological debate has been whether the stratification of social systems is inherent in the nature of social interaction, or whether egalitarian distributions are practicable. From nature's hand the members of the system are unequally situated with respect to the ability to make contributions and in their chances of success. The question is whether social systems "exploit" these diversities to establish an order of social ranking, or whether they attempt to mitigate the inequalities.

According to one school of thought, stratification is inevitable and is a prerequisite to the preservation of social systems, and especially so if the system is society itself. If social systems are to avoid dissolution, they must contain some role incumbents who demonstrate an unusual willingness to shoulder responsibilities and carry out burdensome tasks. The incumbents of such roles must be rewarded for their devotion and skills, and these rewards further a systematic tendency in the distribution of values. Those who possess qualifications to assume responsibility are selected for recruitment to positions of authority and receive esteem and appropriate remuneration for their contributions to the system. According to this theory a prime minister or a company president enjoy high rank in society because great social rewards must be offered if really capable and dedicated actors are to take upon themselves the responsibility and the work load associated with these positions. Likewise, because the doctor's services are indispensible in a modern society and his responsibilities grave, he is accorded high prestige. Thus, there will arise a systematic tendency in the distribution of scarce goods between roles, not merely random variations between individuals.[7]

No doubt, the leaders of some social systems plan the recruitment of personnel in this fashion. They attempt to find the best-qualified recruits for the most responsible positions and for the execution of the most exacting tasks, and seek to attract them by those rewards of esteem, salary, and independence which are required in order to make the positions coveted. The question is, however, whether all social systems possess recruitment mechanisms corresponding to this rational model. It becomes particularly pressing with respect to society itself, as well as in local communities where conscious programming has a relatively limited scope and means less for the actual state of the social system.

Empirically speaking, there exist systems which exhibit large divergencies in social rank, as well as systems where the inequalities of rank are negligible. The rank differences within a ship, a prison, a factory, or even a family (parents to children) are very wide. However, within a work team in an industrial plant, in a school class, or in a hamlet of peasants, inequalities may be very minor. Examples abound of social systems developing ever more steep and refined hierarchies of social rank in response to a certain type of challenge. But there are also examples of social systems "refusing" to systematize and formalize rank differentiation in cases where the tasks at hand seem to demand social stratification. Thus, the solution of leadership problems in communities undergoing rapid economic change may oftentimes be frustrated by the drive towards egalitarian distributions of esteem and, especially, of power.[8]

If the emergence of a system is due to the creation of a network of roles around a clearly defined task, it is often exposed to strong forces pulling in the direction of inequalities of power and prestige, and also of remuneration. A hierarchical design of the system with a centralization of power at the top and with clearly defined relationships of superordination and subordination throughout the system has proved to be effective in modern production, administration, and marketing. When the role incumbents have unequal power they will also tend to receive differential remuneration. According to available English studies there is a widespread belief among the employees of industrial firms that payments ought to be adjusted according to the amount of responsibility and independence associated with a position.[9] If the remuneration associated with a position depends upon its power, esteem is likely to follow accordingly, and we get a systematic type of stratification.

The stratification assumes varying "geometrical" forms. One man may have been authorized to lead a group whose members are otherwise equally situated. If this is the case, a flat pyramid results. However, a steep and narrow pyramid may emerge in organizations where no one is in command of more than a handful of subordinates, but where the chain of command comprises a large number of links. Such is the situation in the army, to some extent aboard ships, and also within many other types of economic organizations.

In systems which have arisen spontaneously and where personal and intimate contacts characterize the social life, the tendency towards egalitarianism is at its strongest. In some cases this may also be due to the mode of production. Local groups of peasants or of fishermen often exhibit a very strong preference for an egalitarian structure in the local community. Such groups are especially loath to accept an increase in the power of individual members of the group, even if there is a pronounced need for local leadership in the community. In territorial groups with a strong preference for egalitarian distributions of authority and wealth, the members are tied together by the bonds of proximity and equality. Apart from the marriage market, they do not today have significant relationships to each other based upon complementarity, since they do not sell goods or services to each other. Rather, the produce of the community is exchanged with the outside world. This may point to a statistical regularity or even lawfulness in social life. If the system is based upon complementarity, within a division of labor, and consequently upon inequality, a systematic stratification is likely to emerge. If, however, the system has arisen on the basis of proximity and similarity, random differences will be evened out by the system so as not to result in a systematic social stratification.

111

Dichotomy and hierarchy

Differences in rank lead to the establishment of social strata by which are meant categories of actors who are equally situated with respect to wealth, esteem and power. Much interest has been focused on the question of how many social strata there exist in a given social system. Wealth as well as power and esteem lend themselves to an endless differentiation. Nevertheless, a society is regularly assumed to be divided into a finite number of strata. Of particular interest is the question whether the stratification of social systems is based upon dichotomy or hierarchy. A dichotomous stratification implies a systematic ordering of contributions and sanctions establishing two—and only two—relatively clearly distinguished strata in the system. The term "hierarchy" refers to a type of social structure where the strata have the characteristics of steps on a ladder, each one above the other, without any one decisive breaking point or cleavage in the system.[10]

A quite general problem met with in attempts to describe structures of stratification derives from the fact that social systems are located inside each other, so that a smaller system is part of a larger one. Thus, questions may often arise concerning which social system should be taken as the frame of reference for the analysis of stratification. When analyzing the ship and its structure of stratification, are we also to consider that it belongs to a shipping company? If we do so, the ship's officers seem to be closer to the rest of the crew than to the management and functionaries on land in terms of rank. If we consider the ship as such, without considering its belongingness to the company, the gap in rank between the officers and the crew becomes more pronounced. The system referent ought always to be specified in descriptions of a structure of social stratification.

In a school classroom we indubitably find a dichotomous stratification. Between teacher and pupils there is a profound gap, an inequality in power, esteem, and income. The difference in rank is inherent in the functions performed by this type of social system and can be seen as a consequence of the type of recruitment required by the purpose of education. If, however, the school is taken as the frame of reference, not the individual class, there appears a hierarchical ordering of the pupils among themselves. The rank of the pupils increases with age and with class level.

The dichotomous division characterizing the classroom in school is also found in many other organizations that are established to solve specific problems. It is so in prisons, where the distinction between guards and inmates is basic, and also in hospitals and factories. True, there are many levels of rank and authority in an industrial plant. Nevertheless, the distinction between management and workers has a significance which does not pertain to the other distinctions found. The gap between the two groups is apparent in incomes, power, esteem, education, style of life, patterns of consumption, and in many additional traits, all of which are statistically related to the actor's general social rank. Were we, however, to observe an office organization, for example, in the civil service, we should not find a corresponding dichotomous structure of stratification. The distinction between superordinate and subordinate is quite clear on each level of command in the hierarchy, but there is hardly any single distinction representing a definitive gap which determines the patterns of interaction as the gap between workers and management does in the factory.

Whether the stratification of a social system is to assume the characteristics of a dichotomy or of a hierarchy depends very largely upon the purpose of the organization and upon its means of production. It is, above all, the large physical means of production, like a factory or an agricultural estate, which have fostered dichotomous modes of social stratification. The natural and technological foundations of the enterprise encourage egalitarianism within large groups of mutually interacting subordinates. An office organization, the output of which consists of decisions, orders, letters and other documents, usually exhibits tendencies towards a hierarchical social stratification, the manager on each level supervising and directing only a small number of subordinates. If the administration is charged with extensive tasks, necessitating a large personnel, the solution is to build in height, establishing new levels in the chain of command. Since the subordinates receive orders from their superordinates, the execution of which is independent of the large physical plant, the separate groups of subordinate office workers are often quite isolated from each other, while maintaining continuous rapport upwards in the system.

If we look at the most important types of social systems in the economic sector of society, the outlines of a certain lawful development in stratification structure seem to emerge. We are now concerned with the structure within the single enterprise, not with society as a whole. There seems to have been a movement from the dichotomous types of social stratification in the direction of prevalent hierarchical ones, partly due to the increasing level of processing of the raw materials. Peasant societies of the last century exhibited rather clear-cut dichotomies between employers and employees, or between freeholders and tenants. Similarly dichotomous relationships were found quite generally between masters and servants, a constellation of roles which is now becoming decidedly dated.

The transition from agriculture to industry, from primary to secondary occupations, implies an increase in the size of the enterprises. However, the dichotomous stratification structure has also been prevalent in industry and is expressed in the gap between management and labor. With the development of the service sector of the economy, and especially through the growth of office organizations, the hierarchical stratification structures are predominating in important sectors of the economy. With increased automation this tendency may also spread to industrial plants because the machine operators tend to become fewer, more specialized, and more highly skilled. This situation may also induce a closer relationship to managers and white-collar workers. Simultaneously we may witness a tendency in the opposite direction in so far as the "industrialization" of some office organizations may lead to the establishment of large groups of subordinates who are very similarly situated and are in steady contact with each other, thus favoring a dichotomous stratification. Generally speaking, however, the technological and social changes of our day seem to favor more hierarchical structures of social stratification at the cost of the previously prevalent dichotomous ones.

Social mobility[11]

The stratification systems we have just dealt with must be thought of as structures consisting of roles. Therefore, a snapshot of the status system at any one point of time fails to give adequate information on the location of an individual inside the system. A time factor must be added if we want to place actors more accurately in a stratification structure. In some systems the individuals tend to be chained to the roles once entered, while other systems exhibit a great deal of movement, for example, a high rate of upward social mobility. In European industrial plants there has traditionally been a very limited amount of social mobility among the workers, while there has been considerably more among the office personnel.

The rate of social mobility is related to whether the system has a dichotomous or a hierarchical structure of social stratification. Within hierarchies one is apt to find considerable upward mobility due to promotions, while it is unusual for a subordinate in a dichotomously organized system to pass the basic line of division in the system. The hierarchical ordering of ranks permits a gradual, often imperceptible, increase of power, income, and esteem, while the dichotomous structure presents more formidable problems to those who might wish to pass from one camp to the other. For this reason a dichotomous design of a system fits best into a society where social mobility, generally speaking, is of limited scope. The two layers of the system will tend to be recruited from separate strata of the population. The recruits will retain their social rank within the system they have entered and have their previous social belongingness reaffirmed by the rank they obtain in the sub-system. If, however, social mobility in the society outside the sub-system is of considerable scope, dichotomous structures of stratification will be less attractive, forces inside the system will be induced to transform the structure into a more hierarchical type of stratification.

Social mobility raises a question concerning the basis upon which higher ranking positions are being recruited from the incumbents of lower ranking ones. Relatively pure principles of seniority may be found in some military organizations, in some branches of the civil service, and in the primary schools. Promotion up to a certain level is normally to be expected and requires no more than conformity to a minimal level of performance. One implication of applying seniority rules is a reduction of the amount of control which the manager can exercise over his subordinates. Promotion follows from a near automatic application of rules, relatively independent of the supervisor's evaluation of the performance. Where seniority is accepted as the proper basis of advancement, it is easy to make decisions concerning promotion, and control of the propriety of the decisions is facilitated. Such a practice may also induce the majority of the members of a system to attach themselves more or less permanently to the system because of the advantages inherent in being an old member. This principle may tend to repel some able and ambitious members and those who believe themselves capable of a more rapid qualification for superior positions if seniority were set aside. They may be more attracted by other systems, provided that they are in a position to choose freely.

Advancement on the basis of inherited qualities is a normal event in agricultural communities when the son ceases to be a hired hand on his father's farm and becomes a free-holding farmer on the basis of an inherited property right to the farm. The situation is similar when the son of a manager or owner of an industrial company advances from inferior positions in the firm to one of managerial responsibility. Outside the agricultural sector inherited qualities have become somewhat discredited as a basis for social advancement. If such qualities are overtly attributed importance, it is usually in conjunction with other qualities which refer to criteria of performance and achievement.

The prevalent ideology of mobility prescribes that everyone ought to have equal chances for social advancement and that promotions ought to be based upon achievement or upon a mixture of achievement and seniority. Level of education, graduation, and grades are symptoms of the kinds of performance most emphasized in this context today. In order to reach the higher positions in a modern society it is, in most areas, a requirement to have undergone higher education and to have graduated with a certain distinction. A higher education may qualify a person for immediate entrance into

116

the higher strata of a social system. The engineers start their careers in a firm as members of "the management," without necessitating any "start at the bottom," although a previous apprenticeship may have been required to enter a school of engineering. It is likewise with the recruitment of academic manpower to hospitals, schools, government departments, and to many private office organizations. However, some important channels of social advancement still remain relatively independent of formal educational requirements, as, for example, party politics, sports, and the world of the arts and entertainment. If the party bosses, the electorate, or the audience likes and trusts the actor, his advancement may be secured however humble his educational achievements. But it is quite conceivable that these openings for social mobility are in the process of being gradually closed or that the gate of entrance is at least being narrowed.

Achievement was, of course, also recognized as a plausible basis of social advancement before the advent of industrialization. We find a pointed expression of the opportunity for social mobility in the saying at the time of Napoleon that "every French soldier carries the marshal's baton in his knapsack." The able, energetic, and ambitious had a chance to rise in the army, in politics, and inside the large merchant houses. Advancement was dependent upon the employer's appreciation and his choice of standards by which the subordinate was to be judged. The criteria of promotion lacked the objectivity and uniformity which are being sought in modern examination systems or seniority rules. The superiors were free to attribute weight to subjective factors such as the loyalty and personal devotion of the subordinate. Employees did not have any right to *demand* promotion once certain definite criteria were fulfilled. The old-fashioned type of social mobility according to achievement did not reduce the superior's power to control social advancement, as the standardized modern principles of achievement tend to do. On the other hand, the old-fashioned type of occupational advancement permitted the employee to improve his qualifications without incurring great expense.[12] Qualification through education often requires that the individual at an early stage, before he himself can muster the necessary economic means, must enter an institution of higher education. It is therefore not possible to infer from the general development just outlined whether or not the rate of social mobility in a society has been increasing. We have merely been discussing a transformation of the norms of social mobility.

Mobility over two or more generations

So far mobility has been described as a phenomenon taking place within one social system and limited to an individual actor's life cycle. If the perspective is expanded to encompass the entire society, it is also reasonable to expand the time perspective to encompass mobility from one generation to the next, or even to those which follow. Most human beings develop higher social rank as they grow older, at least to a certain point. This point of rank culmination may vary from individual to individual and may also vary systematically between different types of societies. Societies exist in which age as such bestows high rank upon the actor. In modern industrial societies rank seems to be somewhat reduced when the age of retirement is reached. This is due in part to the loss of professional influence and sources of income.

It has been a common practice in sociology to look at the stratification of society at large as an order of nuclear families and not of individual actors.[13] From this point of view age and sex would not be highly relevant to social rank. It is true that the various members of the same nuclear family are similarly situated with respect to many aspects of consumption, domicile, style of life, and social circle, although the individual esteem of the children is much lower than that of the parents, and the husband often has more power and prestige than the wife. From some points of view it may be proper to deal with families as the units of stratification structures, while this is entirely misleading from other points of view. It would also be misleading to equalize two careers, although completely similar within the adult life span of the two actors, if they came from two families of orientation belonging to different social strata.

Social mobility over two generations can be measured by the social distance between the social rank of the father and that of the son if each is measured at the peak of his career. Similarly, we can measure the amount of mobility over three or more generations in terms of the relationship between the son's rank and that of his grandfather or great-grandfather. Upward social mobility ought to be studied in conjunction with movements downward in the system, social *degradation*. Actually, much more information is available on social advancement than on degradation. In all such studies the most commonly applied criterion of social rank is occupational position.

Within the occupational structure of most modern societies, sex is a factor which influences social rank a good deal. Men occupy far more positions of leadership than women. The occupations in which women are most amply represented require less educational background, are less well paid, and enjoy lower esteem than the most nearly comparable occupations for men. The occupational position is not, however, as decisive for the social rank of a woman as it is for the rank of a man. The wife of a man of high prestige, a company president or a high official of the civil service, may work in a much less prestigious occupation. The woman's occupation would tend to place her in a relatively low-ranking social stratum, while her unconstrained participation in the social circle of the husband suggests that husband and wife ought to be ranked at the same level.

The nuclear family's composition of actors who need each other precisely because of their diversity presents some problems. The differences of sex and age in the family have great significance for the ranking of the individual inside social systems other than the family. If the family is to achieve a sufficient amount of cohesion, husband and wife must have approximately the same social rank, either by birth, or because of similarities of achievement, or simply due to social norms which bestow equal rank upon spouses as a direct consequence of the marriage itself. It must further be a plausible expectation that the children, when grown, achieve approximately the same rank level as that of their parents. If not, the tensions between the generations may be sharpened by the presence of interest conflicts also related to social class. The problem has usually been solved by *de facto* preferential access of a son to the social strata of his father and of his family of orientation. The daughter's problem has usually been solved through the *de facto* operation of principles of mate selection which make it probable that she acquire a husband of a rank similar to that of her father.

A stable family structure seems to presuppose a systematic interplay between occupational structure and social stratification. This interrelationship may, however, be put into effect in different forms. We may distinguish between three principles, roughly speaking, temporally subsequent upon each other. According to the first principle the father's occupation is inherited by the son, and the daughter marries a man from her father's occupation. According to the second principle the son inherits his father's rank, but is faced with a choice between many different occupations, all of them, however, belonging to the same social stratum as that of the father. Likewise, the daughter may choose between prospective spouses from diverse occupations but of similar social rank. The third principle is put into effect when the social strata of a society have become equalized to the extent that it is improbable that the son should be able to find an occupation which status-wise differs much from that of his father. The daughter is in a position to choose a husband irrespective of occupation, since occupations are not much stratified. The last principle is not put into effect in any known society, while a development in this direction may be observable in some modern societies.

The problem inherent in the relationship between social mobility and family structure is revealed when, for instance, the student or graduate is forced to choose between his childhood environment and values, and the new milieus to which his education admits him. Specifically, the problem may be encountered in the choice of spouse, of political conviction, and of general style of life. Social advancement of this kind is often accompanied by geographic migration, tending to ameliorate the latent conflicts inherent in the situation. Visits during the vacations may turn out to be the major type of contact preserved with the childhood environment, and these do not necessarily force the rank problems upon the socially mobile individual and his family of orientation.

Social strata as systems

Social strata have not been defined to make it necessary for them to constitute social systems. No requirements have been specified with respect to contact, cohesion, or communality of interests among those equally situated in the stratification structure of a social system. Categories of social rank have been defined in terms of their similarity with respect to important social contributions and sanctions, especially power, wealth, and esteem. If social systems emerge on the basis of stratification, they do so because of *proximity* and *similarity*. Complementarity is often excluded as a cohesive force in this context by the very definition of social stratification. Actors belonging to the same social stratum do not specifically need to interact because of their capacity to supplement each other. If they need each other, it is because they collectively are able to do more of what each member could do on his own. Social stratification is most likely to induce the creation of social systems when conflicts of interest prevail between different categories of social rank. The germ of the conflict is inherent in the very concept of social stratification, and more specifically in the uneven distribution of power and authority.

When social strata are turned into systems it means that the members establish relationships of interaction with each other, aiming to take care of common functions, while interaction with other actors with reference to these tasks are less frequent and less important. The lower social strata in the peasant societies which preceded the industrial revolution did not constitute social systems. Tenant farmers and agricultural workers constituted a category exhibiting considerable similarities in terms of general living conditions and occupied roles with similarly low social rank. However, mutual contacts and the germs of organization were frustrated by the poor development of the means of communication, by the low level of education, and by other factors. Travel was cumbersome and costly, illiteracy was quite common, and there was a lack of newspapers and leaflets to transmit messages within the agricultural proletariat. The close ties between the peasant and his hamlet and the landowner, based upon complementary needs, made it a remote possibility that he should orient himself towards a wider circle of fellow peasants and workers.

Spasmodic upheavals in the countryside suggest that there were tendencies towards system formation even among the European peasants of the nineteenth century. However, not until the growth of industry had reached a certain magnitude did there emerge a firm basis for the development of stable social systems in the shape of voluntary organizations founded upon membership derived from a definite social stratum. The nucleation of population, fostered by industrial enterprises, led to an increased opportunity of interaction among workers, at the place of work as well as in their leisure time. The industrial development was also accompanied by, or even preceded by, great improvements in the means of communication on a national scale, facilitating travel and providing the basis for a network of information and propaganda. Factors other than these were also contributing to a situation where social strata assumed the characteristics of social systems with the implications of mutual interaction, common ideology, centralized leadership, and collective action to achieve common goals. For one thing, the scope and strength of other kinds of social bonds were of great importance. Some developing industrial centers had a stable local population of workmen, and the owners of the industry exerted their authority in conformity with a traditional paternalistic pattern. Under such conditions a working class, with strong ideological commitment and militant leadership, was less likely to emerge than in those districts where the labor force had been more mobile and where the owner was absent or impersonal.[14]

Social class

If we take our point of departure from the writings of Karl Marx, we may distinguish between several stages in the emergence of social systems founded upon social strata.[15] *A social system founded upon a social stratum in society at large will serve as our definition of a social class.* The first precondition for systems to emerge on the basis of social stratification is that the similarities and dissimilarities of rank are being perceived by the members. Social rank must be psychologically salient and no mere statistical construct based upon differences observed only by the sociologist. In less cohesive societies, geographically disconnected or divided into different ethnic and linguistic groups, it is sometimes doubtful exactly what psychological significance the patterns of unequal access to scarce goods have on a national scale. The answer depends upon what comparisons are relevant to the members of the society in question, what reference groups the actors choose. They may have a frame of reference which is limited to local communities or to ethnic groups, making the stratification of society less relevant than it is in societies where the consciousness of national membership is highly developed.

When actual, observable similarities become psychological realities to the actors, these may refer to diverse criteria of social rank. Marx emphasized especially the distribution of property rights in the system of economic production. Property rights give rise to wealth in the sense of permitting a high level of consumption. More important, however, the ownership of large means of production provides an opportunity to command a group of workers and to control the values they have created by their labor.[16] Even if the workers enjoy full freedom of contract, they are often dependent upon employment in an industrial enterprise. This was especially true during the industrial revolution. For this reason, those in command of the productive machinery were able to employ subordinates who became obliged to obey their directives. The inequalities of power and authority between the "exploiters" and the "exploited" became the crucial criterion, around which were crystallized the most important social systems emerging on the basis of social stratification.

An awareness among members of a social stratum that they have approximately similar rank, that they share the same conditions with respect to the access to power, wealth, and esteem, implies that a reference group has emerged. A reference group is not, however, an interacting group or a social system. Marx claimed that the equality of position in the apparatus of production would lead to a communality of interest, above all in the sense that the workers, objectively speaking, had a common interest to protect against the assault from the owners of the means of production. The latter proposition does not follow by any logical necessity from the fact of equal location in a structure of social stratification. The prospects of improving conditions depend upon diverse strategies in differently situated enterprises.

Traditionally there have been many differences in this respect between workers and functionaries, differences related to the dissimilarities between dichotomous and hierarchical structures of stratification. The clerk who found himself in economic circumstances very similar to those of the laborers might have prospects of rising in the office hierarchy, an advancement which was denied the laborers within their system of production. Besides, the clerk would often represent his boss, for example, in relation to the workers, thus bestowing upon himself a reflection of superordination. Eilert Sundt, one of the earliest empirical sociologists in Europe, classified the clerk, "the black-coated worker," as a member of the "propertied class." [17]

Much in the social development which has taken place in industrial societies during the last century can be interpreted in support of Marx's claim that the industrial workers, together with other members of the lower social strata, objectively speaking, had crucial interests in common. It is not, however, an easy task to show empirically whether this has been so or not, or to what extent his claim has been substantiated. It is, above all, the widespread subjective experience of a communality of interests that has become a driving force in the development of so many societies. Contact and social interaction were a prerequisite to the spread of this belief in common interests. These interests could be experienced as being communal, as goals best achieved through collective action, because of the concomitant development of the means of communication and the growth of the school system. Conversely also, the emerging class consciousness facilitated the contact among class fellows, who at times even became comrades by virtue of belonging to the same class.

Once this interplay between a perceived communality of interests and social interaction has been engendered, a social class is emerging. The developing class consciousness is supported by the creation of interest organizations, lobbies, labor unions, and political parties. Not until these organizations are welded together on a national scale under common leadership, accompanied by a distinct ideology and strategy, do the underprivileged strata of a society turn into a real social system. The significance of ideology lies in its capacity to structure the perceptions of the individual members of a social stratum to clarify for them the nature of society and of their own location in its stratification. Whether factual or fictitious, the notion that society has a dichotomous structure of social stratification, has, at times, contributed a great deal to an approximation of the preceding model in reality.

Marxism is not merely a sociological theory with its strong and its weak points, it has also been one of the great motivating forces in recent developments of societies all over the world, in many cases something of a "self-fulfilling prophecy," but at times also a self-defeating one. In the Scandinavian countries the Marxist ideology of the Labor parties seems to have contributed to make the working classes cohesive and to set the stage for a dichotomous political struggle, out of which the working class emerged victorious in many respects. But this very success, in conjunction with the general technological development, has in recent years led society away from the dichotomous class structure of the years between the two World Wars.

Nations have often been welded together as systems under the influence of external threats, in times of international conflict, or in periods of war with other nations. Likewise, social strata have gained in internal solidarity and have achieved a clearer demarcation, more firmness in organization, and a more militant leadership when engaged in struggles with other social strata. Before the Second World War, strikes and lockouts seemed, symbolically, to affirm the view that there were only two important social classes. Since the interests of the rich and the poor, the capitalists and the workers, were diametrically opposed, any possibility of bridge-building between the two was excluded. Since that time the dichotomous theory of social classes has lost ground in the United

States and in Western Europe. The situations where such a theory might be confirmed are fewer and also less dramatic, which is related to a leveling out of the distribution of scarce goods.

The emergence of classes as social systems based upon stratification has here been described, as it were, from "below." Historically speaking this may be misleading. In most countries the upper social strata probably constituted interacting social networks for a long time before the lower social strata assumed the character of interacting systems. Such a pattern follows almost by definition when the borders of the national state are defining a society. The state is a system of offices; officeholders tend to occupy roughly similar positions in the structure of social stratification, and are simultaneously tied to each other by organizational bonds and often also by kinship.

This connection can be seen very clearly in Norway, which was founded as a modern state as late as 1814. Its upper classes consisted especially of civil servants, dispersed all over the country, but tied to each other by common economic interests, by similar education and style of life, and related to each other by kinship, marriage, or social milieu.[18] The first organized opposition to this upper class were the farmers in Parliament who represented the higher strata of the local communities in the countryside. This antagonism corresponded to a Marxian scheme in so far as it was based upon a conflict between two relatively distinct social strata, defined by their relationships of superordination and subordination, and upon the incompatible interests arising out of this situation. However, the social system setting the frame of reference for this inequality of power and authority was not the private economic enterprises. It was within the state, in relation to politics and public administration, that the farmers represented the underdog and felt alienated. The difference in power did not spring from an inequality in terms of property rights to the means of production. It sprang from an unequal access to the decision-making machinery of the state. While this factor seems to have been the decisive one, it is also true that civil servants and private entrepreneurs in the nineteenth century constituted one social class, characterized by intermarriage and kinship, by a common social milieu, and by mutual trust and cooperation in the execution of many tasks.[19]

The social preconditions for the emergence of upper- and lower-classes respectively are not quite parallel. The opportunities to interact and communicate tended, at least up to the present time, to be more favorable in the upper than in the lower classes. There are fewer members of the upper class than of the lower class. The superior social rank and the greater access to resources bestow an organizational advantage upon the higher strata of a society, further reinforced by the fact that their members often have been shaped by common experiences in terms of training and shared membership in a sub-culture and a common milieu. Schools and universities have in modern times played an important part in the formation of homogeneous and cohesive national upper classes.[20]

On the other hand, there may occur a greater and more apparent differentiation and individualization in the higher social strata. Competition on a geographical, a professional, or some other economic or political basis may also be most marked in the top layers of a society which frustrates attempts at cooperation. The gap between the landed aristocracy and the industrialists in England put its stamp on political conflicts for a long time. During the period of rapid industrialization many societies have witnessed considerable fission in the upper classes. Such a fission in the upper classes may easily induce similar divergencies in the lower classes because the competing factions of the upper class seek to ally themselves with parts of the lower class. Thus, the Tory worker emerged in England, while the class formations in the Scandinavian countries have been less characterized by these internal factionalizations and alliances across class lines.

VI

CONFLICT

AND DEVIANCE

In the preceding analysis the main emphasis was put upon those factors which tie individuals and roles together in systems and which provide for social order. We are now going to deal with factors which may destroy social bonds, frustrate social interaction, or threaten to dissolve social systems. Conflict as well as deviance imply a lack of complementarity in the relationship between expectations and responses. Ego expects something which Alter is unwilling or unable to contribute. Whether this state of the relationship between Ego and Alter ought to be termed a conflict or an instance of deviance may at times be hard to determine. The solution will depend upon the point of view of the observer.

If we look at a crime from the standpoint of society and its legal agencies, it is a deviant act, behavior contrary to the norms prescribed and enforced by the social system. As viewed through the eyes of the criminal, however, the situation looks more like a conflict. The offender is at odds with society. As a rule, it will be natural to speak about deviance when a single actor, or a few, act contrary to the norms of the system. If, however, a system fails to comply with the expectations of another system, or if a number of actors oppose each other inside the system, it may be safer to describe the situation in terms of conflict. For a conflict to deserve the label "deviance," a third party must be capable of judging one of the contestants right, while simultaneously branding the behavior of the adversary as contrary to the norms of the system. Such a third agent provides the foundation of intranational police actions, while often being absent in tense international situations, especially in times of war.

Conflict

The term "conflict" is not unequivocal. It is used to refer to states of a neural system, to intrapsychic processes, and to individual behavior at a choice point. The conflicts which concern us here, however, are those which obtain between actors, roles, or systems. Social conflict may be defined as a state of the relationship between two or more role-players. The state must be characterized by overt symptoms of hostility, tension, or antagonism. The minimal requirement is that one of the actors, Ego, in word or deed gives evidence of a wish to frustrate Alter, and/or that he, through his actions, actually causes Alter some harm. A state characterized by Ego's vain attempts to frustrate Alter will be subsumed under the concept of conflict even if no harm is actually done to Alter. A state in which Alter suffers a loss because of Ego's behavior will also be classified as a conflict even if Ego felt no animosity towards Alter and did not wish to inflict any harm upon him.

The very state of conflict should be distinguished from the causes of conflict. When referring to the source of the conflict we have in mind the characteristics of the relationship between Ego and Alter which have led to the overt signs of hostility or to frustration. The last chapter showed how it is necessary to distinguish between the source of the conflict, the interests of the antagonists, and the actual conflict behavior, in the study of social classes and of the class struggle. The state of conflict and the conflict behavior must, furthermore, be kept apart from the subsequent course of events and the termination of the conflict. Most conflicts disappear in the course of time. This may often happen simply because one of the adversaries is removed and the relationship between Ego and Alter comes to an end. Those modes of termination which release the mechanism of *conflict resolution* are of greater interest. All methods facilitating a reduction or amelioration of the tension between Ego and Alter, or which actually bring the conflict to an end will be considered conflict-solving mechanisms.

A question may arise whether the prevailing relationship between two parties in violent conflict constitutes a social system at all. The antagonism does not necessarily deprive the relationship of the characteristics of a social system when the conflict falls short of being total, that is, when it leaves some reciprocity of expectation and action. Simmel, and later Coser, have enumerated the positive functions that conflicts may serve in a social relationship.[1] A state of conflict may establish bonds upon which a relationship may rest. Let us, however, look at the extreme state of a war. An intensive overt interplay is taking place between the nations at war with each other. The movements of one of the armies have vast repercussions upon the army of the adversary. Mutual sensitivities are sharpened to the utmost. A continuous and mutual adjustment of moves and countermoves is taking place. What is the sociological nature of this interaction? Can it be described in terms of an exchange of contributions and sanctions, which provides a basis for treating two nations at war as elements of a social system?

Some further conditions need to be fulfilled in order for mutually contingent acts between two role-players to constitute a social system. A certain agreement concerning the terms of exchange must be present, at least a minimal consensus on the give and take, on what is gain and what is loss, and on how one can go about measuring the magnitudes of costs and benefits. Such a mutual understanding may prevail between the army commands on both sides. Since, however, the purpose of war is to destroy the enemy, a consensus concerning what would constitute equal gains or equal deprivations on both sides cannot provide a basis for making decisions in the course of the conduct of the war. Both sides attempt to choose battlefields, strategies, and weapons with the purpose of inflicting heavier losses on the enemy than on their own army. The adversaries must protect as secrets the very expectations they entertain vis-à-vis the enemy as well as the response they are preparing for enemy expectations.

The communication of expectations and norms, such a vital ingredient of normal relationships between Ego and Alter, is in the case of war very largely obliterated. Instead the belligerents try to deceive each other concerning their own moves and expectations. To some extent the situation is ameliorated by the warring nations' common interests in saving sick and wounded, in preventing the use of certain types of warfare, and in protecting the civilian population. Thus, the belligerents attempt to convey to the enemy that they will refrain from the use of certain means of warfare and expect the adversary to do likewise. Based upon such covert messages, unwritten agreements may also be reached in times of war, thereby bestowing on the combatants' reciprocal relationship some system characteristics.

When, however, the extremes of a conflict lead to situations where the relationships between adversaries lose the characteristics of a social system, it is due to basic incompatibilities of interest. Ego can expect no other gains than those which represent loss to Alter, and the adversaries are by and large unwilling to convey their expectations and their future contributions and sanctions. Thus, they are debarred from reaching an agreement on the terms of settlement based upon a confrontation of mutual expectations.

Underlying these brief remarks on war is a distinction between two types of conflict which are suggested by the terms "conflict of interests" and "lack of consensus" (disagreement). Next, we are going to deal with this distinction between two basic types of conflict.

CONFLICT OF INTERESTS

A conflict of interest derives from a situation of scarcity. Ego and Alter want the same thing, but there is not enough of it to satisfy all desires. Such a basis of conflicts is very common in interpersonal relationships. In most instances of selling and buying there is some cause for a conflict of interests. The customer would like to acquire a larger quantity of the commodity at the price he is paying, and the seller would like to obtain a better price. However, when a fixed market price prevails, these incipient divergencies of interest will normally not develop into conflicts, as that term has been defined (p. 129). If there is no fixed price on the market, a conflict between seller and buyer is more likely to emerge, although usually not of a serious kind.

Even if a source of conflict is present in commercial dealings, in marketing and selling, the conflicting interests are not wholly incompatible. It is true only to some extent that the gains of one party must become the losses of the other. There usually exists an area where the interests are overlapping, that is, where both parties have an interest in the completion of the transaction. The seller has no interest in remaining saddled with a huge stock of goods which he is unable personally to consume. And the buyer is not interested in saving his money if he consequently is unable to make the necessary purchases. The relationship between Ego and Alter is characterized by partly incompatible and partly overlapping interests.

A similar situation normally prevails in group tensions between nations or between employers and employees. In historical wars one nation's defeat has been regarded as the victory of the enemy nation. Both parties to an international conflict share, however, an interest in preventing war since it is apt to be costly not only for the vanquished, but also for the victor. In industrial conflicts, such as strikes, both parties are interested in preventing a long-lasting stoppage of work which reduces the output.

In those relations between Ego and Alter, where interests are partly incompatible and partly overlapping, negotiation presents itself as a normal procedure to resolve the conflict. Since each party has something he may gain from the adversary, the actions of one are calculated to extract concessions from the other. Ego will attempt to motivate Alter to increase his contribution or reduce his demands by a promise to offer Alter some reciprocal concession. Ego and Alter search for a solution through a compromise. A fundamental motive underlying such negotiations and determining the strategies chosen by the parties is the wish to minimize the risk of a maximal loss (the minimax principle).[2] This desire leads to sacrificing the chance to obtain the maximal gains in order to achieve security against inviting the worst calamity. The operation of this motive is clearly seen in the acquisition of insurance, which implies that people willingly assume the burden of some certain, but limited, payment to obtain security against a much greater, but perhaps unlikely, loss. By and large, people are willing to buy security against catastrophies whenever possible, even if this pur-chase debars them from achieving the maximal gains.

As with so many apparently universal tendencies in human be-havior, it is here also possible to point to deviant cases, namely, to situations where people search for uncertainty. The very great attraction of betting, gambling, and other games of chance sug-gests that this attitude is rather widespread. In most cases, how-ever, the immediate and certain loss is small and quite calculable, limiting the operation of the attractive uncertainty. In negotiations concerning a sale, a loan, or some other business transaction, Ego and Alter are apt to behave more or less in accordance with the minimax principle. Since very often the least desirable alternative is that no transaction will take place, both parties are motivated to make concessions and yield in relation to their initial prefer-ences. They may be willing to concede on some point even though concession may bring them to feel that the terms of exchange are becoming unfair, that is, contrary to the demands of justice. Ne-gotiations often lead to solutions of conflicts precisely because the parties adopt a morally neutral attitude to the transactions they are engaged in.

When a conflict is being solved through negotiations between the parties, it is not necessary to arrive at any agreement regarding the factual origin and development of the conflict or the norms that are applicable to the case. Consequently, a great freedom of movement is bestowed on the negotiators. Strictly speaking, the parties need not reach agreement on anything beyond settlement of a point where the demands of both sides meet, that is, where they would rather accept the solution offered them than face a broken relationship and no agreement at all. To arrive at this point may be easy in some situations, as it is between experienced hagglers in an Eastern market, or it may be very difficult, as the endless negotiations between the chief antagonists in the cold war suggest. The advantage of negotiated solutions is that they need not leave any marks on the normative order of society. The solu-tion does not become a precedent for later solutions to similar conflicts. Therefore, the adversaries need not fear the general con-sequences of the settlement. However, from another point of view a weakness develops from this kind of settlement because a kind of predictability is often needed which would result if the solution could be interpreted as the application of a norm generalizable to other similar cases.

So far we have dealt with conflicts where the interests are partly overlapping and partly contradictory. There are, however, also situations where the incompatibility of the interests is total with regard to a specific set of values. What is a gain for one side must necessarily appear as a loss to the other side. One example is the type of sports where achievement is measured exclusively in terms of a ranking between the competitors; for example, in football, basketball, ice hockey, boxing, wrestling, tennis, and yachting. In most types of track sports like distance running, high jumping, and javelin- and discus-throwing, the situation is less clear, as is also the case in skating and cross-country skiing. The defeated as well as the victorious may have aimed towards a good result as measured by the clock or some other instrument in addition to victory or a very high rank. Conflicts between rivals in love is characterized by the total incompatibility of interests. If one of the rivals wins the girl, it means defeat for the other one. Such is also the case in many types of competition for positions and in the electoral battles of politicians. If one of the candidates wins a seat in the national assembly, it necessarily implies that someone else loses that seat.

When gains and losses are evened out in this fashion, the relationship has been described as a zero-sum game.[3] The competition as such does not generate value; it merely serves to distribute existing values on the basis of an either-or choice, where a benefit on one side reappears as a cost on the other side. Such conflicts are not so readily solved by means of negotiations between the contestants. In the examples enumerated above, a third party intervenes in the conflict and makes a decision in favor of one side: the track umpire, the girl, or the electorate. Negotiations are not ruled out, however, disregarding the world of sports where agreements between the participants in a competition are banned as unlawful or senseless. Two rivals may reach an agreement on who is to win the girl, provided that she cares for both of them, and two politicians may agree on some kind of electoral cooperation and mutual accommodation. A motive to initiate such negotiations lies in the burdens imposed upon both parties by intensive competition. For the most likely loser there are additional advantages in yielding freely and gracefully rather than facing unmitigated and involuntary defeat. For these reasons it is difficult to find the pure zero-sum game in actual social life other than the sports world, and the reality rarely represents more than an approximation of this model of conflict.

In economic transactions a relationship may be transformed from a non-zero-sum game to a zero-sum game if disastrous events intervene in the relationship of exchange. This transformation may occur if the commodity representing Ego's contribution disappears after the contract is signed, but before Alter has received the commodity. Assume that a car salesman has parked a sold car outside the house of the customer, but that the car has disappeared before the buyer has returned home. Who is to carry the loss? The interests of the parties are diametrically opposed to each other. If the buyer already has paid for the car, his interest will prompt him to negotiate in order to recover his money or to get another car. The salesman's interest, however, lies in a rejection of further negotiations because the present status quo, from his point of view, represents the best obtainable result. It is inconceivable that he should gain anything by negotiations. If the car had not been paid for, the situation is completely reversed: the buyer is the one who has no interest in carrying on negotiations since they could only lead to a loss on his part. When we reason this way we assume, somewhat unrealistically, that the parties to the contract have no enduring reciprocal relationship making them interested in future transactions with each other.

It seems that negotiations are a less than adequate means of solving conflicts where the interests are contradictory to the extent that gains and losses must cancel each other, where, in other words, we are faced with a zero-sum game. Society has not been willing to accept settlements of conflicts, like the one between the buyer and seller of the lost car, by the hazards determining which one is lucky enough to retain the profit. In such situations the parties may bring the case to the courts and demand a legal settlement. The courts will then solve the conflict in accordance with principles very different from those governing commercial negotiations.

VALUE CONFLICT AND DISAGREEMENT

A conflict of interests does not presuppose a disagreement between Ego and Alter over values or factual matters. On the contrary, competition rests upon consensus about the evaluation of a scarce good. Jealousy springs precisely from an unfortunate consensus over the value of a woman. Neither would rivalry over positions of leadership arise if the contestants had not tended to evaluate incumbency of the position in rather similar terms. This agreement tends to draw Ego and Alter together; the conflict thus emphasizes their communality of value premises. In the very source of a conflict of interests lies the germ of mutual understanding and the chance of reaching a solution.

A conflict of values means that Ego and Alter have different attitudes to a value. They are in disagreement over the valuation of some benefit or burden. The disagreements over factual matters concerning what has actually happened or the explanation of facts are quite as important as this normative dissension. Dissension over values or facts does not necessarily imply that Ego and Alter clash with each other in a conflict. Rather, the disagreement may tend to keep them away from each other and reduce the probability of a clash if for other reasons they are not brought in touch with each other. In the very source of conflicts over values and what is the truth of a matter lies a factor which may prevent the overt and destructive consequences of the antagonism.

This, notwithstanding, dissension often leads to conflict behavior, to political struggle, or to ideologically determined wars. These kinds of aggression may arise because competing interests are hidden beneath the ideological veneer. Even if, originally, no such interests were present, ideological confrontations tend in their turn to become a source of interest conflicts, that is, in so far as both parties will attempt to secure for their side positions of power and authority from which the ideals may be defended and propagated. Since power is a scarce resource, the ideological struggles over political issues are normally converted into a competition for positions of leadership.

Conflicts about values or about the truth of facts are different from the conflicts of interest and are not amenable to the same types of resolution. Conflicts over values and facts are more public. A solution implies a stand on what has actually happened or on what norms ought to be applied to conflicts of this kind. This has implications for the solution of other, similar disagreements. Actors, other than those directly engaged, have a stake in the outcome because a certain definition of the truth of a factual matter or of a point of value can come to mean something also for them. For these reasons and others such dissension over facts or values is not so readily amenable to negotiation between the conflicting parties. The antagonists have no private property rights to values or to the truth of the matter at issue. Here lies one of the roots of resentment against "horse-trading" in ideological matters. "Values are not for sale" and "One cannot compromise with the truth." At any event, compromise does not present itself as the obvious solution, as is so often the case in commercial negotiations.

Disagreements over facts or values may be settled in many different ways. A third party usually participates in the solution in one form or another to determine the outcome. Feuds between politicians are solved directly or indirectly by the electorate, or occasionally by appeal to the court of history operating through the judgment of posterity. In principle at least debates between scientists are solved by reference to objective methods which may be applied by other persons as well as the protagonists themselves. Conflicts over guilt and responsibility in private matters may be solved by delegating the decision to a court of law. This legal method is the one most clearly and minutely elaborated.

LAW AS A MEANS OF RESOLVING CONFLICTS

When a case is dealt with in court, the conflict between the parties has been formulated as a controversy over facts and/or norms applicable to the case. In criminal proceedings the court decides whether the defendant has committed the crime he is accused of, and in civilian litigation it must decide whether a contract of specified content has actually been entered into or whether a certain amount of injury has been caused. The court is further invited to decide what norms have validity and what inferences are to be drawn from the norms when the specific suit at hand is subsumed under them. Irrespective of the source of the conflict between the parties, it must be formulated in court as a disagreement over norms and/or over factual matters.

The verdict of the court has an either/or character; the decision is based upon a single, definite conception of what has actually taken place, and upon a single interpretation of the legal norms. When a conflict of interests passes from the stage of negotiation to that of litigation, one of the parties must be prepared to suffer a total loss. He runs the risk that the judge will make no allowance for his demands and will decide wholly in favor of his adversary. In addition the loser may have to pay the legal costs. This raises the question of why all civilian suits are not settled out of court after negotiations.

One reason is that there may be considerable uncertainty about who is most likely to win the case and both adversaries overestimate their chances of victory in the legal battle. Aggression and unwillingness to meet the antagonist in negotiations may play their part. Some feel that concessions in the course of negotiations are symptoms of moral weakness and that a defeat at the hands of the judge is preferable. If Ego represents interests which he shares with others, like his family, colleagues, or partners, he may prefer to run the risk of an adverse verdict rather than accept some voluntary sacrifice. In the latter case, he might be rebuked by his relatives or colleagues for having sold out. If the government, an insurance company, or a bank is party to a conflict, the desire to achieve certainty with respect to future claims may gain overriding importance and reduce the significance of a possible loss in the present suit.

There are, in other words, many reasons why adversaries choose to accept the increased risk implicit in litigation, provided that the prospects of a compromise solution are dim. However, the fear of an either/or solution if the conflict is brought before a judge is, no doubt, one of the most important reasons why people attempt to settle their controversies out of court. In the course of such settlements no one needs to take a definite stand on what is right and what is wrong, and on who is responsible; neither is it necessary to find the one proper interpretation of the relevant legal rules. This flexibility gives to negotiations a somewhat less moralistic flavor, a more matter-of-fact character than that associated with litigation. An important task for future research is to discover under what circumstances a solution of conflicts through negotiations is most appropriate, and under what conditions litigation is preferred. The problem is relevant to conflicts between individuals as well as to tensions between groups or nations.

INTERMEDIARY MODES OF CONFLICT RESOLUTION

We have compared with each other two ideal types of conflict resolution. On the one hand, we have the pure conflict of interests where the contestants are engaged in unprincipled haggling until they find a point of equilibrium sufficiently satisfying to both parties to make them accept the outcome and forego further hostile acts. On the other hand, we have a conflict which, although it may also have a source in incompatible interests, is solved through a formalized battle over norms and factual matters, leaving the decision to a third party. In real life these ideal types almost always appear in some kind of combination and mixture.

Even in the most blatant kind of horse-trading it is hardly feasible to keep out all references to opinions concerning what, objectively speaking, constitutes reasonable and just terms of exchange, like pointing to the current market prices. Conversely, even in law suits before a court, the judge is at some liberty to balance gains and losses to make the outcome closer to a compromise than legal form would lead one to believe. Compromise may occur when the court grants the plaintiff his claims for compensation in spite of some uncertainty with respect to the injury, while reducing the claim correspondingly as a concession to the interests of the defendant.

Modes of conflict resolution are to be found, however, that explicitly recognize a combination of elements from both the ideal types. The judge is often authorized to attempt mediation between the parties and thus cancels the demand for a strict application of legal rules and canons of proof to the facts of the case. Situations also exist where negotiation is the normal mode of conflict resolution, but where the adversaries may use a third party as mediator. The mediator cannot decide how the conflict is to be settled, but he may, by virtue of his authority and the counsel offered to the parties, influence them to reach a compromise agreement. Labor arbitrators may play an important part in the settlement of an eventual impasse during wage negotiations, although the negotiating parties in the end have to sign the agreement.

Another intermediary form of conflict resolution is found in the use of arbitration tribunals, private courts, whose members are appointed by the parties. Arbitration grants the possibility that the interests of the parties may be represented on the tribunal. The arbitration council is not obliged to follow the same procedures as the regular courts and are not strictly bound by the law. The decisions of arbitration tribunals may put great emphasis upon the accommodation of interest conflicts by choosing some middle ground, although they are, like the courts, apt to stress the clarification of facts and norms more than the parties would have done in the course of negotiations.

The Scandinavian Labor Courts are in principle regular judicial bodies and bound by the law. The recruitment procedures are different from those prevailing in the rest of the judiciary: each one of the main adversaries (labor unions and management associations) appoint some members of the court. Since many of the issues on which the Labor Court is invited to pass judgment are of a discretionary character, the stress on compromise may play a greater part in the judgments of this body than it does in other courts.

Deviance

The concept of conflict does not presuppose that the observer has chosen a definite point of view when describing the interaction between the parties. A definite point of view is presupposed when the term deviance is used. A group norm must be known and recognized in order for the behavior of a member to be labeled as deviance. This label does not necessarily imply that the sociologist accepts the majority norm of the group. He may very well believe that the minority is right and still characterize its behavior as deviance. Deviance is conduct contrary to the prevailing norms of a group or a system.

Deviations may be classified in terms of the type of norm which they violate, or the type of institution to which the norm pertains. The following kinds of deviants exist in relation to the norms of the family: the divorcee, the unmarried mother, the old bachelor, the spinster, and the bigamist. The last one among these deviants is also a criminal, while the other social types do not represent behavior contrary to the laws. The legal norms permit most of the patterns of conduct just enumerated, while the informal norms inside and outside the family exert pressures, supported by economic sanctions, to reduce the incidences of divorces, unmarried mothers, and spinsters.

Inside the school system types of deviance are found like laziness, obstinacy, disobedience, truancy, and stupidity. The school strives to prevent the occurrence of these deviant forms of behavior and to punish deviants when norms are broken, ordinarily without the aid of the police or the courts. Inside the systems of economic production we find absenteeism, neglect of work, and pilfering as important categories of deviance, but also strikebreaking and apple-polishing. Apart from pilfering, these activities are of little concern to law enforcement personnel. In the two latter instances the action does not constitute a breach with the norms of the firm, but represents deviation from the informal rules of the workers' collectivity. The traitor is a classical deviant in terms of political norms and institutions, while the rebel, the revolutionary, the radical, or even the liberal represent variations on the same theme. In religious institutions the heretic and the sinner are two of the most important prototypes of deviants, differing widely between themselves. With regard to the norms of social stratification, the snob and the *nouveaux riches* on the top and the poor at the bottom represent recognizable forms of deviance.

Inside science and the arts, deviance assumes a meaning very different from the one it has inside the institutions we have dealt with. Science and the arts are founded upon norms which explicitly demand, encourage, permit, and often reward deviation from traditional beliefs and patterns. The inventor, the discoverer, the original scientist, and the pioneer in a branch of the arts are, at least retroactively, heroes rather than villains. When innovation and breach with the tradition is encouraged, one may raise the question whether the term deviance is appropriate to the situation.[4] Whatever the answer to this terminological question, it is important to register, analyze, and explain the kind of trespassing upon conventions which is not met by penalties and social control. Here lies one of the sources of *social change*.[5] The process of social change today is all pervasive in modern society, and not at all limited to the arts and sciences.

Social change implies a modification of previous norms, and the substitution of new roles for old ones, or the creation of entirely new role patterns and system structures. The changes are often precipitated by technological innovations and by alterations in the material rewards offered to actors. It becomes advantageous to deviate from traditional norms, such as those which define proper and prudent behavior of rural folk, and instead take up a new way of life like that found in the cities where employment opportunities are better. What originally emerged as the consequence of an opportunistic strategic choice may soon become ensconced in norms and role patterns which define the new behavior as proper and moral, as well as being lucrative. However, norms may create a resistance to change, and sometimes this resistance can only be broken if normative patterns are first loosened up.

Criminality is the type of deviance which has been taken as the very prototype of conduct contrary to society's norms. Crime is deviation from legal norms to which the threat of penal sanctions are attached. In contrast to this type of deviance is illness, the deviations from norms concerning sanity and health. Crime and illness represent polar opposites in many respects. A closer inspection of some of the types of deviance that have been touched upon would reveal, however, that they borrow traits from the criminal as well as the sick in varying combinations. We shall now consider the criminal and the sick as two social roles which may be entered into as a consequence of definable social criteria.

TWO MODELS OF DEVIANCE[6]

The criminal law is one among several mechanisms designed to order the priorities between values or between means to obtain values. The criminal law puts Ego's wish to live above Alter's desire to get rid of him. It gives preference to the owner's access to his property at the cost of the thief's access to it. This characteristic of penal laws bestows upon criminals a quality of being actors in search of valued goals. Whatever theories one may entertain about what a delinquent really achieves, the assumption that he was striving to consummate some desired goal is a prerequisite to his being branded as a criminal.

Medical science defines illness without requiring that the criteria refer to the priority of values or to actors' opportunities to consummate goals. The one necessary value premise inherent in the social definition of illness is that it ought to be negatively valued. To become sick is to undergo a change for the worse. It is normally assumed that the onset of a disease occurs in spite of, not because of, goal-striving, which is the effort to stay well and sane.

In those instances where the criteria of the deviant action are impossible or difficult to recognize, a deviation from what is normal may assume an ambiguous position. Whether a given case of deviance should then be labeled a crime or a disease is largely dependent upon the situation in which the deviation took place, including the social characteristics of the deviant as well as those who administer the social control.

Any situation where the actor's withdrawal may present itself as an advantage because it would relieve him of responsibilities makes a claim to be ill suspicious. Service in the army is such a situation, for withdrawal may present itself as attractive to the draftee. This is so universally recognized that any claim to be sick in the army or when appearing before the draft board is met *a priori* with scepticism. Absence from the school, the factory, and other places of work and responsibility is similarly countered with suspicion.

Examples of the obverse situation may also occur, since it is easier to have a claim to being ill honored when the sick role would lead to deprivation of the role-player. When a child is on his way to a party, his claim to being ill is readily believed since it must override his desire to participate in the party. If he had been on his way to school, or about to get up to go to school, the burden of proof would once more have been sharply reversed.

The present point of view also implies that the criminal nature of a certain action is rendered dubious in any situation where it seems that the goal must be worthless, or even repellent, to the actor. Pilfering or shoplifting committed by well-to-do elderly ladies often falls into this ambiguous category. Apart from cases where insurance is involved, arson is another type of conduct where the breach of norms is as readily perceived as a symptom of disease as well as a criminal act.

FROM CRIMINALITY TO ILLNESS

The evolution of modern penal ideologies is, in part at least, a concomitant of the ambiguities of deviations. The approach is now to treat the deviant, not to react to the deviation and, more specifically, that offenses ought to be viewed as symptoms of disease. There are several reasons why such an approach should gain ground in the course of a search for rational solutions to the problems of deviance. The most profound reason is probably the one anchored in the need for predictability.

As a model of deviance, crime is in some respects unsatisfactory and even threatening. This is not simply due to the criminal's capacity to injure, but also to the legal decision's inability to lay down with any measure of certainty what the convict's future behavior is going to be like once he is out of prison. He may commit new crimes in the future, but he may also have reformed or he may never have been the type to commit such offenses because his crime represented an exceptional straying from the narrow path. Neither the law, nor the particular sanction, gives any definite answer to the questions arising out of this ambiguity. Law and juridical decisions in their pure forms aim at retroactive justice, not at prediction of the future. However, in a society where science is used to make predictions and control the future in ever increasing areas of social life, the lack of predictability of the criminal's future behavior cannot easily be tolerated. It is in this situation that the science of criminology developed, which attempts to explain and predict criminal acts by referring to processes of cause and effect.

A simple way of rendering criminal offenses predictable is to establish a connection between them on the one hand and stable, although not necessarily unchangeable criminal traits on the other. Such schemes of interpretation and explanation have developed from Lombroso's theories[7] about the decisive impact of inherited organic traits to the modern theories relating crime to psychopathologies and deviance caused by factors in the social environment. Since such theories receive much of their support from a social need, they have tended to take an everyday logic for granted. According to this logic a negative outcome, such as crime, must have negative antecedents and causes, such as defects in the offender. In other words, the criminal must be sick, or his state is at least strongly suggestive of a disease. Such a definition brings his deviant behavior into the scope of comprehensive theories, whose predictions are based upon a biological and psychological model of man. In principle, the behavior of the offender appears now to be predictable.

If deviant acts are to be expected, there arises a need to deal with the problem before the harm is done. Since the legal system is mainly oriented towards the past, it is not well suited to take care of this need. Therefore, psychiatrists and psychologists are brought into the legal orbit to fill a gap in the juridical method. The demands for prediction and for preventive action are also associated with a need to understand and explain. In modern societies purely moralistic or legal interpretations of delinquency appear unsatisfactory and out of tune with the scientific ethos of the times. If it can be determined that the offender is sick, his deviance is at least made explicable in principle, like other diseases, although there may still be some undiscovered "virus."

The analogies with the sick and with the patient have made their appearance accompanied by an increased emphasis upon a humane reaction to the criminal. In the Scandinavian countries, for example, this humanitarian trend has led to a far-reaching liberalization of the penal sanctions which are applied. At the same time the public has been witnessing an increasing crime rate, particularly among the young. It has been widely thought, although not necessarily correctly, that the liberalization encouraged crime. Whatever the truth of this is, there has been mounting pressure to apply stringent measures once more, but now in the apparently humane form of preventive detention or "treatment," based upon the analogy with illness.

DECISION-MAKING IN SOCIAL CONTROL

It has been shown in the foregoing section that the concepts of disease and criminality are sometimes interchanged and that doubts may arise about whether a deviation is a criminal offense or a symptom of disease. These doubts have philosophical implications, and they also have important practical consequences. If an instance of deviance is a pure crime, it belongs within the orbit of the legal profession and the reaction is to be determined through a legal decision, ideally by a court. If, however, a transgression of norms is conceived of as a symptom of illness, the medical profession, including psychiatrists and psychologists, are the legitimate authorities to make decisions about the proper reaction to the deviation. The deviance falls within the scope of one or the other of these models of decision-making, depending upon how it is being classified. The decision models exhibit many important differences. We are now going to contrast them with each other.

THERAPEUTIC DECISIONS

When the physician describes and classifies his patients, he does so on the basis of traits and symptoms that are spatially located *in* the patient, often clearly limited to a distinct organ, such as the heart, the skin, and the digestive tract. Whether the symptoms are specific or general, like fever or feebleness, they are assumed to have been caused by some disease agent. The practice of medicine rests upon the assumption that it is possible to modify or even prevent the symptoms causing the patient trouble or pain through intervention in the process of cause and effect. Healing is conceived of as a process stretching over a certain span of time, marked by

146

graduated stages of improvement. The doctor is charged with the task of deciding on how the patient is to be treated. In this decision we may distinguish three separate elements: the diagnosis, the prognosis, and the choice of cure or therapy.

The physician is responsible to the patient for his decisions and the application of treatment. Normally, the patient comes voluntarily to the doctor, asking him to perform an investigation and make a judgment which is in the patient's own interest. The physician is also answerable to his professional organization and may be exposed to disciplinary measures; at worst he may be expelled from the medical association. He may also be tried in a court of law for malpractice, and he may be punished by fine, imprisonment, or by having his license revoked. These sanctions are almost wholly derived from the physician's responsibility towards his patients.

The physician is responsible for the future consequences of his decisions upon the patient's state of health. The success or failure of the cure is the criterion in terms of which the esteem and career of the medical doctor will be determined. Because the physician is responsible for the future effects of his decisions, he is obligated to follow the patient's process of healing with care and to observe the future course of the disease.

The more important or difficult therapeutic decisions can be rendered only by professionals who have undergone a specific type of higher education. Although laws against quackery prohibit everyone else from making such decisions, we are willing to accept the participation of laymen even in very intricate legal decisions.

Medical decisions are secret. The laws on medical practice in most countries stipulate the doctor's obligation to keep secret what has been confidentially conveyed to him in the course of medical investigations and during the cure. Without this basis for a relationship of trust between patient and doctor, the medical profession would be unable to fill its social function.

Therapeutic decisions are limited to problems concerning the patient's health and cure. The physician is not at liberty to found his decision upon any conceivable consequence which may flow from the decision. Nor is he held responsible for effects of the cure which transcend the state of the patient's health. Evidence for this can be found in the doctor's duty to give medical aid to enemy soldiers in times of war. Whatever the implications of such medical aid may be for the balance of forces in a battle, they are irrelevant to a medical doctor. In situations where the physician is asked to treat criminals sentenced to die, or dying individuals who seem to have little to look forward to, it is neither his right nor his duty to evaluate the total balance sheet of the patient's happiness or distress. His decisions are concerned with the patient's state of health, and his responsibility is limited to implications for the recovery and sanity of the diseased.

The decision of the physician in one specific case of illness need not be equal to the decisions in other similar cases of the same disease. Each separate case may be dealt with as unique, that is, in terms of its own peculiarities. Other similar cases are to be considered in medicine as no more than empirical data for possible generalization. The medical decisions should not, however, assume the character of precedents, of decisions worthy of compliance merely by virtue of having been established, as the case often is in law.

In each individual case the doctor is supposed to do his utmost for the patient, disregarding the fact that patients of other doctors may possibly have received less appropriate attention and have been victims of faulty diagnosis and ineffective cure. Equality at the doctor's office is not a social ideal of the same kind as equality before the law, although modern medicine is not removed from principles of justice. However, the responsibility for considering equality and justice rests primarily with the agencies of public health and not with the individual doctor or with medicine as a science.

LEGAL DECISIONS

While reasoning in terms of cause and effect and processes in time and space characterize scientific decision-making, as in medicine, legal decisions are characterized by comparisons of actors, confrontations of rights and duties, judgments on guilt and merit. The latter characteristics of decisions are also found outside the juridical orbit, that is, in most human relations where considerations of justice are held to be relevant. The principle of equal pay for equal work implies precisely this, that decisions on economic rewards are to be made by comparisons of performance, achievement, and quality on the one side, and of wage levels on the other side. Seniority principles imply, likewise, that decisions on promotion and wage increases are to be made with reference to comparisons and not to effects.

Legal decisions spring, normally, from situations where two or more actors are engaged in a conflict of interests. The decision made is a choice with respect to the priority of these interests. However, the juridical decision-maker is not merely responsible to his "clients" for the decision. The judge has no duty to further their interests if this does not happen to coincide with his obligations to other sources of norms. The judge is answerable more to the law than to actors who make laws. He answers to the Supreme Court, or other superior courts of appeal, in the sense that they may set his decisions aside and thus administer a certain kind of rebuke. The judge is responsible to society at large which is represented by other public authorities and by legal symbols.

This very general kind of judicial responsibility is related to the fact that an actor may be exposed to a legal decision without having asked for it, or even by compulsion. With few exceptions this is the situation in criminal cases, and it may also be true in civil litigation where one of the parties wanted to avoid the court proceedings. However, civil suits do not arise unless at least one of the adversaries, the plaintiff, has asked for a decision, just as the patient asked the physician to make a decision. This private demand for a service from the judiciary establishes no particular relationship between the judge and the plaintiff. The plaintiff does not become *his* client the way the sick person becomes the particular doctor's patient, that is, not just *a* patient. While the doctor is supposed to receive a fee from the patient, a similar honorarium paid to the judge by the plaintiff would be termed a bribe and would represent a severe breach of the norms of proper conduct in court.

To a much lesser extent than is the case in medical decisions, the judge is responsible for the future consequences of the decision. His responsibility is primarily retroactive, attached to factual matters which belong to the past. It is his duty to describe these past facts truthfully and precisely, and he is obliged to make a reasonable estimate of the probability of guilt or some other operative legal fact. Next to his responsibility for a correct description of past facts, the judge is supposed to make the proper choice of legal rules under which the facts are to be subsumed. Having succeeded in presenting the past facts of the case, and having delivered a verdict based upon a correct application of the appropriate rules, he is more or less without blame irrespective of the accruing future consequences of the decision.

The basis for the judge's lack of responsibility for the future is to be found in some of the fundamentals of legal thinking in the Western world. While the intervention of the physician often is assumed to cause the cure of the patient, it is not commonly assumed that the judge creates law, rights, and duties. The judge does nothing but record and formulate rights and duties that had already been established by the adversaries prior to the court proceeding by their own contractual arrangements or by breaches of the law.[8] If the verdict is formally impeccable and retroactively valid, the responsibility for subsequent implications are assumed to rest with the parties themselves. The ethics of medicine take the responsibility for the future off the shoulders of the diseased when he becomes a patient, transferring a good deal of the concern with the future to the physician. In law the contrary holds. The responsibility for the future remains with the litigating parties, and the judge is being spared the responsibility for the future as long as he deals appropriately with the past and the present.

Contrary to the situation which obtains in medicine, laymen participate in a large number of important legal decisions. Such participation is no doubt related to the compulsory element in law. In medical treatment the people delegate the right to make decisions directly by the patient's individual consent to be treated by the physician. This individual act of consent is necessarily missing in many legal proceedings. Because the law is an aspect of the state, procedural legislation has been strongly influenced by the general political currents in which democracy, representation, and the protection of individual rights are basic demands.

As long as non-professional justices or jurors participate, legal decisions cannot to any large extent be founded upon expertise and specialized scientific knowledge. The lay participation makes it mandatory upon legal thinking and terminology to preserve strong links with the vernacular and to communicate effectively with laymen. It prevents the courts from becoming too narrowly absorbed in strictly juridical matters and in the ways of thinking of the legal profession. Traditionally, the lawyers have been a rather unpopular occupational group; their skills have been variously feared and scorned. They cannot be compared with physicians in the eyes of the mass audience, although representative surveys have shown the justices, especially those of the Supreme Court, to be highly esteemed members of society.[9]

The institution of the lay judge or the juror is not the only lay element in the law. The professional judge is in most respects a layman when it comes to the technical and scientific aspects of his case load. Judicial tribunals tend to be relatively poorly specialized in terms of factual problems. One judge may preside over cases ranging over large areas of social life with links to numerous scientific specialties, like cases involving patents, bankruptcies, copyrights, and the like. It is clearly impossible for any one justice to master them all. The weaknesses inherent in this situation are readily visible, but the law has at least two important functions which obstruct a far-reaching specialization of the judiciary.

In the first place, the demand that the law ought to be one and the same for every citizen would be more difficult to meet if the courts were more specialized in terms of personnel and objective standards of decision-making. In the second place, it may be doubtful that experts are always the ones best qualified to make decisions, even within their own field of competence. An expert may find some problems so dubious that he is incapable of rendering a decision. In any event, his specialized insight may create psychological inhibitions against making the claim that the conclusion he arrives at is *the* correct one. The lawyers, and especially the judges, seem to fill a societal need for a group of actors who are willing and capable of making, and justifying, decisions where it is impossible or very difficult to reach a scientifically correct conclusion on short notice.

Medical decisions are secret, while legal decisions are public and sometimes highly publicized. Publicity is related to the same complex of considerations underlying the institution of the lay judge and the juror. Since the individual may be involuntarily exposed to legal decisions, the public must have access to the proceedings and to the grounds of the verdict so as to be able to exert a measure of control on the administration of justice. However, as with the principle of lay participation in the judiciary, the principle of public proceedings will also impede the further specialization of the courts and the introduction of more expertise into the judiciary.

The physician may ignore considerations which fall outside the scope of his expertise and do not directly pertain to problems of health. Problem-wise there exists no such delimitation of the relevant factors when the judge makes his decision. He is, however, entitled to disregard anything that is legally irrelevant, and he has no duty to make a survey of all the factors which may impinge upon the consequences of his decision. He is constrained to a consideration of those criteria which are part of law and which are relevant: legislation, custom, and precedents. These criteria may belong to any number of scientifically delimited fields, like chemistry, geology, medicine, economics, or psychology. However, the principles underlying the choice of relevant criteria has this in common with a scientific theory: they simplify a complex reality, thus making it possible to act.

If the patient can be accorded a more adequate treatment, the regard for equality should not influence the therapeutic decision. When legal decisions are made, however, precedents are of paramount importance and comparisons with other similar cases are eminently relevant. Equality before the law is a fundamental requirement in the sense that similar cases ought to be treated equally, although investigations have suggested that reality sometimes falls short of this ideal. The design of the judiciary as one pyramid of norm sending and sanctioning, with one legislative body and one Supreme Court at the apex, assures a certain degree of uniformity in the enforcement of the law. The ethos of science, on the other hand, is unresponsive to the notion of one single highest scientific authority. The centuries-long struggle against the unchallengeable authority of Aristotle established a firm conviction on this point in the scientific community, although in practice many a scientific proposition has been accepted on faith or authority and has sometimes frozen into dogma. But let us say again that the treatment in this chapter has been one in terms of ideal types suited to bring out regularities and patterns. It has been impossible to cover every nuance of empirical reality.

VII

THE STRUCTURE
AND FUNCTION OF
SOCIAL SYSTEMS

GENERAL NOTE

The sole purpose of this chapter is to illustrate the application of theoretical concepts and to demonstrate a mode of analysis. To increase the reader's empirical knowledge of the institutions discussed is not its goal. For this reason, I have deemed it appropriate to retain the examples which were originally assembled for the Norwegian edition of the book, based upon native data. For an audience with a different society as their primary and spontaneous frame of reference, some of the reported relationships would seem inadequate or misleading if they were directly transferred from the Norwegian context. Although institutions have many common features across national boundaries, the structure of the inclusive society has influenced the characteristics of its specific institutions. A description of an institution, purified of all the features which pertain to a specific inclusive society, would belong on a higher level of generality than that which has been aimed at here.

It has proved necessary in many instances to retain in the presentation descriptive properties of the particular empirical system which has provided the basis for the analysis. The goal of the presentation of the factory, for example, is to enumerate traits which are characteristic of factories as a *type* of social system. However, it has proved impossible to avoid references also to some characteristics which pertain to the particular factory studied by Lysgaard, and which cannot be generalized to apply to all factories, not even to all Norwegian factories. The reader will probably be able to make the distinction between that which is limited to a particular empirical instance of the system type and that which has a wider application.

The differences between the American and the Norwegian frameworks are particularly striking in relation to the isolated hamlet and the ship. At the present stage of social analysis it is hardly possible to sketch the elements of a local community structure without including some references that are nation-bound and inapplicable in other countries. The merchant marine is, relatively speaking, so much more important in Norway than in the United States that the national coloring will seep through in the presentation, despite the fact that the formal structure of the ship is developed within a cosmopolitan milieu. The remaining three organizational types may have more in common across this particular national boundary. Even so, it is quite clear that the American prisons function in a way which differs considerably from the function of Norwegian prisons. The terms of imprisonment are much longer in the United States and the security measures often more drastic than they are in Norway. The mental hospitals in the United States show a greater spread of types than they do in Norway. Hospitals may be found in the United States which are more wholeheartedly devoted to therapy and active psychological guidance than are any found in Norway. But it is also easier to find the purely "case"-oriented detention hospitals in the United States than in Norway. Considering the higher degree of industrialization and automation in the United States, as well as the considerable political differences between the two countries, American and Norwegian factories must be expected to exhibit important differences.

A cross-national comparison of institutions like the five discussed in this chapter could probably lead to new insights into the differences between the structures of inclusive societies. Because these institutions are sensitive to the influence of general features of a country's social structure, such comparisons would certainly be a worth-while task for sociological analysis. However, we must leave it at that. This headnote was merely intended to sensitize the reader to the difficulties of using data from a specific national society to elucidate conceptual and analytical methods which are applicable beyond the confines of any nation.

Sociology can hardly claim to have become as international a discipline as economics and psychology. European students of sociology have had the opportunity to learn a good deal about American society while being introduced to the general works on methodology and theory which have been written against the background of American society. But they have also had the problem of determining how these methods, concepts, and theories apply within their own national framework. It is not always easy to distinguish between those findings which are truly general and international, and those which are nation-bound. This chapter will present an American audience with similar problems. In the long run, only a process of communication in which data are conveyed from one country to another with at least a modicum of reciprocity can provide a basis for developing the language of sociology to become truly international.

THE PRIMARY aim of the first six chapters was to provide an introduction to some basic sociological concepts and to show how they can be used to classify social phenomena. The purpose of sociological analysis, however, is to establish dynamic relationships between variables and to discover the causal or functional relationships between various aspects of a social system. In a few examples such analyses have been broached. In this chapter we are going to deal in some more detail with five social systems in a comparative perspective. The social systems which will be compared are those of the factory, the ship, the mental hospital, the prison and the isolated rural hamlet. Comparisons are required to bring out the mutual interrelationships among the different characteristics of any one system.

The purpose will be to show how the function of a social system determines its internal structure. The term "function" refers to the way in which the aims of the system are put into practice. A function is an effect of a social phenomenon such as a norm, a role, or a system, measured against a preconceived standard derived from the system itself.[1] However, the main emphasis will be on social structures and the interplay between clusters of structural elements. By structure is meant the patterns of characteristics which pertain to a set of roles constituting the system, including also the systematic choices made by the actors within the framework set by the roles. Structure represents the static picture of the system, while function points to a movement, a drive towards goal consummation.

The five systems presented in this chapter are chosen because they are clearly delimited and relatively easy to survey. They exhibit a sufficient variety of goal settings to enable us to analyze the impact of varying functions upon system structures comparatively. The analyses in the following discussion will be rather abstract, but they will not lack an anchoring in empirical experience. Although the systems chosen are important *per se,* the selection has not been strongly influenced by this consideration. Other types of systems of similar or even greater social significance could be found. The purpose is to demonstrate a mode of social analysis, not to provide representative knowledge on any particular society. The latter study would demand another volume.

The analytical scheme

An implicit hypothesis underlies the previous discussion of attributes of social relations. It is as yet the unproven assumption that these attributes are useful in the search for invariance and lawfulness in social life. On a modest scale these assumptions will now be put to a test to see whether the choice of variables seems to be fruitful. Comparisons of the five chosen systems may suggest how the classificatory analyses in the preceding chapters serve as means to expose the regularities of social life. The comparisons may demonstrate that the occurrence of one structural characteristic is dependent upon the simultaneous occurrence of other traits relating to the structure of the social system. A description of one single system at any one time can rarely answer questions about the regularity, or even less about the functional necessity, of established relationships among the structural properties of the system.

The possibility of comparing social systems, and not merely individual actors, is circumscribed by several factors. As a rule, the available investigations of relatively complete social systems have been planned and executed without any explicit concern for a comparison with other systems of a similar or different type. Occasionally, hamlets or villages have been studied with a side glance to similar studies of other local communities, but almost never with any reference to studies of factories or prisons. However, precisely by means of such contrasts can sociology, at its present stage of development, find a fruitful avenue to further advances in analytical technique. The clear-cut contrasts reveal massive regularities in social life, although they are often of an apparently trivial kind. A scorn of the trivial may, however, be out of place, for, if similarities are found between systems as different as those surveyed here, the implication may be that we are facing some of the fundamental invariances of social life.

The following analysis of types of social systems continuously refers to some treatment of a point in previous chapters and such references provide new connecting links between what has up to now been separate. As a point of departure some basic concepts from Chapter IV have been chosen, especially the three criteria: proximity, similarity, and complementarity. The purpose or the function of the systems will normally account for the state in which these variables are found in the various system types, and thus provides us with an opportunity to draw the contours of the social systems in simple lines. Given a definite purpose and a specified condition with respect to proximity, similarity, and complementarity, how are the prerequisites of social systems fulfilled? What about recruitment, socialization, and production? The analysis is still kept within the confines of Chapter IV. The next step is a renewed debate of the questions raised in Chapter V with respect to social stratification. It leads us to some hypotheses about the dependence of stratification structures upon the varieties of system goals and upon differing states in social attributes which have already been dealt with.

Our procedure does not imply the assumption of a one-way theory on the origin and development of social stratification or of any other social phenomenon. The relationships carry throughout the characteristics of feedback and mutual reinforcement rather than those of unilineal causality. A property which, in one analytical perspective, appears as a cause may in a different context be dealt with as an effect. From social stratification the comparison is carried further to conflict and deviance, resuming the analysis of Chapter VI in a more specific form. Cases of deviance and conflict, and the way they are dealt with, are now treated within the framework of the specific system where they occur. Finally, some remarks on normative orientations will link the analysis to the discussion of the pattern variables in the very first chapter. This discussion will reveal that the phenomena used there as the simplest building bricks of social systems are themselves fully intelligible only as consequences of the total structure of a social system or even of society itself.

An extraneous element of chance and of subjective preferences may have influenced the selection of structural traits in this design for comparative studies of social systems. Other sociologists would have attacked the task in a different manner and might have chosen to substitute the selected variables with different ones, at least in part. The purpose of the following comparative venture is not, however, to establish certain knowledge, but to demonstrate a method of analysis. For this reason, no attempt is made to draw definite conclusions from the comparisons. The claim made is the more modest one that if sociology is to develop the state of knowledge on how systems function, and not merely on how individuals behave and think, it must be by putting more emphasis on the use of such comparative designs. The following discussion is, above all, an exercise in a theoretical method of analysis, and as a method it is no less important than the more highly developed techniques of data gathering and statistical processing of the empirical sociological materials.

The analyses of two of the systems, the ship and the peripheral hamlet, are based upon first-hand knowledge of the data. Otherwise, the analyses are based upon published reports and oral information conveyed by colleagues. My indebtedness to the published reports appears in footnote references, but these do not fully convey the scope of a debt which extends beyond the reports to include also the more subtle process of communication within a research milieu.

The factory[2]

PROXIMITY

The great majority of the employees are assembled inside the same physical plant. In contrast to the proximity found in the following four systems, however, this proximity is temporally limited to a certain period every day, namely, during work hours. The system operates on a diurnal basis. Most of the employees share work hours. If, however, the workers are singled out for special consideration, we see that the majority of them work on shifts. The size of the factory, the dispersal of personnel upon shops and sections, as well as the varying time rhythms, establish barriers to interaction inside the factory. However, inside a section, and among the fellow workers on the same shift, ecological conditions encourage social contact. The employees live in the city where the factory is located, and many of them are born and have grown up in this local community. Extensive periods of employment in the factory is normal; the majority consider their membership in the system as a lifelong relationship. Since the firm plays the dominant role in the life of the small city, the conditions of social interaction inside and outside the factory are bound to affect each other. The proximity is not limited to physical closeness inside the factory but extends to neighborly relations in the local community.

COMPLEMENTARITY

This system is founded upon dissimilarity with respect to professional qualifications as well as with respect to authority and leadership. The product sold by the firm can only be completed by the cooperation of workers and functionaries representing many different skills and several levels of superordination and subordination. A system as large as this one, built up to achieve very specific aims, cannot function without a leadership structure based upon a skewed distribution of power. As a system the factory is founded upon shared interests, not primarily upon the communality of values. However, the purpose of economic production does not exclude the sharing of common values among the members. For other reasons, however, processes arise in the factory and generate dissimilarities in some important evaluations.

SIMILARITY

Large groups of employees are similar in significant respects, whether they perform the same work operations or differing tasks. This similarity springs from the technical requirements of mass production which demands many workers without much formal schooling but capable of doing manual labor. Large groups of subordinates will tend to have similar social characteristics at the time of employment in the factory. This correspondence is due to a similarity of rank in the stratification structure of the local community with the further implications of shared values. The similarities are, however, emphasized and elucidated as a consequence of the proximity in the factory with the ensuing encouragement of social interaction. The similarity in terms of access to authority, or rather the lack of power inherent in a shared subordinate position, forms the basis for the experience of a communality of interest and a common social belongingness. These interests are experienced and clarified in encounters of workers with their superiors on the side of management. The conflicts are not overshadowed by encounters with customers or others which might put them in the position of firm representatives, thus tying them closer to the management, as sales personnel often are.

Based upon proximity and similarity inside the system, the subordinates' collectivity arises as a sub-system of the factory.[3] To what extent, and by what mechanisms, an eventual "managerial collectivity" arises is less well known. Proximity and similarity must be assumed to operate also when these personnel categories face the workers' collectivity in negotiations and in strikes or lockouts. However, the preconditions of system formation are not the same within management or within groups of white-collar workers as they are among the workers of the factory. The leadership group is often highly differentiated in terms of professional competence as well as in power. Besides, the top management is engaged in vital relationships of social exchange with actors who do not belong to the system, customers, suppliers, banks, shareholders, and competitors who represent factories in the same trade. Vis-à-vis these actors the management will tend to represent their firm as a unit, emphasizing the dependency of top management upon the whole system, workers and all, and also the responsibility towards all members to "keep the wheels going." This inter-system aspect of managerial functions may, however, further emphasize and develop the managers' membership in larger social systems in which the workers or other subordinates do not take part. These external activities underline the role of the executive as a member of the business community, of manufacturers' associations, and quite generally as esteemed members of the higher social strata. What has been said here about the executives applies also, with the proper modifications, to the workers' representatives such as the shop stewards who are tied to nationwide trade unions, but to a lesser extent to the regular workers.

RECRUITMENT

Because the factory is making money on its products, it can attract personnel through its capacity to offer the recruits remuneration. We may assume the recruitment is voluntary and the employees freely join the system, while mutual rights and obligations are established by contract. Membership can be terminated when the employee so wishes, although the factory operates under some constraints if it wants to fire an employee. Due to the situation on the labor market during recent years in the most highly developed industrial countries, possible applicants for jobs have considerable opportunity to choose when deciding to join a specific firm or not. Under conditions of full employment the factory has been less able to pick and choose amongst applicants for subordinate positions. The degree of freedom of choice on both sides concerning inclusion of a new member in the system is less regulated by norms than it is exposed to the vagaries of the trade cycles and economic trends. This is characteristic of social systems designed for economic production and is not the case with respect to inclusion in other types of systems.

To a certain extent recruitment to various positions in the factory may be determined by birth. This type of recruitment takes place on the basis of ascribed criteria. The norms which state that this ought to be so are now in decline, while norms advocating open competition for all jobs have gained ascendancy. It is assumed that achievement, examination grades, stamina, skills, and abilities ought to determine how the various positions in a factory are to be filled. Since industry needs an accumulation of capital and well-educated leaders, those who can furnish the capital and pay for the education are more likely to see their offspring in top positions than are those who lack the means. The technical, commercial, and administrative leaders of industry are very largely recruited from similarly situated families of the upper or middle class. Thus a blend of achievement and ascription determines business careers.

The systems of promotion in industry have been characterized by some impassable gaps in the hierarchy. It is a rare exception for a worker to rise above the level of foreman and enter the managerial ranks. It is also exceptional for a blue-collar worker to become a white-collar worker in the same firm. Disregarding these big, but rare, jumps on the ladder, the conditions of promotion are rather different among workers and functionaries. The workers belong to a few large categories and rise relatively early in their career to the level where they must expect to remain for the rest of their lives. There exist finer gradations among the white-collar workers, admitting of more chances of promotion and spread over a larger span of their careers. The limited opportunities for advancement of the workers are not necessarily due to a wish of the managerial groups to preserve high ranking positions as a class privilege. Industrial leaders may be prepared to set such considerations aside if they believe that the interests of the firm and the shareholders are better taken care of when rewards are held out to the most capable, loyal, and energetic workers, and when the top positions are filled by those most qualified, irrespective of background. The workers, however, protect the cohesion and solidarity of their collectivity against the threat of members being tempted to leave their ranks. They meet such threats, for example, by breaking off social contacts when a fellow worker is promoted to foreman and thus becomes the "company's man." [4]

SOCIALIZATION

All the members of the system, whatever their rank, have completed a certain amount of schooling. The primary schools offer the children training in elementary skills and in accepting the principles of achievement, specificity, and universalism which prepare the ground for participation in the factory. Without such preparation it is difficult to find suitable recruits even for subordinate positions in industry, and the demands for education are steadily increasing. The demands also increase as we pass from the lower to the higher ranks in the factory, since formal schooling is a crucial criterion for employment in executive positions and, quite generally, for career expectations.

As mentioned previously, promotions "from the bottom" meet with insuperable barriers in the factory. A concomitant of this condition is that socialization for top positions to a great, and increasing, extent takes place in educational institutions such as technical schools, colleges, commercial schools, and the universities with their schools of economics, of business administration, and engineering. Contrary, however, to the situation in hospitals and prisons, employment in a top position in the factory is not formally dependent upon academic training. Managers and presidents may be appointed on the basis of an individualized judgment of their qualifications, ranging from technical and commercial skills to economic power and family connections. One reason why this is possible in the factory, while impossible in public bureaucracies, is that the board of the firm usually has no formal responsibility to more inclusive systems, within which all directors could be compared to each other. Another reason is, of course, that property rights traditionally have played such a large part in the recruitment to positions of leadership in economic production.

A considerable amount of socialization takes place in the factory. New recruits are guided and supervised in their work, in part through apprenticeship or trainee jobs, and partly through courses organized by the factory. Since we are dealing with a large factory, the size of the system permits these internal educational efforts, and the long duration of employment in the firm makes it economical to sacrifice some personnel, time, and resources to provide for better training. One contributing reason why these efforts to train personnel are so poorly developed in the merchant marine is that the systems are small and the turnover is very high.

PRODUCTION

The purpose of the factory is to produce. This does not imply, however, that each actor is motivated to produce as much as he is

164

able to. In large systems of production there is a very complex relationship between that which is profitable to the system and that which is profitable from the individual actor's point of view. The management judges the successful completion of production targets on the basis of output, surplus, and profit. Managers have an interest in promoting a system design which would permit these criteria to have direct effects upon wages and other benefits of the employees, thus giving them a direct stake in the success of the firm. However, due to internal cleavages and the formation of sub-systems, especially of the workers' collectivity, the subordinates have favored a wage policy which does not foster inequality and envy amongst them, but which is designed to protect those who are weak or less qualified. While the purpose of the factory as a system is to produce as much as it is profitable to sell, some of the members may well see some advantage in a limitation of production.[5] For example, the workers' collectivity has often enforced a production ceiling, marked by a norm establishing an upper limit of production and individual effort. For reasons related to taxation, the top management may also be interested in a production ceiling, since further output would increase taxes more than profits.

The employee in modern industry is often at a loss to find adequate criteria for the evaluation of work well done. He does not know how much he has achieved because his efforts do not result directly in a finished marketable product. They rarely constitute more than a minute contribution to the collectively achieved targets. Subjectively speaking, the main criterion for having done one's duty is the feeling of exhaustion or fatigue when the day's work in the factory is completed. The achievement is measured by its cost. Nevertheless, industrial production provides the employee with more easily recognizable criteria of positive achievement in the work situation than does the type of production carried out on board ships, in prisons, or even in mental hospitals.

STRATIFICATION

Some factors associated with the social stratification and rank relationships of the factory have already been mentioned. Internal and external rank relationships seem to coincide rather well in this case: the social rank of the worker inside the factory corresponds with the rank accorded him in the local community. This relationship is also true of the upper echelons of the firm. The general social rank in modern industrial societies based on esteem, power, and wealth is closely associated with the occupational hierarchies, and especially with the occupational ladder inside the large systems of economic production. They form, as it were, miniature models which approximate the social stratification of society at large. It seems, however, that the stratification inside the firm has a more clearly dichotomous character than does a modern society, which exhibits a gradual transition from the lowest to the highest social strata.

Positions belonging to different levels of authority in the factory are largely recruited from different social strata and classes; the differences are preserved or reinforced by membership in the system. For some functionaries with working-class backgrounds, however, employment in the firm may launch them on careers providing for considerable social mobility. For some workers employment may become the point of departure for elective office in the local union shop, thus initiating political careers. The possibility of such careers implies social mobility in terms of increasing power, prestige, and conceivably also remuneration.

The most important implication of the rank structure of factories is the contributions made to a dichotomous structuring of the national system of stratification. The great and militant industrial organizations were formed around the workers' collectivity on the one side, and the management and the owners on the other. One outcome of the political struggle is that the workers as a class have been undergoing a considerable amount of collective upwards social mobility, thus becoming more nearly equal to the upper social strata in income, power, and esteem. The lack of internal mobility, resulting from the dichotomous structure of industrial plants, has been strongly mitigated by this collective mobility, implying as it does that the very ladder of rank in society has taken on new form. The equalization of incomes implies that the pyramid of rank distribution has also been somewhat flattened.

We have already seen that antagonism exists inside the factory, although exhibiting great variations from firm to firm. Of all intranational group conflicts the ones taking place between workers and management have been among the most important. When bitterness at times has characterized these conflicts of interest it is in part because they originate in systems based upon proximity and complementarity. The mutual dependency of the parties upon each other provides them with strong means of sanctioning. If other social agencies kept out of the conflict, each one of the parties would be capable of inflicting great economic loss upon the other, although usually at similar economic costs on either side. The owners had the sanctions implicit in the power to control the use of the means of production, although dependent upon society's general ability to protect the property rights through which the owners exert control. In order for the workers to achieve a similarly powerful position, enabling them to sanction undesirable steps of management, the manpower had to be made irreplaceable. This enforcement of solidary action among the workers who discovered they had very strong common interests was based upon a similar position in the productive process. And the workers were not merely alike; they needed each other in order to fully harvest the fruits of the performance which each one of them was capable of.

The conflicts in industry are by and large solved through negotiations, having been conceived of as conflicts of interest, as competition for scarce goods and not as disagreements over values. Due to the mounting concern of the rest of society to prevent strikes or lockouts, and the ensuing loss of wages and commodities, third parties have not infrequently been mobilized to participate in the settlement of such conflicts. This may occur through mediation, arbitration, wage councils and labor courts. The latter tribunals deal with industrial conflicts in legal terms, establishing the facts of the dispute and applying legal rules to the facts; the verdict is made irrespective of whether it may present itself as an acceptable compromise to the parties. However, even the labor courts are not formed wholly according to the standard judicial model, since both of the main parties have appointed their own justices.

The methods of conflict resolution that have developed to take care of industrial disputes seem to have had an integrative social function. They have brought the individual industrial firms into new types of cooperation with each other and with public institutions of various kinds. They have also fostered stable and enduring relationships between the negotiators and representatives on both sides. The requirements of the negotiations, in which the representatives of the parties come close to each other and become professionally similar to each other, create a communality of outlook across the lines of the interest conflict. The negotiators share the grave responsibility of preventing the often catastrophic consequences for the economic life of a country if negotiations fail.

Another aspect of the situation is that the conflicts in factories induce a need for alliances on both sides. The cleavage created in the system because of the conflict must be weighed against the integration which it has induced across the borders between competing enterprises and across the borders between local communities. Thus, by contributing to a division of society into social classes, industrial conflict has simultaneously generated a mechanism of cohesion, tying nations more closely together across the differences between economic fields and between geographic subdivisions or local communities.

When industrial conflicts are brought before a labor court, they are viewed from the angle of deviance. One of the parties must answer for having broken an agreement or transgressed a law. Apart from these cases, the most common forms of deviance inside the factory are absenteeism, drunkenness, pilfering, and embezzlement. The normal sanction, enforced with greater or lesser leniency, is to fire the employee, that is, to expel him from the system. The actions mentioned will normally also represent deviance from the norms of the sub-systems of the factory. These norms have in addition branded some acts as deviance which would be acceptable to the factory as a system. Such deviants are those who overcomply with the demands of the firm by being strike-breakers, scabs and apple-polishers. These deviants are castigated by the workers' collectivity and become the targets of informal social controls like

168

ridicule, the cold shoulder or, in critical times, violence. These informal pressures from fellow workers and associates constitute a very effective source of social control.[6]

NORMATIVE ORIENTATIONS

Achievement, specificity, universalism, and affective neutrality are generally assumed to characterize the norms of modern industrial life, especially inside the factory. A change has taken place since the old days when many industries were run according to a paternalistic pattern. The manager, usually the owner, was considered to have the right to know everything, including the control of the food the workers brought with them to the factory, and to make friendly inquiries about the family and other personal matters. The professional delineation of what is relevant to the execution of the job has become sharper and more strictly enforced in present-day interaction between superordinates and subordinates. The workers' collectivity, even more than management, sees to it that the norms of specificity, universalism, and affective neutrality are adhered to. However, there is some dissension concerning the norm of achievement or performance. The management often wants to reward individual performance, while the workers' collectivity prefers the equality of pay and other benefits for carrying out equal jobs, irrespective of individual performance in the role.[7] The dissension concerns in a sense whether the reward system should be entirely oriented towards roles or whether it should also discriminate between incumbents. The attitude represented in the workers' collectivity is determined by several considerations. One is that the rewarding of individual achievements may in practice lead to particularism, that is, the firm is suspected of a proclivity to reward those who are loyal and accommodating even more than those who are capable and conscientious.

Inside the workers' collectivity we find norms which differ from those applied to relations between superordinates and subordinates. Diffuse and many-faceted human relations, loyalty to friends and the opportunity to give vent to emotions are, to some extent at least, permitted or even encouraged among fellow workers. The general amelioration of class conflicts in recent times increases the likelihood that the norms of equality will also be practiced between different levels of authority and command in the factory.

So far, the deviations from specificity, universalism, and affective neutrality have been represented in new welfare measures of limited scope, as, for example, by a social worker who is authorized to pay attention to considerations which are ignored by the management. The same is true of the roles of factory doctor or industrial psychologist where these new welfare measures can be found. It is characteristic of the lapses from the four norms we have discussed that they are represented by roles in the factory which are kept clearly outside the line of command responsible for keeping the wheels going and achieving the production targets.

The ship[8]

The purpose of the ship is the same as that of the factory, that is, to produce. In describing the industrial plant, the structure of a social system has been sketched. We shall now present the ship as a system by comparing it with the factory.

PROXIMITY

If the shipping company were compared to the factory, we should have to conclude that the employees of the merchant marine have considerably less opportunity to interact than do the employees of an industrial firm on land. The sub-systems, the ships, are dispersed in foreign waters all over the world, while the various factory sections usually are found adjacent to each other. If we take the ship as our point of departure, however, the members are assembled in close proximity to each other over fairly long periods of time and without interruption. The system is not intermittent like the factory, which goes into a latency phase each day after work hours. The most obvious and significant difference between the ship and the factory is that the seaman lives at his place of work and spends most of his leisure time there, with superiors as well as with fellow workers. This constant proximity bestows upon the ship the character of a "total institution," sharing important traits with the psychiatric hospital, the prison, and also with the army camp, the monastery and the boarding school, and to a lesser extent with the isolated hamlet in the countryside.[9]

The enduring and uninterrupted proximity on board a ship has as its counterpart a similarly enduring separation from the family, home community, and the society to which the system belongs. The crews of some ships are recruited from amongst the inhabitants of the same local community, such as a small coastal town, thus establishing links between the social life on board the ship and interaction patterns outside of the system. Today, however, this situation is becoming the exception rather than the rule, implying that interaction patterns on board have no counterparts in the structure of society at large. The roles of the occupational organization are of decisive importance for all aspects of the interrelations among crew members, including those aspects normally considered part of private life. Places to sleep, to eat, and to spend leisure time are rigorously determined by the actor's role in the ship's system of production. Occupational labels commonly replace given names when the crew members speak to each other, not only during working hours but also during their off-duty hours. One important consequence of the physical proximity between the social system of production and leisure-time interaction is that each actor has his identity and self-perception more closely attached to his occupational position than industrial employees on land.

The members of the community of the ship do not have the daily opportunity of leaving the territory of the system. On the other hand, the turnover in the merchant marine is probably much higher than it is in factories or industries. For example, on a Norwegian ship sailing outside territorial waters, it is normal for a seaman to remain no more than six months to a year on board one ship; it is somewhat longer for officers than for crew members. Social interaction patterns on board are, consequently, transient, thus giving to leisure-time activities a flavor somewhat different from the one in the local community with its relatively stable neighborhood relations. The proximity which extends all day on board the ship does not constitute a favorable condition for the development of friendships.

COMPLEMENTARITY

The members of the crew are reciprocally dependent upon each other for the fulfillment of the function of the system. They need each other also in a more profound sense since all of them are, as it were, "in the same boat." Due to the special relationship between the ship and the conditions of nature: wind, climate, temperature, visibility, and harbors, and similarly due to the total character of the ship which provides the seaman also with his home, the sharing of a destiny extends beyond the common economic interests. In critical situations it is even more essential that members of the system rely upon each other. In this respect there are similarities between the ship and the isolated hamlet exposed to the hazards of an inhospitable and dangerous nature, as well as with military units in war operations. The paramilitary structure of the community of the ship has one of its sources precisely in this mutual dependency in times of stress.

The formal role structure of the ship gives evidence of the operation of complementarity as an organizing principle. Due to the turnover of the crew, the structure is formulated explicitly and in detail to give every actor a clear direction for role performance rigorously tied to a formal position. This condition has contributed to define each position on board as in some respect unique. The division of labor is more highly formalized, more closely associated with regulations and organizational blueprints, and less dependent upon discretionary decisions by supervisors from day to day than it is in industry on land.

SIMILARITY

Complementarity implies dissimilarity in some respects. At sea it results in a number of barriers to interaction and identification due to the compartmentalization in deck, engine and restaurant personnel, the division between officers and crew and between those who work during the day and those who are allocated to watches around the clock. Incomes and power are sharply differentiated, and few members of the system are complete equals; this counteracts the formation of firmly coherent workers' collectivities in the merchant marine. The complementarities which obtain between the ship and the company have similar implications, since everyone on board, including the captain, senses that they share some common interests and are equal in some respects, despite inequalities of rank. Everyone on board a ship, from the mess boy to the captain, is in the same category in the sense that all of them are labelled "seamen" or "sailors." This phenomenon has no parallel in industry.

The proximity on board establishes certain limits beyond which the growth of internal dissimilarities is prevented. True, the inequalities of work and authority flow into and "contaminate" most human relationships on board an isolated, oceangoing vessel. But all members are equally deprived of a large number of privileges and benefits enjoyed by people on land. In significant respects living conditions are similar for everyone on board regardless of rank. However powerful and well paid a captain may be, he is bound to be frustrated in some of these more important respects. These similarities, and the accompanying contrasts to people on land, provide for a common ground among seamen with respect to value orientations and place the seaman in juxtaposition to the landlubbers. However, the captain, who is the company's representative on board, establishes a firm link with the systems of economic production in the home country, as does the crew's membership in national unions with the main offices back home. The ship is a part of society and outside of it at one and the same time.

Due to the international nature of shipping, the encounters with foreign ports and with crew members from different countries on board, a seaman is apt to make certain comparisons and find some reference groups which would be alien to an industrial worker. When contrasted with a foreign milieu shared national belongingness, language, and "style" furnishes a reaffirmation of national identity which would otherwise be difficult to keep up because of distance from home. The member of this social system meets foreigners and new experiences not only as a seaman, but as a seaman of a specific nationality. Due to the high rate of turnover among seamen, he is in a position also to make comparisons of ships and of shipping companies, comparisons which are hard for industrial workers to make with their more limited range of occupational experience. While the structure of the ship discourages identification with equals within the system, the turnover is apt to encourage such identifications within the framework of the merchant marine as a more inclusive social system.

RECRUITMENT

The major principles of recruitment are similar to those found within industry. New recruits join the system voluntarily, although the term "shanghaiing" is a reminder that this freedom was not always as self-evident as it is today. Due to the continuous geographic mobility of the ship, and also because of the high rate of turnover, employment is organized through semipublic hiring offices. This hiring procedure deprives the employer of some of his freedom to choose recruits, as well as depriving applicants for jobs some of their freedom to choose ships. But the ship also has two other types of implications for recruitment which we shall now turn to.

Because the ship is separated from society and physically remote from the local community, possible applicants for jobs have difficulty forming any clear and realistic impression of this particular place of work. Myths, stories, and rumors have to a large extent influenced the perceptions of the ship's community and the life of the seaman, thus also channelling the motivation of prospective recruits. Since the ship is a total institution, entrance into the merchant marine implies more than a mere occupational choice. It means choosing a way of life, although frequently only for a limited period of time. Enlistment in the merchant marine may express a wish to escape from the present environment, but may also spring from a positive desire for the kind of life sailors are assumed to lead and a preference for a closed and intimate milieu with a clear-cut structure of authority and responsibility. This is not to deny that the economic rewards of sailing weigh heavily with young men who contemplate a sea voyage. In any event, available data suggest that the merchant marine attracts and absorbs a disproportionally high rate of deviants, although some deviations probably are to be interpreted as effects, rather than as causes, of life at sea and in the ports.[10]

The vast majority of recruits to the merchant marine are very young boys, which implies that the social system of the ship has few members capable of interpreting their common experiences within a general framework of occupational and other social systems. Older seamen have wide experience from many ships and contribute to making the sub-culture of seafaring fairly uniform even across national boundaries and at the same time different from other occupational sub-cultures.

The officers are recruited by the same general mechanism, beginning their careers in subordinate crew positions. This kind of recruitment indicates a very important difference between the factory and the ship: the top positions inside the factory are largely recruited from outside the system amongst the graduates of institutions of higher education. The ship's officers are required to complete several years of sea duty before they are admitted to nautical schools where they spend only a year or two. It seems that the social background of the officers of the merchant marine is rather wide. This fact implies that the chances to rise in the ship's hierarchy are open to many capable young seamen, not only to those previously designated by parents or the shipping company to serve an informal apprenticeship before they join the officers' ranks.

The distinct career patterns in the merchant marine must be viewed in conjunction with other dissimilarities between the ship and the factory. For one thing, the isolation of the ship from the local community, the fact that the two systems are kept apart by the distance, reduces the importance of the inherited social rank of the officer. Second, the high rate of turnover reduces the opportunities to make those comparisons to other workers, which cause such obstacles to an industrial worker who qualifies himself to join the management side. At sea the passing of the line between crew and officers is usually invisible because promotion is preceded by an interruption in sailing due to school attendance, and also because the new officer normally is employed on a ship other than the one he served in a subordinate position. Third, it has often been claimed that the preparation of an officer for his role should not be limited to acquiring the proper technical skills by schooling, but that he ought to grow into the role through actual experience as a seaman. However, the most important practical reason for the democratic career system of the ships is the large demand for officers in a rapidly expanding merchant marine. In addition, the type of life which is imposed upon the seaman by the very conditions of sea transport imply deprivations most acutely felt by mature men. If the recruitment had not taken place at a very early stage, we may suspect that it would have dwindled at a later one.

SOCIALIZATION

The social system of the ship lacks those highly educated experts who are found among the functionaries and leaders of industrial factories. The ship's officers have spent a few years in nautical schools, but many of them never graduated from a high school or a junior college. The completion of higher general education is largely prevented by the mode of recruitment typical of the merchant marine. The ships have been able to function without highly educated personnel because the ship is directed from a distant office to a larger extent than is the factory. Since the ship is a very costly and complicated means of production, the upkeep and repairs of it take place in ports where docks, engineers, and other technical facilities are available.

Contrary to the situation in the English merchant marine, Norwegian ships have no formal role for apprentices. The new recruits are largely left to their own devices; the assumption is that general and unguided participation in the social system serves a socializing function and "turns boys into men." Implicit in this idea is the notion that socialization does not aim at rigorous occupational specificity, but comprises larger sectors of the personality. The truth of this notion, as it is applied here, emphasizes further that very characteristic fusion of social identity and occupational role. One implication of this truth is that someone who has gone to sea remains an "old seaman" long after he has entered another occupation on land or possibly for as long as he lives. The phenomenon has a parallel in the assumption that once a criminal, always a criminal; criminality has become a characteristic which is glued to the actor's social identity.

A great majority of those who are recruited to the merchant marine as boys leave the occupation after a few years in favor of different employment. What, then, are the implications of this brief experience for adjustment to other systems of economic production or for general social adaptation? In a country like Norway, where nearly one-third of all young men serve for a time in the merchant marine, the problem is not insignificant. There is some evidence that the experiences as seaman, when combined with the missed opportunities for other kinds of training, may create considerable difficulties when the seaman seeks employment on land. The difficulties are especially marked amongst sailors who have spent many years away from the home community and who not infrequently feel themselves alienated from normal life. The abnormally broken and intermittent relationship to the family[11] or the lack of a family may reduce the wish as well as the opportunity to start afresh on a different type of career.

The nautical schools in which future officers are trained concentrate on technical and theoretical skills. Quite as important is the implicit preparation for superiority by facilitating the passage from the collectivity of the crew to the ranks of the officers. The promotion is preceded by an experience in an educational system where proximity and similarity tie together groups of aspiring officers, thus easing the transition even further.

PRODUCTION

The purpose of the ship is the same as that of the factory, namely, production. The ship does not create material products, however, but provides movement and transportation of cargo or passengers. The very foundation of the ship as a total institution must be sought in this specific productive purpose and in the available technical means to further the goal of sea transport. The total character of the ship is mitigated by the extent to which it transports passengers, especially for those officers who dine with the passengers. Transportation of oil, on the other hand, tends to reduce the contact with the environment to a minimum because oil is shipped over large distances and almost exclusively in foreign waters or on the high seas. The crew of tankers rarely set their feet on land, as loading and unloading is carried out with great rapidity and takes place at installations located far from inhabited areas. The dangers of fire on board lead to further restrictions upon the behavior of the crew and upon the opportunities of social life.

The fulfillment of production targets at sea is, above all, marked by the keeping of a schedule and arrival on time or ahead of time. Today keeping a schedule is mostly dependent on the efforts of the engine crew and officers who, thereby, get some standards by which to measure efficiency. Similarly, the deck officers may see an opportunity to gauge skills and achievement when navigation takes place in bad weather, storms, or reduced visibility. The crew on deck, however, who are mainly charged with tasks of repair and upkeep, are often unable to see any relationship between input of labor and output of economically measurable results. The restaurant personnel under the direction of the steward are in the position of having their products consumed inside the system. This situation may cause considerable friction on board many ships because of adverse criticism by the crew.

STRATIFICATION

The internal and the external rank relations among crew members do not correspond as well as those of factory employees. As seen from the inside, the ship appears to be a high and narrow pyramid of rank, divided into a large number of clearly defined steps of income, prestige, and authority. From outside the system, the distances between officers and crew members seem to be smaller than the differences between management and the workers in the factory. In this sense the rank system of the ship appears somewhat "artificial," created merely to further the specific goals of production, and less obvious in its relation to the social environment.

The rank orders of factories tend towards dichotomous structures, while this tendency is weaker in the ship system. The hierarchical nature of the ship, characterized by fine gradations of power and rank, is further emphasized by the opportunities to climb the whole ladder in the course of a career in the merchant marine without meeting any insuperable barrier. In this respect the ship is more like an office organization than the technical division of a factory. The lack of a clear dichotomy is related to the complicated types of multiple membership in personnel categories on board. Membership of a sub-system, such as the engine section, may in conflict situations take precedence over belonging to the managerial group or to the subordinate group. In some relations the captain alone represents management and the company vis-à-vis everyone else on board, while in other relationships everyone on board, including the captain, face the company on the basis of shared interests and common values. The upward mobility favors a sense of equality across all categories of rank, all of which counteract and weaken those tendencies towards a dichotomous structure which no doubt are also present on board many ships.

The ship provides for opportunities of social mobility that are ruled out in the factory. The income of captains, as well as their general esteem in the home community, place them above crew members and other workers on a general scale of rank. This relatively high rank may be reached by men who came from working-class backgrounds, and it is further transmitted to their offspring. Thus, the ship's officers seem not infrequently to have represented intermediary stages in an upward social mobility over three generations, starting in the working class and ending in the higher social strata of businessmen and academically trained functionaries. To the extent that this is so, the career system inside shipping has contributed to strengthening an hierarchical image of society, while, as we saw, the factory has probably been a main source of the spread of a dichotomous image of society.

CONFLICT AND DEVIANCE

The conditions of conflicts on board ships differ from those in factories. Disputes arising out of the conflicts of interest between crew and company have not taken place to the same extent inside the ship as a system. The officers have to a large extent been organized in the same national unions as the crew members. Otherwise, the solution of conflicts follows the same pattern as that established for the solution of industrial conflicts on land.

Recruitment to the ship takes place on a voluntary basis. But the ship has at times been used as a place of banishment and as a penalty, that is to say, as social control of deviants. Both in this respect, and to the extent that the ship attracts deviants, deviations are a more dominant theme in shipping than they are in the factory. Since the ship is not only isolated but has a paramilitary discipline, it has been considered an appropriate institution for the detention and reform of criminals. It was at one time a common practice to send unruly boys to sea to make human beings out of them. This tradition lingers on in courts which sometimes attempt to use the ship as a reformatory for juvenile delinquents.

On the other hand, it is clear that deviant behavior may cause a disproportionate amount of trouble inside the closely knit community of the ship. Drunkenness, fistfights, high accident rates, relatively frequent suicides, psychic breakdowns, and the abandonment of sailors in harbors have led to some efforts to prevent deviance on board ships. The ship is no longer conceived of as a suitable place to detain the deviants of society, but rather as a system in need of developing new means to keep its own deviance under control. The most important disciplinary measure in the merchant marine today is black-listing, debarring the seaman from hire for specified periods of time. Black-listing is decided upon after a quasi-judicial procedure, leaving room, however, for the play of discretionary, personal, and even random factors. Attempts have been made, through extensive psychological surveys, to develop principles of preselection which might prevent potential deviants from being employed in the merchant marine. These attempts, which have not as yet led to decisive measures, are closely related to the total character of the ship and to the fact that the recruit chooses a way of life, not only an occupation, when he joins the merchant marine.

NORMATIVE ORIENTATIONS

The social system of the ship is governed to a considerable extent by the normal occupational norms of modern industrial society with their prescriptions of achievement, specificity, universalism, and affective neutrality. However, the structural peculiarities of the ship cause some deviations, at least in nuances, from the situation in the factory. Achievement is less important at sea in the sense that highly educated experts are absent. On the other hand, achievement orientations are more consistently applied in promotion policy, since this is less dependent upon inherited or other ascribed characteristics of the employee than it is in industry.

It is difficult to stick to specificity in relations between executives and subordinates when large sectors of private life are included in the productive system itself. The officers have access to a wide range of information concerning the life of subordinate crew members. The inspection of living quarters is one example. By regulating the sale of liquors and by the consumption patterns on board, by withholding parts of the payments, and by the reporting system practiced on board the officers are in a position to control much more than occupational behavior. On board a ship there are no clear lines of distinction between what is relevant to performance of the job and what is not.

A principle of equal treatment of everybody on board has some validity but is difficult to put into practice due to the many cleavages in terms of rank and function. To some extent informal norms are apt to stimulate individual idiosyncrasies because they may contribute to enlivening the atmosphere on board. The establishment of particularistic bonds between officers and crew members is discouraged; the crew condemns and ridicules fellow seamen who "run on the midship" to please the officers. The fear of "espionage" from the management's side is even stronger in the crew than among the workers of the factory, possibly because eventual "secrets" cover a wide area of life and because the problem of privacy becomes particularly pressing on board a ship. The relatively stable interaction patterns arising between an officer and a man on his watch could make room for some particularism, and may counteract effective enforcement of the norm of universalism in relations between superiors and subordinates. The norm seems, however, to be applied with vigor to relations among equals in the crew. The instability of social bonds and the stress of "seeing the same faces day after day" encourage a matter-of-fact tone in friendships on board, even to the extent that special friendships may be looked at askance. On the whole, it seems that the ship favors a certain approximation of the norms of private life to those applicable on the job, because the transition from one sphere to another is imperceptible and is not symbolized by the physical movement back and forth between the place of work and the home.

The handling of emotions is more problematical at sea than it is in the factory. The dense and closed nature of the milieu, the accidentally composed crew, added to the continuous frustrations of sexual and other social needs, create problems and tensions. The incidence of deviant forms of behavior generates some anxiety on board, and there exist norms against a display of emotions, as well as against conduct which might provoke these forms of deviance. Drunkenness and fights are banned on the ship, but permissible in ports, where violent behavior is sometimes perceived as a necessary safety valve for aggressions accumulated at sea. These aggressions are also directed against superiors. At sea, however, it is important to encourage affective neutrality and to prevent the discharge of pent-up emotions because the system is ill-equipped to channel and handle strong expressions of feeling. Such a situation exists despite the fact that the system constitutes the whole social world where the individual actor must seek the satisfaction of most of his emotional needs.

The mental hospital

This social system has a purpose different from the two preceding ones: social control instead of production. It is charged with the task of offering a solution or an amelioration of such interpersonal conflicts and deviance which have their origin in a diseased state of the potential patient's mind. The control aspect is especially apparent in cases of compulsory hospitalization, and in the presence of the means of compulsion such as straitjackets, enforced isolation, and closed wards. However, the hospital also serves the function of socialization: teaching the patient new patterns of behavior through habit training, individual and group therapy, work training, and general participation in the social life of the hospital. The psychiatric hospital is supposed to combine the achievement of the two purposes of treatment and control. Many of the internal tensions of this social system derive from this dual, and in part contradictory, definition of goals.[12]

The members of the system are gathered inside the walls of a hospital which is sometimes isolated from the nearest cities and urban settlements. In comparison to the isolation of the ship, the separation of the hospital from the community was once considered a means of reaching the hospital's goal. The hospital has the character of a total institution for the patients, as does the ship for the crew. Usually, the patients spend day and night for several months inside the system; in the case of the chronically ill, even for many years; and in extreme cases for the rest of their lives. The rate of turnover of the majority of the patients seems to correspond rather well with that found among seamen. Hospital personnel leave the place of work every day, but many of them live near the hospital and some even live on the hospital grounds. This proximity tends to create a total hospital community, although less dominated by the occupational requirements than the ship's community, if only because many units consist of personnel with families.

The proximity is accompanied by complementarity and the dissimilarities between patients and treatment personnel. Each division, or ward, of the hospital represents an effort to gather patients who are somewhat similar, in the sense that they need similar types of treatment or can be exposed to the same kind of routine in terms of regulations and the degree of freedom offered. Proximity and the ensuing interaction among patients and personnel are considered a means to achieve the curative purpose of the system.[13] Since, however, this type of interaction contains much stress and may be threatening to the nurses and doctors, some of them tend to withdraw a little and to isolate themselves from the demands of the patients. Proximity and interaction between the patients have also come to be viewed as a therapeutic lever, although not without some reservations. Under some circumstances isolation cells are used; the patient is removed from the ward and excluded from interaction with others. When removal occurs it is often equivocal whether the intervention is to be perceived as a penalty or as a therapeutic device.

Outside the hospital the homes and relatives of the patients are dispersed over large areas, or sometimes spread all over the country. The break with the home community is often even more drastic than it is in the case of seamen. Some hospitals attempt to keep up contact with the patient after his discharge through after-care and rehabilitation measures of various kinds. A hospital environment is not necessarily a prerequisite for cure and healing, although therapeutic methods outside the hospital have to take different forms.

COMPLEMENTARITY

The patients need the personnel of mental hospitals to protect vital interests, while it cannot be assumed that the personnel who administer treatment need the patients in the same sense as management needs the workers. True, without patients there would not be incomes for doctors, nurses, and other staff members. Nevertheless, a real, and not merely apparent, absence of qualified recruits for the mental hospital would imply the fulfillment of the goals of psychiatry and could not be regretted by those responsible for financing the mental health program of a society. The customer, in the last analysis the taxpayer, does not need mental patients in the same way as the ordinary customer and buyer need the worker who produces a commodity. The patient is not a "worker," rather a "raw material" to be "processed," although modern ideologies try to implement a partnership between psychiatric personnel and their patients.

From this difference in purpose springs also a sharp difference in the preconditions for the termination of membership in the two kinds of systems. If the factory fires an employee, it is often caused by his failure to comply with the requirements of the system. When a hospital discharges a patient, it implies, as a rule, that the patient and the system jointly have achieved the purpose of the system which is to cure illness. The former patient is thereby disqualified from continued membership. When, however, a patient sometimes leaves the hospital at his own request, against the advice of doctors, his reasons may spring from a dissatisfaction with membership somewhat parallel to that of an employee who decides to quit his job in the factory.

The members of the personnel group are tied to each other by a mutual dependency which is normal in work organizations. But due to the dual purpose of treatment and control, as well as to the rapid changes of treatment methods in recent years, there is considerable uncertainty and dissension about the relative competency of the different members of therapeutic teams. Competition has at times been a substitute for cooperation. For example, there may be doubts whether the professional differences within the personnel contribute to the functioning of the whole system, or whether they represent mutually exclusive approaches, facing the members with the need to make a choice. The relationship between doctors and psychologists is at times beset with this ambiguity.

SIMILARITY

The goal of the hospital furnishes a basis for a dichotomous division into patients and personnel, a distinction between those who are ill and those who are experts in healing illness. It is usually considered as particularly disqualifying for membership on the therapeutic side to possess the attributes of the patients. This sets the hospital clearly apart from the ship, although the folklore surrounding mental illness sometimes tends to assume a similarity between mental patients and psychiatrists. It seems that the total character of the mental hospital has led to the assumption of a transfer of qualities from patients to staff.

Excepting some minor deviations, the patients form a mirror image of society regarding the distribution of previous social rank. Most symbols of inequalities of rank are, like other individualizing attributes, stripped off the patient together with his watch and his clothes upon his entering the institution. The hospital shares this aspect with other total institutions, all of them demanding a certain amount of uniformity and subservience to a regime. Patients on each floor are assumed to be treated approximately as equals, while members of each sex are separately located. Some observers have depicted the patient's introduction to the mental hospital as a process of degradation, mortification, and loss of individualization which aims at an extreme degree of equality and uniformity.[14] This applies especially to the equal deprivation of influence and self-determination, since each patient is exposed to the same routine which practically regulates his whole life. On this point the situation in the mental hospital is even more extreme than it is on board ships at sea, where, after all, a certain amount of privacy is respected. The life of the mental patient inside the hospital is, in principle, subject to complete control. The permission to have a private life and some secrets is not granted as a self-evident right, but rather as a privilege which recognizes some improvement and success in the cure. The control exerted by the hospital does not simply follow from the opportunities of supervision and inspection offered by the total institution and from the disciplinary requirements. It follows also from the prevailing theory that the personality of the mentally ill, and above all his ability to make rational choices, is affected by the disease. This theory bestows upon the personnel an unusually wide responsibility for intervention in the patient's life, and also implies that therapeutic efforts may be directed towards any aspect of the individual's life.

Differences are found between floors or wards, which appear to the patient to constitute a hierarchy within which they may move from "worse" to "better" levels depending upon their progress. These differences provide for visible signs of the patient's general state, and more particularly of his standing with the hospital authorities. The latter may be measured to the extent that a move to a "bad" ward is perceived as a punishment. As the modern dynamic treatment theories have gained ground, and as the introduction of psychopharmacology has reduced the need for many disciplinary and protective measures, the idea of individual treatment has gained ascendancy at the cost of the old conception of the patient as a "case." In these modern ideologies lie also the germs of inequalities of treatment inside divisions and on the same ward. Here lie also the roots of a tension between the kind of equilibrium established upon considerations of justice and the concern with effectively achieving the hospital's therapeutic purpose. This purpose demands inequalities in distributing treatment according to the patient's peculiarities.[15] It seems unlikely that these dissimilarities should induce inequalities of rank, but such an interpretation may lurk in the background, causing patients as well as nurses to react against special privileges for a single patient.

The basic dissimilarity in the mental hospital is the one between patients and staff, particularly regarding independence and authority. A dichotomous structure is even more clearly suggested by this cleavage than by that of the factory. To what extent this leads to the formation of interacting sub-systems is, however, more dubious since many factors counteract the formation of a patients' collectivity parallel to that of the workers. The very condition of mental patients tends to inhibit interaction, identification, and co-operation with other actors in spite of extensive similarities and a shared experience. The inequalities of social rank outside the system may linger on also inside and form obstacles to identification in spite of the apparent uniformity. The state of illness is defined as temporary, making it appear less rational to strive through collective action for an "improvement" of the conditions of patients. The individual solution, where the patient responds to the cure and becomes well, is presented as the proper escape from the inequities of the patient's situation. The close and extended contact with staff members provides a basis for identifications across the basic cleavage and counteracts the formation of militant groups of patients. Thus, too, many patients come to realize that the conflicts of interest between patients and staff are less real than apparent.

If we regard the staff as a sub-system of the hospital, many structural similarities with the factory appear. There is a small executive group on the top, the doctors, who possess an expertise based upon extensive education, and there is a much larger group of subordinate personnel, such as nurses (male and female), kitchen personnel, and work therapists who have normally received much less education. The inequalities of rank loom large within the staff hierarchy, although it is doubtful whether this leads to any clearly dichotomous image of the staff system among its members. In part, this sub-system dichotomy is counteracted by the basic cleavage of the hospital system, and in part the dichotomous development is hampered by the fact that the executives of the hospital usually lack the independent economic power which pertains to factory management. In state-operated mental hospitals the fulfillment of the hospital's goal does not result in any surplus or profit which may be distributed by the chief psychiatrist, the director, or the hospital board. Thus, a very important source of economic conflicts of interest is absent in the mental hospital, although many other kinds of conflicts may occur within the staff. The rate of turnover among doctors is relatively high, preventing them from remaining so long in the system that they acquire great vested interest in its operation. This, also, may prevent subordinate staff members from perceiving the hospital as belonging to the main experts of the system, which is in contrast to the workers' perception of the factory as belonging, not only to the owners, but also to the hired managers.

RECRUITMENT

Since the psychiatric hospital has as one of its goals to control deviance, admission has not been based exclusively, or even predominantly, upon voluntary recruitment. Compulsory hospitalization following upon a formal declaration of insanity, or formally voluntary hospitalization which covers a reality of compulsion, are common types of inclusion in this social system. To an increasing extent, however, mental hospitals base their recruitment practices upon voluntary applications from prospective patients. This is a concomitant of the increasing emphasis upon the therapeutic purpose of the hospital.

The recruitment situation contains a paradox, since labeling a person mentally ill carries with it a suspicion concerning his ability to make rational and sensible decisions. This leads to much ambiguity about the grounds for hospitalization. Many patients believe they have been confined against their will because others wished to have them under control and observation, or because society considers them to be "criminals." Simultaneously, the patient is apt to experience aspects of the hospital and of staff demeanor which must be interpreted as signs that the hospital is there to aid him and not to deprive him. Both these interpretations of the aims of recruitment, which in combination add to the confusion of the mentally ill, differ from those underlying recruitment to the factory and the ship. The factory does not lock one up, but neither does it operate solely for the benefit of the workers.

The termination of membership in the hospital occurs in two different forms, voluntarily if the patient was hospitalized on his own behest, but according to the hospital's judgment in cases of compulsory hospitalization. In both cases termination of membership is a sign of success or improvement, the only certain criterion of achievement applicable to the work of the hospital. From this criterion may arise occasional conflicts of interest between the hospital and the patient, since the hospital leadership is at times tempted to discharge patients in order to lift the pressure from waiting lists. The obverse situation is, however, more common: the patient wants to leave the hospital while the doctors want to keep him on because the cure is incomplete. The environmental conditions awaiting the patient may also be considered more demanding than he can take for the moment, or the doctor may want to ease the stress upon the relatives of the patient for a longer period of time. The sources of conflicts between the mental patient and the doctor are more numerous and more significant than they are when the disease is somatic. The decision on discharge is very different from the decision to fire an employee from a factory, in which case the possibility of finding a satisfactory substitute for the fired man is the only important system consideration. Discharge is, however, the last chain in the very process of "production" in the hospital, bringing the highest expertise to bear upon the proper timing of the termination of membership.

Promotion across the basic cleavage between patients and staff is not an eventuality that has to be considered. Nor is the mental hospital in other respects conducive to social mobility, since the top positions are recruited from amongst graduates of medical schools and other faculties of universities. It is common for members to begin work in the system at the approximate rank level where they remain for the duration of their membership in the system, although there are promotions such as those from nurse to head nurse.

A failure in the prior process of socialization is the most important qualification for becoming a patient in a mental hospital. On the other hand, one of the most extended types of education in modern societies is the precondition of membership to the top layer of the system, that of doctor or psychotherapist. The hospital has a socializing task in recovering the patient's faulty socialization outside the system. Before this process can get started, the patient must be socialized to life in the institution. The new recruit must learn to play the role of the patient, adapting himself to the hospital routine with its distinctive daily rhythms of sleeping, eating, play, and work, and to arrive at an accommodation with his new neighbors and superordinates. Above all, the patient must gain some insight into his illness; he should learn to perceive himself as being sick and thus acquire the proper therapeutic motivation.

For many patients this perception represents a difficult and painful transition. Since many psychotics suffer precisely from a weakness of the ego, the attachment to the hospital may contain the germ of their first secure social identity; their self-perception is now based upon their role as patient.[16] Socialization for life in the hospital is not, however, a goal of the therapeutic process. Quite to the contrary, adjustment to the social environment in the hospital may present obstacles to the preparation for life in society outside the hospital which is the aim of resocialization. The staff of the hospital is usually aware of this particular obstacle to treatment and attempts to deal with it accordingly.

It has been said that the leaders of the mental hospital need to undergo a very extensive socialization for their roles, which takes place outside the hospital in medical school and elsewhere. The last stages are, however, represented by internships in hospital divisions. There are also interns in psychiatric hospitals who do not intend to become psychiatrists. They merely spend a brief period in the mental hospital on their way to a different kind of medical career.

The mental hospital does not participate in economic production in the strict sense. It supplies, however, a service for which there is an urgent demand. Unlike the situation of other kinds of hospitals, the demand does not come primarily from the patients. Most psychiatric care is publicly financed; the government or other public agencies represent the demand side in this exchange. The criteria of successful completion of production targets are more uncertain and in more dispute than they are in other hospitals. Therapeutic theories and clinical practice vacillate between the application of highly specific types of intervention, like the administration of electroshock or medication, and diffuse personal treatment and psychotherapy. A temptation exists for physicians to use their specifically medical knowledge and skill to achieve some affirmation that they satisfy normal professional requirements and make use of their tremendously costly education. It is a source of great difficulty that the final production result, the healthy adjustment of the released patient to his social environment, is so hard to observe and measure, while the course of treatment and progress inside the hospital is readily observable and simpler to gauge. For this reason the mental hospital is bound to generate a certain amount of ritualism, a displacement of attention from final goals to compliance with prescribed methods. The use of tranquilizers and the rapid discharge of patients are favored by internal system pressures, whether or not they are equally suited to obtain the declared external goals of the system.

Patients and therapists are not defined as colleagues or co-workers in the usual sense, although the staff encourages patients to "collaborate." The healthy, cured, or improved patient is the "product" of the hospital in most cases, while detention and care may be all that the system can achieve with those defined as chronically ill. This latter production target may be overshadowed by the therapeutic goals because its achievement does not to the same extent depend upon the application of expertise and current theories, and because it is difficult to perceive the differences between more or less successful detention. The ambiguous situation for the patients as simultaneously products and collaborators makes it difficult for them to assume their role, which is unlike all other roles they are familiar with. The closest analogy is the role of the child when it is being told that the parents exist for its sake and are willing to do everything for it, but that they must, nevertheless, make great and partly unintelligible demands upon it.

STRATIFICATION

With some reservations it may be claimed that the patients of a mental hospital are a representative sample of the population in terms of occupation.[17] The great internal rank differences between staff and patients do not correspond to parallel inequalities of rank outside the system, as they do in the factory and, to some extent, even in the ship. The mental hospital is a social enclave where many norms of society are set aside, amongst them some concerning the attribution of social rank. Some patients enjoy higher rank outside the hospital than do many staff members, perhaps even higher rank than that of the chief psychiatrist. In this context it should not be forgotten that a certain ambiguity prevails with respect to the meaning of the hospital hierarchy, since the therapeutic personnel are the superiors of the patients and at the same time their servants.

It is difficult to make any general statements on how mental illness and the more or less publicized fact of having been a mental patient influence the esteem and the general social rank of an actor. In many instances the mental deviance will tend to reduce the performance and thereby the rank of the actor. For some the stamp of insanity will lead to a social location at the bottom of the rank hierarchy with criminals, bums, drunkards, and prostitutes. The majority of those who have been in a mental hospital seem, however, to recover previous social rank in accordance with their income, occupation, and family connections. Thus, cases may occur of rather sharp inconsistencies of status, like a low ranking in the hospital combined with medium or high ranking outside the system. For subordinate staff members the obverse may hold; their influence over patients bestows upon them a rank inside the hospital which is belied by their modest rank in the stratification of society according to income and esteem.

It has been pointed out that the hospital does not furnish a particularly convenient channel for social mobility, disregarding the fact that the internship is a necessary stage in the careers of the physicians. The obverse question is more important, whether hospitalization and the concomitant removal of the patient from normal social relations facilitates a downward mobility, whether, in other words, the hospital may serve as a vehicle of social degradation. In those cases where the individual is judged insane, degradation does occur. In other instances the hospital stay facilitates an adjustment to the disease and possibly a socialization for a more modest occupational role in which the disease symptoms will be less incapacitating and the stress lessened by comparison with other occupations of higher social rank.

CONFLICT AND DEVIANCE

Mental illness is often brought to the surface during conflicts with others, especially with close relatives or with colleagues and superiors at the place of work. The initiative for hospitalization comes frequently from these Altera who find Ego's conduct threatening, provoking, or incomprehensible. The part played by Altera in the process of hospitalization often leaves the patient with a feeling of having been indicted and then sentenced by the hospital authorities to confinement without that access to legal counsel which is open to defendants in criminal proceedings. The model underlying the decision on hospitalization is one of deviance and not one of conflict, assuming that the trouble, like a somatic disease, can be located inside one of the conflicting parties. *He* is the one to be treated, not the conflict. Since it is in his own best interest to receive treatment, even though the illness may prevent him from realizing this, no real conflict of interests is present as it is in a criminal case. Neither is it necessary, therefore, to provide for the elaborate legal guarantees granted to defendants. In spite of this, we find a certain legal element also in the control of the mental hospital, based upon the assumption that some sources of conflict may be present. A great many difficulties in public mental health can be traced back to this ambiguity in the very grounds for initiating treatment, which gives rise to dissension between patient and doctor about whether deviance or conflict is the proper way of classifying the difficulty.

Neither the conflict between the mentally ill and his social environment, nor that between the patient and the treatment staff, have much chance to develop into systematic group conflicts. There are no organizations of mental patients or ex-patients established with the purpose of defending the interest of their group against the psychiatric personnel. Neither does this field show many examples of the voluntary associations which abound in other medical fields, such as those of the blind, the deaf, or the disabled. On the contrary, the occupational organizations of nurses and doctors see it as one of their main tasks to propagate the interests of the patients vis-à-vis society at large and more specifically in relation to those who control the appropriations to public health purposes. The situation is radically different from the one found within industry, although it may be faintly reminiscent of the very earliest stages of labor organization, when the initiative to improve the workers' conditions was sometimes taken by paternalistically motivated employers.

The suffering of mental disease assumes an equivocal place among the types of social deviation. Unpredictability, withdrawal, hallucinations, and aggression can be interpreted as capriciousness, negligence, dishonesty, and wickedness. If so, the conduct is perceived as a breach of moral norms, which is parallel to a crime, and may in fact often constitute a crime. These patterns of behavior may, however, also be viewed as symptoms of a state over which Ego exerts no control and for which he cannot be blamed. In this case the model of illness is applied to the conduct when it is classified in order to decide on the proper remedies. The ambiguity flows from a more pervasive pattern of contradictions in the role of the mentally ill.[18]

The ambiguous aspect of the situation not only concerns the role of the deviant from general societal norms, it is also present in cases of internal deviation from the hospital regime. When the staff at times insists upon the need for order, discipline, and justice in the administration of therapy, the patient's violation of the disciplinary prescriptions is interpreted as a moral transgression amenable to sanctions. However, such deviance from the rules of the system may be interpreted quite differently, namely, as more or less inevitable symptoms of the patient's disease. The deviation calls for a causal explanation and for individualized therapeutic measures that are not designed to re-establish discipline by meting out just sanctions. Breach of the discipline is in a sense used positively for diagnostic purposes in order to understand more profound and more important phenomena, and may even be a welcome pretext for initiating new therapeutic measures.

NORMATIVE ORIENTATIONS

Many aspects of the structure of mental hospitals prove to be different from those of ships or factories. Systematically related to these differences are also some dissimilarities of normative orientations. No positive achievement is demanded of those recruited to the hospital as mental patients. The most common interpretation is that the recruit was included in the system as a consequence of processes beyond his control. The role is an ascribed one, based upon the negatively valued qualities of the mentally ill. Hospital staffs make a point of reducing demands upon the patient, exempting him from many of the pressures of society. This "vacation" aspect of the system has a therapeutic purpose. Nevertheless, there is no doubt that the hospital demands a certain performance of the mental patient, encouraging some kinds of behavior, while discouraging other kinds. The most important type of upgrading is the discharge, which depends in some measure on the performance of the patient, such as his eagerness to "collaborate." However, compared to the situation of subordinate employees in business firms, the role of the patient is less oriented towards achievement. For staff members, on the other hand, the degree of achievement orientation hardly differs much from what it is in the factory.

The perceptions of the mental patient waver between specificity and diffuseness. The sick condition may be caused by specific biochemical or physiological processes, and a cure is promised in terms of similarly specific types of intervention through medication or the administration of insulin or electroshock. The disease may also have been precipitated by highly specific traumatic events, suggesting that a reconditioning of the patient's behavior is possible. At the same time it is a widespread notion that mental suffering is expressive of a state of his whole personality and even of his general existential situation. Thus, his disease must be met with a very broad and diffuse register of therapeutic measures, employing "interpersonal relations" and the "therapeutic community" as techniques of healing.[19] This is also very different from what is found in systems aimed at economic production.

The notion of interpersonal relations, especially those between staff and patients, as a therapeutic weapon must also favor particularism. The therapeutic personnel may attempt to offer the patient individual care, permitting the relations to assume a flavor of friendship. The concern with equilibrium and tranquility on the ward may, however, lead to demands for justice in the administration of burdens and benefits, irrespective of therapeutic justification.

The psychiatric hospital is a social system designed to make room for individuals whose emotional expressions have proved intolerable to society outside the system. Many eruptions of emotion, but also an apparent flatness of feeling, which would be considered shocking outside the hospital, are here accepted as matters of fact. Direct emotional expressions are encouraged or, at least, permitted to an extent unheard of in the factory or on board ships. In spite of this many attempts are made to control affects, especially by means of tranquilizers. They have the effect of reducing emotional expressions of anxiety or aggression, but without explicit recognition of norms condemning eruptions of feeling.

The prison

The purpose of the prison is to exert social control through the punishment of deviants. In recent years, especially, more emphasis has been put upon the resocializing function of prisons, although it still plays a much smaller part than socialization does in the mental hospital. In what follows we shall deal with prisons as well as institutions of preventive detention, although the latter affords a closer approximation to the psychiatric hospital.[20]

PROXIMITY

The prison is an isolated institution, sharply separated from the rest of society. Isolation by means of physical barriers is intrinsic to the very aim of the prison, which is to deprive the convict of his freedom. The immediate goal of the prison is to prevent the inmate from free communication with the social environment through incarceration, and the strict control of both visits and the written exchange of messages. While the isolation of the psychiatric hospital has traditionally been achieved by a suitable location in the countryside, many prisons are located in urban centers and are isolated by heavy brick walls, locked doors, and barred windows. As a result, the personnel are able to leave the system in their spare time, obviating the necessity of living inside the community of the system.

The internal conditions regarding proximity and interaction vary a great deal according to whether the prison is based on a cell system or is designed to permit group formation when the prisoners work, eat, or spend their leisure time. The development of the prison has led away from the cell system, although the inmates are usually still forced to spend a great deal of their time in isolation. In any event, the interaction between prisoners is highly controlled and regularly supervised by guards. The institution of detention offers greater opportunities of social interaction than the prison does.

Contacts between staff and inmates are more limited and more circumscribed by rules than they are in a mental hospital. Only limited efforts have been made to use interpersonal relations as a means to further the function of rehabilitation in the prison. The security system of the prison imposes barriers of interaction upon all human relationships inside its walls.

The proximity inside the prison is usually of limited duration, as terms have tended to become shorter than they used to be, although with considerable variations between different types of prisons. The social system of the prison does not correspond to any part of outside society. The relationships between staff and inmates are usually strictly limited to the prison. However, a certain tendency may be observed for the criminal offenders of some types to congregate outside the penal institutions in cliques or in a more or less loosely knit "underworld," characterized by its own interaction patterns and social norms. Criminality seems to be spontaneously conducive to group formation, unlike what we find among mentally ill patients.

COMPLEMENTARITY

The prison assumes a unique position among the systems of society, for at first glance it offers no opportunity for reciprocity of exchange and mutual satisfaction of needs. The situation is parallel to that of the psychiatric hospital in that it would be desirable for the clientele to completely disappear. Assuming that the clientele exists, the two types of staff have become dependent on the supply of patients and inmates for the perpetuation of their jobs. At this point the similarities cease, for the inherent characteristic of the penalty as an evil inflicted with the intention of frustrating the convict[21] deprives most offenders of any motivation to become inmates. The inmates do not need the prison and its staff. The institution was established not to satisfy their needs but, on the contrary, to frustrate their wishes, especially the wish to be free. In this lies the unique nature of the prison as a social system.

In actual practice this image of the prison is not applicable without modification. There are instances when the criminal seems to have longed for imprisonment, or when he accepts his stay in prison as a temporary solution to an otherwise insoluble predicament. Within the formal framework of the penalty, as established by law and prison regulation, the staff is often moved by a wish to satisfy the needs of the inmates. In spite of these modifications the formal model is of decisive significance for any attempt to understand the functioning of this social system.

The termination of membership in the prison system does not correspond to the situation in the factory, where a normal precondition for being fired is a failure to comply with the demands of the system. Nor does it correspond to the situation in the mental hospital where the discharge of patients implies the reverse, namely, a fulfillment of the system's purpose. Termination of a term in prison bears little connection with what has taken place during the stay, apart from the fact that the term has been served and that good behavior may shorten the stay. By definition, expulsion from the system is unsuitable as a punishment for deviance in prison and presents itself rather as a reward. Since the time for the discharge from prison is normally determined in advance, with only limited room for adjustments, it does not necessarily imply that the offender has been in any way changed, healed, or rehabilitated.[22] He may, or he may not, be a different person from the one who entered the prison.

The staff as a sub-system shares many traits with other personnel groups in industry as well as in hospitals. The division of labor and the amount of specialization are poorly developed; the expertise, derived from the purpose of the prison, is simply to guard and keep watch. Since the execution of power is the dominant task, law enforcement is the crucial type of expertise, usually represented in the figure of the warden. Other staff members ordinarily have a rather limited education, except for the few psychiatrists, psychologists, and social workers who may also be found in the prisons. The relationships of complementarity between the professionals of the prison system are unclear. This is due, in part, to current competition over the proper allocation of decision-making power in prisons and detention institutions, for example, that between psychiatrists and lawyers.

SIMILARITY

The role pair of the prisoner and his guard exhibits one of the most clear-cut dichotomies in terms of power and rank. If any social system is designed on a dichotomous model, it must be the prison, since all the power apparently lies in the hands of the staff and since the inmates are deprived of all influence and self-determination. Several studies suggest, however, that this omnipotence of the staff may in many situations turn into a powerless condition.[23] This condition is due in part to the constraints which prison regulations impose upon the guards in their administration of discipline. In part it is also due to the difficulties of finding the proper negative sanctions in the prison, where deprivations already are so great, or to finding rewards other than giving the inmate his freedom, which guards are prevented from doing. This certain lack of power does not obliterate the dichotomy, but it narrows the gap a little, as does the lack of complementarity, which may imply that the inmate and the guard share the wish for a speedy release. The gains of the inmate need not be a loss for the guard.

The inmates do not constitute a representative sample of their native population, as the lower categories of rank seem to be heavily overrepresented in the prison clientele. The criminals and the prison inmates are, as such, often perceived to represent the lowest social stratum or the "underworld." [24] In most instances this rank corresponds fairly well to their actual situation in terms of occupation and income. The uniformity which results when an offender becomes a "number" in prison is, therefore, not likely to eliminate as much social inequality as the loss of individuality in the mental hospital does, although the process is carried to even greater lengths in the prison.

In spite of a loss of individuality, the prison community also exhibits a differentiation of social rank which is in part associated with the type of crime for which the inmate serves time. Economic crimes that require courage and technical skills rank at the top with the safebreaker as the leading figure, while sexual delinquents rank near the bottom in the prison community.[25] Age is probably important, although it does not seem to be a universal norm that the young admire and take after the older and seasoned criminals as role models. In countries with a high degree of professionalization among criminals, the prisons may tend more to assume the character of schools of crime. The personality of the inmate and the degree to which he invites trust and confidence is probably decisive for the esteem he receives. The "rat," the person who reports on fellow prisoners to the guards is, of course, not at all popular in the prison. The norm on which such reporting is condemned is similar to norms found in the factory and on board the ship. However, it carries even greater weight because secrecy is a professional weapon among the members of this particular social system. Crime is a type of activity which requires deception and concealment if its purpose is to be achieved.

Within the staff there are great inequalities of rank. The warden, the doctors, and psychologists have completed university educations, while the guards have very little formal schooling. The opportunities for social mobility inside the system are usually limited. The executives of the prison tend to be oriented towards colleagues outside the system, those in the department of justice, in the courts, in the police department, or in other similar institutions, and will rarely conceive of their position as one of lifelong duration. The prison is to a very large extent, and much more so than the mental hospital, dependent upon decisions made outside the system with respect to the fate of the inmates.

RECRUITMENT

No one can voluntarily join the prison as an inmate. If someone wants to be imprisoned, he has to commit a qualifying crime and then be convicted of it. Recruitment is compulsory, but the qualifying characteristic of the recruits is assumed to be caused by a voluntary act or choice. The inclusion of the new member is due neither to the need of the system for the inmate, nor to the offender's need for the prison, and the one held responsible for the imprisonment, the convict himself, is usually assumed not to want the inclusion to take place. The court, making the decision on imprisonment, neither wishes nor has the final moral responsibility for the fact that a new recruit is included in the prison. This lack of positive motivation in recruitment is intimately connected with the lack of complementarity and the apparently meaningless nature of the institution. The prison assumes meaning only as an appendage to society at large, which utilizes the prison for specific purposes of social control.

The representatives of the system do not normally participate in the decision on inclusion, although they may at times be consulted. Since the courts have made the decision on recruitment, the relationship between the system and the member bears no trace of a contract relationship. This condition is clearly different from that of the psychiatric hospital where hospitalization is often based upon

201

an agreement between the patient and the hospital or, if not, upon a unilateral decision of a responsible psychiatrist. There exists no basis of mutually, or even unilaterally, incurred responsibility as a basis for interaction between prison staff and inmates in terms of recruitment. The interaction is forced upon both parties, which is an essential reason why it usually is so limited and so unsatisfactory.

Recruitment is undertaken on the basis of considerations for others, not to aid the recruit, since imprisonment originates in a conflict between the criminal and the victim, a conflict in which responsibility and blame is assumed to rest with the offender. However, because the source of the trouble is a conflict between two actors, it is considered in advance problematical whether a type of deviation which qualifies for imprisonment is actually present. The origin in a conflict has led to surrounding imprisonment with an elaborate procedure, which is also aimed at safeguarding the interests of the defendant. It is, therefore, unlike most other types of recruitment. In criminal law and through the rules of criminal procedure the conditions for recruitment to the prisons are laid down in great detail. They permit the judge, however, to pay some attention to the possible effects of imprisonment on the convict as well as on outside society.

The last point brings out another distinguishing characteristic of the prison. When recruitment takes place to other systems, it is unusual that attention is paid to its implications for outsiders not directly engaged in the transaction. Criminals, however, are frequently imprisoned because it is considered necessary to deter others from a criminal career. The prison is the negative social system of society, the hidden whip, a system designed to attract no one. Is such a design compatible with the characteristics of a social system? This dilemma may be one of the basic driving forces behind the reform movement in penal administration, which aims at development of the prison into a system based upon complementarity, but nevertheless without encouraging recruitment of inmates. We are thus faced with the question whether social systems are possible if all motivation to recruitment is removed.

The prison is not in principle very different from the mental hospital with respect to recruitment to staff roles. The unique nature of the prison does, however, tend to reduce the incentives to recruitment for personnel. If the prison is to be experienced as an evil and a deprivation by the inmates, the guards will also be exposed to frustrations since interpersonal relations are by definition unsatisfactory in such a social system. A certain parallel in terms of deprivation between staff and inmates follows from the general principle of reciprocity in human interaction. We touch here upon another reason why the prison system generates pressures for reform, since the prison can hardly become a satisfactory place of work for the staff unless it also becomes a more livable place for the inmates.

SOCIALIZATION

Today imprisonment is commonly regarded in terms analogous to recruitment to the mental hospital, that is, as a failure in prior socialization and adjustment to society. It is more dubious, however, to what extent the prisons are charged with the task of re-socialization and therapy, or to what extent they are at all fit to take on the task. A certain amount of socialization is necessary for the inmate to adjust to the prison regime, and the prison usually inculcates the appropriate inmate habits, in spite of the sudden and sharp transition from everyday life. The prison has means of physical coercion at its disposal, enabling it to compel the inmates to a certain degree of obedience, thus making the system less dependent on appeals to motivation. Despite this, the guards and old prison hands argue recalcitrant recruits into "being sensible" and voluntarily accepting the prison routine.

Although socialization to the prison regime is necessary to make life in the system bearable, this adaption may be detrimental to the inmate once he has been released. The situation is parallel to the one found in mental hospitals with the difference, however, that mental hospitals make efforts to mitigate the adverse effects of adjustment to the hospital milieu, while the "prisonization" of inmates[26] rarely can be met with efforts to prepare them for life outside the institution. Many have claimed that the prisons counteract their own intentions because they tend to further disqualify the prisoner for normal life, rather than lead him back to society. Whether or not the claim that prisons are the very schools of crime is justified, it may at least be maintained that the function of the prisons in terms of socialization is equivocal.

With the growing efforts to make socialization a part of the prison's goal, new methods are introduced in the socialization of guards for their changing tasks, like courses in group therapy. It seems likely that an increase in the training of personnel must simultaneously contribute to a shift of emphasis in the system's purpose from detention and guard duties in the direction of socialization. More intensive training in guard duties does not seem to be called for and does not require any specific type of professional expertise. The knowledge of law is of primary significance only with respect to inclusion in the system and termination of membership, but largely irrelevant to a management of the day-to-day functioning of the system.

PRODUCTION

The productive purpose of the prison may be viewed as analogous to that of a warehouse in economic life, since the immediate requirement of the prison is to keep the inmate inside the walls for a specified period of time. In so far as the prison succeeds, its basic function has been fulfilled. If escapes are too frequent, demonstrating a failure on this point, severe criticism is directed against the warden and his staff. It is more difficult, however, to find clear and visible positive criteria that the productive purpose has been fulfilled, or even fulfilled with distinction. If the production targets of a prison are to be positively evaluated in the sense that the results reflect honor upon the staff, they must be differently and less narrowly defined. This consideration may oblige the prison to undertake tasks of rehabilitation and therapy, tasks which might furnish more readily visible and measurable criteria of success. One positive criterion which is being applied is the absence of recidivism or compliance with the laws subsequent upon release from the system. This is even a more precise and more specified criterion than those applied when the cure of mental illness is being evaluated. However, recidivism is a very common phenomenon, whatever the nature of the prison; consequently there is scepticism about whether the prisons can turn delinquents into law-abiding citizens, and thus exempt the prison staff of the responsibility for recidivism.

In addition to the possible consequences of imprisonment for the future behavior of the convicts, the deterrent and generally preventive function of prisons is often stressed. It seems probable that imprisonment has some influence upon the general rate of obedience to the law, particularly within certain areas of conduct. But the impact is even more difficult to measure than the effects of imprisonment upon the released offender. This doubt concerning a production result of the prison contributes to the uneasy attention and debate which is continuously focused upon this social system.

According to a traditional legal way of thinking the inmate is neither a co-worker of the staff nor raw material, since he is not primarily there either to work or to be further "processed." He may be conceived of as a tool to the extent that he is used to deter others like himself. This idea prompted Durkheim and Mead to describe the criminal offender as useful to society.[27] However, from the point of view of the prison system he has no utility, and it is not clear how "processing" of him might take place, if at all. The goal is to become a law-abiding citizen, but there are doubts whether the prison provides the proper climate for the needed processing.

While mental patients are invited to collaborate with the therapists in an endeavor to foster more self-insight, the prisoner and his guard have nothing to collaborate about except compliance with the prison routine. In an institution of forced labor, or when craft production is organized in the prisons, a tenuous basis is laid for the functional interplay between staff and inmate. The work carried out by the prisoners is, however, of a peculiar nature because it is unpaid; the small remunerations are considered marks of deserving conduct. One might, of course, construe the situation to mean that the prison work is the inmate's contribution in exchange for his room and board. However, he did not ask for this kind of room and board, and his labor is stripped of the normal societal characteristics of work and turned into a ritual.

The prison makes room for many different categories of social rank as defined by differences of power, education, and the nature of the offense. Internal mobility meets with an impassable cleavage between inmates and staff, since there are no characteristics more thoroughly disqualifying for membership in the staff than prior membership in the inmate group. Neither have the guards much chance to rise very far in the prison hierarchy. Recruitment to guard positions may imply an opportunity for upward social mobility by providing for a transition from working class origin to the achieved rank of a functionary. It seems that the rank of guard is higher inside than outside the prison, since he enjoys some kind of superiority in prison, while his salary is apt to place him with typically subordinate occupations on the general scale of social stratification.

The rank of the inmate in the prison is very low, as was usually his social rank prior to the imprisonment. Great variations are to be found in the subsequent fate of the general social rank of those who were respected members of society prior to the incarceration. A brief spell in prison for drunken driving need not affect the rank of the offender very much, unless he happens to be a professional cab driver or truck driver, and is simultaneously deprived of his driver's licence. Quite generally, it may be assumed that imprisonment has a socially degrading impact upon the offender, in spite of the commonly held principle that those who have served their term in prison have settled their account with society and ought not to be reminded of the fact.

Imprisonment can be used systematically to reduce social rank, although our legal authorities are not inclined to make use of this weapon. On the contrary, efforts are made to conceal names of defendants from the public so as to keep the general social esteem of the convict unimpeded by the criminal proceedings and the penalty. There are many examples of political trials, however, which have been used to bring the defendant and his peer followers into disrepute. The Nazi trials in occupied countries after the end of World War II offered examples of how punishment was used as a means of reducing the social rank, and especially the power, of those who had illegitimately usurped high social rank during the war. The punishment was designed to bring the offenders back to the rank they enjoyed prior to their treason, but often had the effect of further reducing it. Punishment, and more particularly imprisonment, remains the major institutionalized means by which society deprives actors of their social rank, and some of the downward social mobility in any society is precipitated by imprisonment.

CONFLICT AND DEVIANCE

Criminality is defined as a situation of conflict where the deviance is located on one side and the concern for the victim and for general social interests have decisive influence on the choice of sanctions. The underlying conflict makes it unrealistic to apply pure considerations of socialization to the stay in prison. The inmate is not put in prison for his own sake, which also tends to hinder the prisoner's willingness to accept any measure inside a prison as designed to aid him. Since he has not voluntarily joined the system it is difficult to reach him with offers of, or demands for, collaboration.

The structure of the prison as a social system reflects the conflict which precipitated the incarceration. The inmates find themselves in juxtaposition to the "local" representatives of society and to the victims. However, the conflict of interest out of which the crime arose, such as a theft, cannot be carried on inside the prison walls. The staff is unable to take care of the victim's interests inside the system, since the inflicted retribution obviously cannot wake up the dead, recover lost money, or provide for other remedies. The initial conflict of interest between victim and offender is substituted by another one between guard and inmate, the inmate usually wishing to leave, while the guard is obliged to keep him confined. The chances of compromise are moot. If, however, the confinement is accepted as an accomplished fact, imposed from without and beyond the control of the members of the system, guard and inmate may arrive at a *modus vivendi*. The conflict between them cannot, then, be characterized as a zero-sum game, and the gains of one of them need not impose a loss upon the other. Since the main purpose of the prison is to detain the inmate for a certain length of time, and little beyond that, the guard is not dependent upon his ability to extract much achievement from the prisoner. The absence of a more constructive purpose may bestow more significance upon purely human relationships. Although the prerequisites for satisfactory human interrelationships are hardly present in prisons, the guard as well as the inmate shares an interest in making the most of the situation. One consequence of this wish for a personal accommodation is that the staff is tempted to overlook minor transgressions of the prison routine, which may by way of reciprocation tempt the inmate to relent in his militant opposition to the prison.[28]

Deviance inside the prison can be met in various ways; the sanctions are limited, however, by the peculiar design of the system as a means of deprivation. Since guards are obliged to interact daily with the inmates, the means of sanctions are not quite unilaterally distributed. If guards deviate from the expectations of the prisoners, they can be encountered by inmate conduct which is apt to annoy or threaten them. Those sanctions which in extreme cases are applied to deviants inside the prison have often been interpreted as representing in themselves new instances of deviance from societal norms. Thus, revelations about guard brutality or the use of straitjackets and other means of physical compulsion in prison tend to shock outside society.

NORMATIVE ORIENTATIONS

The crime and the failure to comply with social norms provide the basis for confinement in the prison. Good conduct in prison may sometimes speed up release; apart from this the guards' attitude to the prisoner seems to be marked only slightly by achievement orientations. According to modern theories of crime and penology the attitudes to the offender and the inmate are moving in the direction of putting more emphasis on quality orientations. The transition of the target of treatment from the crime to the criminal implies also a transition from principles of achievement and performance to those of ascription and quality, although this is more apparent in theory than in practice.

The basis for recruitment has traditionally been highly specific, namely the evidence for guilt of a specified kind and the subsequent subsumption under precise rules of law. With the increasing range offered to the judge in his choice of penal sanctions, the basis for incarceration is becoming more diffuse, admitting a great many attributes of the defendant as relevant when the penalty is to be meted out. Inside the prison, however, the regulations often constrain the operation of human considerations in guards' dealings with inmates. The orientation tends to be specific in the sense that the staff behaves in accordance with the implications of one single shared characteristic of all the prisoners: that they are inmates. Neither the attitudes of inmates nor those of outside society vis-à-vis the staff are characterized by specificity or achievement orientation. It is too difficult to measure their performance and almost impossible to delineate an area of relevant specialized competency. The skills of the guard are diffusely defined, and his personality may appear to be more relevant than are his skills and knowledge.

In probably no other institution is the norm of universalism as firmly entrenched as it is with court decisions in criminal trials. Such decisions are expected to be rigorously just and marked by a total absence of particularistic considerations. This is evidenced by the demand for equality before the law, although many inmates have doubts about the relationship between theory and practice. Inside the prison it is even more difficult to practice universalism. Due to the poor development of the functional aspects of prisons and to the difficulties of judging inmates in terms of achievement, personal relations between guards and inmates come to loom larger. The manipulation of these personal relationships remains one of the few levers of social control in the hands of the guards, while being simultaneously the vehicle through which inmates may express approval or disapproval and influence the guards.

Emotional eruption in prison is not assumed to be functional as it may be in the mental hospital, while the causes are amply present. The closed cells lead to outbursts of claustrophobic anxiety, and the quarrels with guards contain the seeds of violent aggression. Homosexuality, which is considered dysfunctional, is also a means of emotional outlet in prison; it is probably less important in a prison system for short-term inmates than it is in systems where there are life-term offenders. The structure of the prison system creates great obstacles to emotional expression, which is, nevertheless, unavoidable; the personnel are rather poorly equipped to handle it when it occurs.[29]

The isolated rural hamlet[30]

The hamlet on the geographical periphery of society is different from the four preceding systems in one fundamental respect: it has not been established in order to fill a specific function. It is a spontaneous social formation, not a programmed system. But the hamlet is not a society, since it could not contain within its confines systems like those we have dealt with. Like these other systems, the hamlet is incapable of self-sufficiency and cannot, by means of its own productive efforts, provide the means of subsistence for its members or for the perpetuation of their culture. This distinguishes it from primitive tribes. No doubt, the hamlet must be seen as a sub-system of the inclusive system, although one which has not been programmed to fulfill any specialized function for society at large. These considerations may serve perhaps as a definition of local communities inside modern societies quite generally. There is some doubt today concerning whether the peripheral rural community is a viable social system at all, or whether it is in the throes of dissolution as a consequence of emigration and a failing resource base.

PROXIMITY

The social system of the hamlet is defined by physical proximity, consisting as it does of neighbors in a fiord, upon an island, or encircling a lake. The conditions of proximity, normally visible by a glance at the map, lead to much interaction inside hamlet borders and to a dip in interaction frequency and intensity at the border. The hamlets frequently coincide with formally defined school districts and census tracts. Kinship is more closely woven inside the hamlet than it is between hamlets, and the inhabitants themselves distinguish between members of the hamlet and outsiders. Although hamlets of fishermen and farmers may at first glance appear similar over large coastal areas, a closer inspection reveals considerable differences between hamlets in terms of economy as well as politics and religion. These differences are utilized by the population to make distinctions between one's own neighbors and people who belong to other hamlets which are often accompanied by rivalries and a certain amount of animosity.

A hamlet is a group defined by domicile or settlement, implying that proximity is not accompanied by separation from the nuclear family as it was with the ship, the mental hospital, and the prison. When a member of the hamlet is in his system, he may also be near his family, although he does leave it for certain periods, as, for example, to participate in the great seasonal fisheries. One may claim that the hamlet is constituted of families rather than individual actors, for the family is the sub-system of the hamlet through which the individual also acquires membership in the hamlet. In this respect the hamlet also differs from the factory, since employment in the factory is unrelated to family belonging-ness.

COMPLEMENTARITY

The hamlet's lack of purpose implies that it was not established by the bringing together of actors whose dissimilarities qualified them for reciprocal satisfaction of needs. The division of labor is poorly developed and reciprocity is not highly characteristic of the social structure. Most members of the system produce similar goods to be marketed outside the hamlet. A shopkeeper and a school teacher, however, have occupations which differ from the rest of the population and which permit them to enter into a reciprocal exchange with the community. The occupational life is to some extent differentiated, but the division of labor is not a response to internal demands for complementarity; it is rather the outcome of the differentiated demands of outside markets and of differences in the access of natural resources.

One important type of complementarity based upon dissimilarity prevails regarding marriage. Due to the small size of these hamlets and some skewness in the proportion of the sexes around the age of marriage, many have to marry outsiders. Because of these limitations on the availability of spouses, quite a few marriages are contracted between spouses who are close relatives, such as first or second cousins.

Mutual dependency is not always and exclusively determined by dissimilarity and the division of labor. Farmers and fishermen may in many instances depend upon their neighbors because of their common stake in the relationships of exchange with the outside society. Since a hamlet may lose its local school if the number of children drops below a certain minimum, the emigration of families with children may deprive the remaining families of their preferred school service, thus creating pressures upon them also to move. Other services, like the construction of roads and the provision of electricity, are dependent upon the size of the hamlet as well as upon its location. All of this engenders a mutual dependency amongst neighbors, although not linked to specific activities or performances. This was somewhat different years ago when the neighbors depended upon each other for specific neighborly cooperation, such as assistance when the boats were hauled ashore. Even today neighbors on the most isolated spots depend upon each other. For example, a man may be unable to leave his home to participate in the fisheries unless a neighbor is able to aid his wife if need be in his absence. The presence of such conditions implies that these small systems may dissolve rapidly because of a chain reaction when the membership has fallen below a certain minimum level.

SIMILARITY

The inhabitants of the hamlet are either born in the hamlet or in another peripheral community with many of the same characteristics, preserving a similarity in culture and style of life. Although many members of the hamlet have participated for shorter or longer periods in different occupations, these are as a rule unskilled and transient, and thus do not induce appreciable differences between the members. Even shopkeepers have a style of life rather similar to their neighbors and often participate in fisheries or in farming as a sideline. The difference between farmers and year-round fishermen should not be ignored, nor should those between the teachers and other municipal functionaries on the one hand, and the remainder of the population on the other. Since a stretch of the coast of Norway was partially populated by Lapps, the amount of Lappishness has been a social characteristic determining interaction patterns and the social identity of the individual up to recent times. Today the ethnic criteria and the reminiscence of Lappish culture are too few and insignificant to play much of a part in the social life of these communities. In other North-Norwegian communities ethnic criteria are still very important.

There are appreciable differences in income amongst members of the same hamlet, while the differentiation in terms of power, superiors, and subordinates, is well nigh non-existent. We find nothing which resembles the sharp dichotomies which characterized at least three of the preceding social systems, although some men control resources upon which their neighbors depend. This statement applies particularly to shopkeepers who may grant credit, and to a lesser extent to teachers, whose verbal skills and knowledge are an important resource in dealings with outside society. Due to previous experiences with powerful local merchants who utilized indebtedness to secure their position of omnipotence, the population is extremely sensitive towards any effort on the part of a neighbor to establish himself in a superior position which might make other members of the hamlet dependent upon him. This sensitivity leads to a strongly egalitarian ethos in the population, an attitude which is supported by the shared conditions of living on the very periphery of society under the reign of a harsh and capricious nature; it even occurs amongst those who are rather dissimilarly situated in purely economic terms.[31]

RECRUITMENT

The four preceding systems receive all their recruits from outside the system; this was initially the case with the hamlet when it was settled by migrating farmers and fishermen. The practice of outside recruitment is continued when marriage brings new female members into the system. The predominant form of recruitment, however, is through reproduction; the birth rate is so high that the communities are able, and even compelled, to let many of their young emigrate to other more centrally located communities. Apart from the supply of immigrant spouses, there is a very limited amount of movement into the system. This, in combination with the strong tendency to emigration, has resulted in a population with declining absolute figures during recent years.

The original recruitment patterns were characterized by the communities' location in an area where the path of immigration of Norwegians from southern Norway crosses the path of immigrant Lapps from Sweden and Finland in the east and north. In some hamlets the present population can be traced back to a handful of progenitors, some of whom were southern Norwegians while others were Lapps. Due to the distances from population centers, the proximity and shared conditions of life, the caste barrier was broken down; the system functioned as a veritable melting pot for Lappish and Norwegian elements. The end result was that the Norwegian language and culture became all pervasive, the local community becoming firmly enmeshed in the wider network of the inclusive Norwegian society.

The system is a producer of recruits to other systems and to a much lesser extent the recipient of recruits coming from other systems. This pattern often leads to a skewed distribution of the population in terms of age and sex, and may also tend to sap the community of some of its most capable members. The imbalance between immigration and emigration poses a threat to those who remain in the hamlet. This threat can hardly be met by developing new incentives to attract recruits from the outside, since the state of the economic resources is very precarious and the community lacks many of the amenities of urban life.

SOCIALIZATION

No educational demands, beyond those which are made of all citizens, have to be met by those who are accepted as members of the system. Due to the isolation and the retarded development of educational facilities, one may still encounter elderly people who have not attended school for more than a few weeks in the course of their life. Even today the majority of the children attend a primary school which is divided into no more than two classes; the teachers themselves have rarely been trained for their profession. In some places the children have to stay in dormitories or with relatives because of the distance between school and home. The difficulties of getting the children to school and the unsatisfactory living conditions for children away from home have often been the precipitating cause of migration. A few people in the hamlet may have attended a commercial or agricultural school in addition to primary school; they may have taken correspondence courses or courses for fishermen or for young people in general, but a complete high-school education is practically unknown in the community.

Under these conditions the spontaneous socialization which takes place in the family or in neighborly interaction is the predominant mode of preparation for adult roles. Today it is difficult for the grown-ups to know what they are going to prepare the young for, whether for the roles available in the hamlet or for any one of the many that are waiting for them in the larger society outside. The parents are at a certain disadvantage in this situation, because they know little about the ways of city life. The upbringing of children of fishermen is no doubt influenced by the fact that the father is absent for extended periods during the year. Due to the limitation of population, the children of these hamlets do not form peer-groups of certain well-defined ages; consequently this source of social norms fails to gain ascendancy as in cities.

There exist hardly any occupational roles in the peripheral hamlets that require a university education. Some entire municipalities may have no doctors, lawyers, or representatives of other professions. Their services are obtained from a neighboring municipality. For a young individual growing up in the hamlet, the choice of higher education implies, then, a decision to move out of the hamlet. In addition, it is unlikely for other reasons that the young would decide in favor of a higher education; for example, they might find remunerative work outside the hamlet as fishermen, seamen, or in some other branch of unskilled labor. These choices have the additional advantage of flexibility, and at the same time they correspond better with the traditional ethos of the local community.

In former times peripheral local communities were not evaluated on the basis of rentability or viability (thus abandoning hamlets if they did not yield some profit), despite the fact that the member of the hamlet was a producer in the strictly economic sense. Relative to the goals of production it seems reasonable to place the hamlet somewhere between the factory and the ship on the one hand and the mental hospital and the prison on the other. Today public authorities attempt to encourage depopulation of some local communities because the prerequisites of rational production are absent. When, generally, hamlets are being more amply sustained, it is not necessarily because the economic conditions are judged to be more favorable. It is because the inhabitants are so strongly tied to their habitat by tradition and by individual economic interests, that the government is unable to cajole them into moving by the means available to influence settlement patterns. The public authorities are not entitled to evaluate the hamlet in the same terms that a shipowner may apply to his boats or that a firm can apply to the unprofitable factory.

Many hamlets are run with a deficit, that is, the population is unable to produce enough to pay for the services which are considered necessities in more densely populated areas. This is to some extent caused by the low income levels, but also by the exorbitant costs of many social services and basic investments, such as road-building, provisions for schooling, medical aid, electricity, transportation and entertainment. The great distances and the dispersed settlement pattern are obstacles to economic growth. From the point of view of the inclusive society these hamlets are being "subsidized," contributing less to society than they receive in return. From the point of view of the local population the obverse seems to be the case, namely, that they make greater sacrifices and efforts than others, while receiving less in return—less than what is taken for granted in more centrally located communities. The hamlet population thinks in terms of distributive justice, while the public authorities apply an equilibrium model to the terms of exchange between the hamlet and the inclusive society.[32] The difference between the two frames of reference permit both sides to find good reasons for their views. When the hamlet's account with the public authorities is settled, it might be reasonable to expand the concept of production to also comprise some elements normally kept outside economic calculations. One such element is the fact that the hamlet delivers a steady supply of recruits to other sub-systems of society. The hamlet carries the major cost of reproducing and of socializing these later emigrants without receiving any explicit remuneration for the execution of this task. One plausible construction of the present situation would be that society is willing to subsidize these hamlets to a certain extent in return for socialized recruits for other systems where they are in demand.

STRATIFICATION

The four previous systems have goals which demand some social stratification, but not the hamlet. Here many factors counteract the development of any marked social stratification. One of these factors has already been mentioned, namely, the sharing of a common fate by everyone living under the same conditions of isolation, nature, and climate, and the sharing also of a common distrust of the government and of city people. The individually owned production systems, like farms and fishing vessels, do not demand much hired manpower and very rarely provide a basis for establishing permanent relationships of superordination and subordination. Political leadership is not organized on a hamlet basis; the nearest centers of political power are located outside the local system. In so far as political or cultural leaders are found inside the hamlet, their influence is derived more from their personalities than from the role, and there seems to be a tendency for this kind of leadership to be rather dispersed.

An important fact with respect to inequalities of income and influence is that they do not coincide with kinship or neighborhood. Close relatives may show considerable disparities in wealth. The marriage market is much too limited to permit endogamous tendencies inside social strata. The closely knit web of kinship presents

217

obstacles to the accumulation of capital locally, as relatives and neighbors expect the entrepreneur to share his growing wealth, and censor niggardly tendencies.

The sharp conflicts of interest which prevail between neighboring hamlets over road building and other development priorities counteract the formation of social stratification and class conflicts. Geographical factors take precedence over rank differences, while factionalism inside the hamlets may thwart the emergence of class solidarity. All this was strikingly different around the turn of the century when prosperous and powerful local merchants dominated many municipalities. They served as a focus of all economic activities, while also being singled out for a concerted political attack from the vast majority of fishermen and farmers who were equals by virtue of their common bondage under these so-called "Island Kings." The first Socialist representatives in the Norwegian Parliament were elected from this area which suggests that a class consciousness had arisen and that it was directed against the local merchants who were perceived as the main enemies of the common man.

Under present conditions this population of independent farmers and fishermen are in many respects subordinated to the decisions of the central authorities, who make the most important decisions regarding public investments, grants of loans, subsidies, and various kinds of pension claims. The influence of local politicians or of local shopkeepers weigh relatively less when compared to the implications of these decisions. The tensions between the peripheral local community and the central representatives of the inclusive society weigh more than the internal social stratification. In spite of this, the hamlets are politically divided into a right and a left, vaguely in accordance with income and wealth. If, however, the antagonisms between periphery and center are the dominant ones, it means that the cleavage does not correspond to the major political divisions in society at large, which follow social class lines.

CONFLICT AND DEVIANCE

As has been mentioned, some of the most important conflicts of interest are found in the competition of neighboring hamlets over appropriations and public investments. The municipal council has the responsibility of channelizing and ameliorating these conflicts, while the actual decisions are often made somewhere else. For an individual to obtain some aid from the county or state, the municipal authorities normally have to make a recommendation or offer some guarantee. Thus, some pressure is exerted upon the hamlet representatives to overcome the conflicts of interest, in order to present a common front to outside society, while the central authorities may, occasionally, have an interest in preserving the conflict on the basis of financially determined tactics of procrastination.

Conflicts may rise to high temperatures in these isolated communities when the interests at stake are vital to the future viability of the hamlet. The closed character of the small, rural system often bestows upon antagonisms a personal element of bitterness. Many local communities around the world are reported to show a strong preference for solving their own conflicts without interference from the inclusive society. The peripheral hamlets dealt with here seem to be more closely integrated in the larger society, in the sense that they often bring their internal conflicts before a larger audience through the press, or even take them to the courts. However, examples can also be found where deviance is treated as a hamlet secret for long periods of time; more centrally located communities would have brought the matter to the attention of the proper authorities at an earlier stage.

Disagreements over values seem to play a much smaller part than the conflicts of interest based upon geography or other factors. However, there is dissension in some hamlets between actively religious people and those less committed: evidence can be found in disputes over the propriety of drinking alcohol and participating in celebrations or parties. Some political disagreements occur as well. There is also a vague but possibly significant difference of opinion between modernists and traditionalists, between those who by and large accept the goals of the inclusive society and those who wish to defend the values of the old rural community against the inroads of modernity and urbanism. These various conflicts of values run, at least in part, counter to each other, thus preventing the cleavages from gaining much structural significance in the hamlet.

Questions arise whether the most isolated homesteads have been recruited by deviants on the run from their own communities, and whether extreme isolation may induce deviant predispositions. Some limited and uncertain evidence suggests that the most isolated households more frequently than others contain deviants, either in the form of incomplete families or mental disease. It is impossible, however, to generalize on the peripheral hamlet as a whole. Unlike the situation in southern mountain valleys, bachelors are not disproportionally prevalent, while another type of deviance from family norms, represented by unmarried mothers, seems to occur with relatively higher frequency than in the rest of the country. It seems likely that this latter type of deviance is closely related to the amount of isolation and to interaction barriers. These deviants are by and large accepted despite the fact that the population seldom entertains norms of family life different from those prevailing in the inclusive society.

NORMATIVE ORIENTATIONS

Since the hamlet systems have their basis in a territorial belongingness and are not established by a network of roles around a task, it is difficult to find any formulation of goals or normative orientation. No blueprints exist. Achievement is unnecessary to obtain membership in the hamlet. A person may not be accepted as a member simply by moving to the hamlet and adjusting to life there. Unless such movement occurs in conjunction with marriage, which somehow reshapes the social identity, there are many indications to prove that even a prolonged residence in the community is not enough to become recognized as a full-blooded member of the hamlet. Traditionally, the home community, the community where the family of orientation lived, was assumed to put its stamp upon the social identity of the actor, a stamp which could only with difficulty be erased. The quality orientation, based upon ascribed traits, was, and still is to some extent, the prevailing one.

The hamlet has no specified purpose. The danger of depopulation leads to a diffuse mutual dependency of the members upon each other. There also exist, however, some specific relationships, such as those between customer and shopkeeper, between fisherman and fish buyer, and between teacher and pupils. In many instances, however, it can be clearly seen how such specifically defined relationships serve to activate a more comprehensive and diffuse underlying relationship between the actors. Some relationships of complementarity seem also to tie in with a more general reciprocity, bestowing upon them the nature of being elements in a system of alliances that have implications beyond what appears to be at stake in the particular transaction. To buy in one shop, or to sell fish to one buyer, may mean that one is tied by a wider bond of loyalty to these other parties and is no mere expression of what seems most profitable and convenient at the moment.

There are many signs of universalism within the hamlets, such as through norms prescribing equal treatment of all those who belong to the hamlet in certain contexts, or through norms which demand hospitality to anyone, including visitors to the hamlet. On the other hand, particularism is self-evidently practiced in many transactions, as, for example, when property rights to the homestead are transferred or when fishing vessels and gear are inherited. It cannot be claimed, however, that kinship is as important in economic transactions of this kind as it is in more typically agricultural communities in other parts of the country.

Compared to the purposively founded sub-systems of society the hamlet offers more opportunity for affective expression, which occurs largely because the hamlet is composed of families. This basic characteristic of the peripheral rural community has an all-pervasive influence in all normative orientations, setting it apart from the four systems described above.

AFTERWORD ON SOCIETY

THE PRECEDING analysis terminates at a point where a new volume might begin. An attempt has been made to furnish a conceptual structure applicable in analyses of society, without our actually trying to analyze either a society or the separate social institutions of which a society is composed. Some institutions have been mentioned, like the family, the school, and the social stratification, but no effort has been made to describe any concrete society or to develop a model applicable to societies in general. We should, however, be equipped by now with the tools needed to examine a concrete society and its institutions. Although I am not proposing to take on this task here, it might be useful to sketch the contours of what we should observe as sociologists investigating a concrete society. This brief sketch may also serve to build a bridge between the present conceptual analysis and those works which present the structure of a concrete society.

It has become a rather common practice when describing a society to order the data according to the institutions under which they can be subsumed. An *institution* has been defined as a set of norms and roles grouped around a task or a function. As a basis for the ordering of sociological items under chapter headings a classification of institutions may be a useful point of departure. It may appear simple to impute a social task to some institutional arrangement, but the actual establishment of the functions served by any institutional item often proves to be a complex research task. There are also some phenomena in any society that are not so readily classified in terms of a specific institution and its norms and roles. Thus, although population trends and internal migrations may well be influenced by norms, the events that take place in these societal fields cannot be exhaustively dealt with simply in terms of norms and roles. This holds true also for the actual distribution of goods, which is of such decisive importance for social stratification. In most instances a mapping of society according to institutions is a practical and didactic device with the aim of providing an overview of society, and is not intended as an effort to settle more profound theoretical issues.

It is reasonable to put the *family* first among the institutions, if for no other reason that life begins within the family. The family institution is a set of norms and roles organized around the function of reproduction, and aimed at the solution of important socializing tasks. Apart from this there is not much that can be said with any claim to general applicability in modern society. True, the family establishes a normative framework for the satisfaction of sexual needs and provides norms concerning the division of labor and cooperation with regard to consumption. But these needs can also be satisfied outside the family, and seem actually to be satisfied more and more frequently in other institutional settings. The normative design in modern societies is marked by the conception of a "normal" family as consisting of a couple with their children, who remain with their parents until they are grown up but not much longer. In many societies incest taboos prevent marriage and social relations only with members of the same nuclear family, and with direct ascendants and descendants. The husband usually works outside the home, while most women do their work in the home, although a sizable minority of married women also are gainfully employed. Men and women have in most respects equal legal rights; the differences that can be observed in actual practice are very largely a consequence of the operation of informal norms and sex role patterns.

The family shares the task of socialization with the *educational* institution, since the socializing functions are gradually transferred to *schools*. The school has become a pivotal institution in modern society. Its position is due to the emergence of a school system of seven, nine, or even more years of obligatory attendance, accompanied by a vastly increasing demand for higher education. The schools socialize for specific, and often highly specialized, occupational roles as well as for general membership in society. One typical aspect of the modern educational institution is the demand by everyone for an equal opportunity to an education, although studies have revealed considerable disparity between consciously voiced ideals and actual practice.

From the family and school the actor is led into the *occupational* role system and is drawn into the orbit of the *economic* institution. It is concerned with the task of production, including primary, as well as secondary and tertiary occupations. The normative framework of the economic institution is very comprehensive, ranging from the constitutional protection of property rights to the rules in limited liability companies and the general law of contracts, as well as legislation on the protection of labor and rules on the settlement of industrial disputes. The framework of the economic institution also comprises the technological rules, the detailed and scientifically founded prescriptions on how specific commodities can best be produced. Although the technical norms do not have the same compulsive formal character as the legal rules, they have come to dominate the lives of modern man no less, nay probably even more, than legal rules.

These three institutions correspond to the three prerequisites of social systems that were discussed in Chapter IV. Chapter VII showed that the problems of recruitment, socialization, and production arise within sub-systems of society just as they do in relation to society itself. It is only in this latter perspective that we may point to specific institutions which satisfy the prerequisites of social systems. Considering society as a whole, it is very difficult to draw clear borderlines around the economic institution, since it is intertwined with two other institutional clusters, those of stratification and politics.

As an institution *social stratification* is less explicit, more covert than the three preceding institutions. There are few formal rules pertaining to the rank order of a modern society, or to the general distribution of goods in society. Nevertheless, differences of rank and the unequal distribution of goods are pervasive features of society, in part even accepted on the basis of prevailing, although informal, social values and norms. In addition, however, one may find a certain amount of social inequality which is largely unnoticed. Some inequalities are fought by social agencies. Whether the solution is judged as good or bad, the stratification structure settles a problem of distribution, and is thus closely intertwined with the economic institution which distributes commodities, services, wages, and profits. One of those resources which is being distributed through the stratification system is power. This establishes a close link between politics and social stratification.

The *political* institution regulates the power relationships in society at large and inside the territorially determined sub-systems of society: the states, counties, or municipalities. Other important power relations exist but are not directly regulated by the political institution. The power relations of economic corporations or associations do not fall completely outside the orbit of the political institution, since they are influenced by legislation and various types of government intervention, without, however, being fully subordinated by the political institutions. Power relationships in the family are very important to the individual but remain relatively untouched by political influence. Like money, and all the things which money can buy, power is a scarce commodity. Most modern, non-communist societies seem tacitly to accept the distribution of power as a more burning issue than the distribution of money, and so make it mandatory that society regulate the relations of power, while leaving the distribution of money largely to the mechanisms of the market. The basic principles underlying the regulation of power are found in the constitution, in legislation, and in parliamentary customs and regulations. Some very important aspects of the distribution of power are, however, left in the hands of private organizations, the political parties, which are largely free to arrange their internal power structures as they see fit. Political life takes place in a field of tension between two norms, one which prescribes equal participation of everybody in the decision-making process, and another one which claims that leadership and centralization of power is necessary if society is to survive.

One particular aspect of the exertion of power is frequently singled out for treatment as a separate institution, *law*. The task of law is to solve conflicts and to prevent deviance, that is, to exert social control, while seeing to it that this is done in accordance with the demands of justice. Some important aspects of the legal institution were discussed in Chapter VI. The legal institution, like social stratification, interpenetrates other specific institutions. Law is engaged in a battle against deviations from the rules of the other social institutions; it also offers a technique for solving conflicts which the separate institutions are unable to settle by their own means. Law thus puts force behind the norms of other institutions. However, while the norms of social stratification accept or acquiesce to the fact that actors in the various sectors of society are ranked above and below each other, law purports to treat everyone equally, even when it is not engaged in an attempt to remedy existing social inequalities. Also, contrary to social stratification, the law has its own specifically designated agencies, such as legislators and judges, and the norms of the law are explicit and formal, while those of social stratification are informal and covert.

The *religious* institution, like the family institution, once set the framework for most of the individual's activities. In recent years they have been reduced to institutions charged with more specific and limited tasks. It is not easy to state what the tasks of the religious institution are, because to do so may demand a stand on religious issues. The church and the ministry facilitate the relationship to the supernatural and to God for the members of society. If we define the functions of the church and of the sects in their own terms, their main task is to sustain man's relationship to God, while simultaneously catering to a great many needs of a more earthly character. The intervention of the church in the life of modern man concerns the crucial, critical situations where advice, admonition and ritual are especially called for.

The task of the *health* institution is to cure illness and, to an increasing extent, to prevent illness through social policies. This latter task has brought new and vast areas of human life and living conditions within the orbit of medical norms. To the health institutions belong the work of physicians in private practice, as well as agencies of public health. In Chapters VI and VII some basic norms of the health institution have been discussed. In conjunction with the development of techniques of production, the evolution of medicine has been a major precondition to the increase in longevity and in population figures.

The *mass media* are not anchored in explicit and coordinated norms, as are the institutions of school, church, law, and health. They constitute, nevertheless, a distinguishable sector of modern societies, charged with the task of emitting messages to large and open audience groups, with the purpose of entertainment, propaganda, or education. The tasks of the mass media overlap in part with the functions of the school and of politics. These functions are fulfilled, however, in large measure by the application of norms borrowed from the economic institution, prescribing an adjustment of the supply in accordance with the demand. No definitive set of norms has been crystallized around the task of the mass media, and there are important differences between mass media in private hands and mass media under government sponsorship, or at least under public control. We find, therefore, substantial disparities in the structure and function of the mass media between the countries.

Science as an institution has traditionally been closely linked to the institution of education, especially to the universities. In spite of this connection, science operates under a set of norms which exhibit some significant deviations from those governing the schools and education, particularly with respect to innovation. The norms of science are marked by a tension between the demand for originality and creation on the one hand and the emphasis upon truth and reliability on the other hand. Although no more than a small number of individuals have so far been engaged in scientific research, this institution contains the germs of far-reaching social changes. These changes have been mediated through the economic institution, through medicine, and the military institution, but to a much lesser extent through those institutions which concern themselves with the solution of social and interpersonal problems, such as politics and the family.

The norms surrounding artistic activities bestow upon *art* a very distinct, and in some ways unique, place in modern society. The norms of art share with the norms of science the emphasis upon creativity and innovation, while putting much less weight upon empirical truth than science. It has been considered the task of art to create beauty and to cater to the aesthetic needs of man. However, literature has also been charged with certain didactic functions, and most art forms have had a nationally integrating function, although it does not seem that modern painting and modern music serve such a function. These latter art forms are non-traditional in that they pay no heed to national values and tend rather to form an element in a growing, uniform world culture. Compared to the other social institutions, art is characterized today by a lack of recognizable social purpose, at least if we adhere to the principles applied to measure the purposefulness of social institutions. It is reasonable to assume that the function of art in modern society bears a specific relationship precisely to this apparent lack of social purpose.

Sports hold a great interest to very large masses in all modern societies. They are one of the few foci of interest which can tie together actors across the many social dividing lines. This bestows upon sports an important integrating function not only nationally, but also on the international level. The task of the sports is to cultivate physical performance and to provide spectators with an opportunity to observe and vicariously experience physical excellence; risk and uncertainty are integrative elements of the experience. The norms are dominated by the basic principle of fair competition and define as irrelevant everything but what directly pertains to the skills and achievements of the participants. A point of controversy is the relationship between professionalism and amateur sportsmanship, as well as that between the mass sport and the star performance. Although participation in sports is no more than a leisure-time activity for most people, it is undoubtedly an important and serious social institution of modern society.

The *military* is the institution charged with the task of defending the territory and, more generally, securing the safety of a national society. As an institution the military establishment has in recent times been intimately linked to those norms which emphasize national values. A soldier in war acts under norms different from those which apply within all other social institutions, permitting, or even encouraging or forcing him to take enemy lives, while he is simultaneously prepared to sacrifice his own life. The development of weapons in the postwar period has led to significant changes in the place and function of the military institution, especially as a consequence of the emergence of atomic weapons. While the traditional army was designed upon the precondition that it might be applied in times of war, it is becoming a widespread view that the modern army is primarily designed to prevent war, and that it may be a poor means of defense should a war actually break out. The prevailing mood of people regarding this very old and significant social institution is characterized by a considerable amount of uncertainty and doubt.

There is no definite, logical end to such a list of social institutions. If the list which has been furnished were to serve as a list of contents for a volume on the sociology of any single society, it would probably cover most of its social life. The purpose of this book, however, is limited to providing the reader with some of the sociological tools which should enable him to study these institutions effectively.

NOTES

CHAPTER I

1 Frantz From, *Om oplevelsen af andres adfærd* ("On the Perception of Others' Behavior"). Copenhagen: Nyt nordisk forlag, Arnold Busck, 1953, 17-19.

2 *Ibid.*, 25. See also Fritz Heider, *The Psychology of Interpersonal Relations.* New York: John Wiley & Sons, Inc., 1958, 79-124.

3 Ralph Linton, *The Study of Man.* New York: Appleton-Century-Crofts, 1936, 115. Kingsley Davis, *Human Society.* New York: The Macmillan Company, 1949, 96-98. Talcott Parsons, *The Social System.* Glencoe, Illinois: The Free Press, 1951, 63-65.

4 Parsons, *Ibid.*, 65-66.

5 *Ibid.*, 61-64. See also Samuel A. Stouffer and Jackson Toby, "Role Conflict and Personality." *The American Journal of Sociology,* 56 (1951), 395-406.

6 Parsons, *Ibid.*, 60.

CHAPTER II

1 Renato Tagiuri, "Social Preference and Its Perception." In Renato Tagiuri and Luigi Petrullo (eds.), *Person Perception and Interpersonal Behavior.* Stanford: Stanford University Press, 1958, 316-36, especially 321-25.

2 Knut Erik Tranøy, "An Important Aspect of Humanism." *Theoria,* 23 (1957).

3 Ragnar Rommetveit, *Social Norms and Roles.* Oslo: Universitetsforlaget, 1953, 47 ff.

4 Rommetveit, *Ibid.*, 44 ff. Cf. also Leon Festinger *et al., Theory and Experiment in Social Communication.* Ann Arbor: Edwards Brothers, 1950.

5 *Ibid.*, 97 ff. David Krech and Richard S. Crutchfield, *Theory and Problems of Social Psychology.* New York: McGraw-Hill Book Company, 1948, 389, 512, 514.

6 Torgny T. Segerstedt, "Social Control as Sociological Concept."

Uppsala Universitets Årsskrift. Uppsala, 1948, 14 ff. Rommetveit, *Ibid.,* 18 ff.

7   George C. Homans, *The Human Group.* New York: Harcourt Brace, Inc., 1950, 1.

8   Eugen Ehrlich, *Grundlegung der Soziologie des Rechts* ("Fundamental Principles of the Sociology of Law"). München and Leipzig: Duncker & Humbolt, 1913, 29-30.

9   Robert K. Merton and Alice S. Rossi, "Contributions to the Theory of Reference Group Behavior," in Robert K. Merton, *Social Theory and Social Structure.* Glencoe, Illinois: The Free Press, 1957, 225-80.

10 Rommetveit, *Ibid.,* 61-69. Festinger, *Ibid.,* 6 ff.

11 Norbert Wiener, *The Human Use of Human Beings. Cybernetics and Society.* New York: Doubleday & Company, Inc., 1954, Chapter 6.

12 Jurgen Ruesch and Gregory Bateson, *Communication: The Social Matrix of Psychiatry.* New York: W. W. Norton & Company, Inc., 1951.

13 Paul F. Lazarsfeld, Bernhard Berelson and Hazel Gaudet, *The People's Choice.* New York: Columbia University Press, 1948, 153-55. Elihu Katz and Paul F. Lazarsfeld, *Personal Influence.* Glencoe, Illinois: The Free Press, 1955, 31 ff.

CHAPTER III

1   Ralph Linton, *The Study of Man,* 113. Robert K. Merton, "The Role Set," *The British Journal of Sociology,* 8 (1957), 106-20.

2   See pp. 9-11.

3   Verner Goldschmidt, *Retlig Adfærd* ("Legal Behavior"). Copenhagen: C. A. Reitzel, 1957, 117-18. An outstanding analysis of the general psychological problems underlying role conflicts is to be found in Leon Festinger, *A Theory of Cognitive Dissonance.* Evanston: Row, Peterson and Company, 1957.

4   Harriet Holter, "Kjønnsroller og sosial struktur" ("Sex Roles and Social Structure"), in Edmund Dahlstrøm (ed.), *Kvinners liv og arbeid* ("The Life and Work of Women"). Stockholm: Studieforbundet Näringsliv och Samhälle, 1962, 71-109.

5   Robert K. Merton, "The Role Set."

6   Erving Goffman, *The Presentation of Self in Everyday Life.* Garden City, New York: Anchor Books, Doubleday & Company, Inc., 1959.

7   Talcott Parsons, *The Social System,* 428-29.

8   Alf Ross, *On Law and Justice*. Berkeley and Los Angeles: University of California Press, 1959, 11-19.

9   Anne Roe, *The Making of a Scientist*. New York: Dodd, Mead & Company, 1953.

10 Robert K. Merton, "Bureaucratic Structure and Personality," in *Social Theory and Social Structure*, 195-206.

11 Vilhelm Aubert, *The Hidden Society*. Totowa, New Jersey: The Bedminster Press, 1965, 275.

12 See Abraham Kardiner, *The Individual and His Society*. New York: Columbia University Press, 1939, and *The Psychological Frontiers of Society*. New York: Columbia University Press, 1945. Erik H. Erikson, *Childhood and Society*. New York: W. W. Norton & Company, Inc., 1950. Erich Fromm, *Escape from Freedom*. New York: Farrar, Straus & Company, 1941. Geoffrey Gorer, *The American People*. New York: W. W. Norton & Company, Inc., 1948. Geoffrey Gorer and John Rickman, *The People of Great Russia*. London: Cresset, 1949.

13 Anselm Strauss (ed.), *The Social Psychology of George Herbert Mead*. Chicago: University of Chicago Press, 1956, 213.

14 *Ibid.*, 215.

15 In the film version of David Howarth's *We Die Alone*. London: Collins, 1955.

16 Cf. Ernest A. Haggard, "Isolation and Personality Change." In Philip Worchel and D. E. Byrne (eds.), *Personality Change*. New York: John Wiley & Sons, Inc., 1964. Zachary Gussow, "A Preliminary Report of Kayakangst among the Eskimo of West Greenland: A Study in Sensory Deprivation." *The International Journal of Social Psychiatry*, 9 (1963), 18-26.

17 Unforgettably illustrated by Danny Kaye in the film after James Thurber, *The Secret Life of Walter Mitty*.

18 Strauss, *Ibid.*, 229 ff.

19 Vilhelm Aubert, *Om straffens sosiale funksjon* ("On the Social Function of Punishment"). Oslo: Universitetsforlaget, 1954.

20 Edwin H. Sutherland, *The Professional Thief*. Chicago: University of Chicago Press, 1956, 200 ff.

21 Norman R. F. Maier, *Frustration: The Study of Behavior without a Goal*. New York: McGraw-Hill Book Company, 1949. Saul Rosenzweig, "Need-persistive and Ego-defensive Reactions to Frustration as Demonstrated by an Experiment on Repression." *Psychological Review*, 1941, 48, 347-49.

22 Erving Goffman, *The Presentation of Self in Everyday Life,* XI.

23 *Ibid.,* 13.

CHAPTER IV

1   Øivind Hanssen, *Skipets sosiale system* ("The Social System of the Ship"). Oslo: Institute of Sociology (Mimeo), 1962.

2   George C. Homans, "Social Behavior as Exchange." *The American Journal of Sociology,* 63 (1958), 597-606, and *Social Behavior: Its Elementary Forms.* London: Routledge, 1961.

3   Ørnulv Ødegård, *Unge tilbakefallsforbrytere* ("Recidivist Juvenile Delinquents"). Oslo: Det norske videnskapsakademi, 1941, 41.

4   Vilhelm Aubert, *Om straffens sosiale funksjon* ("On the Social Function of Punishment"), 11 ff. and 112 ff.

5   Robert K. Merton, "The Self-fulfilling Prophecy." *Social Theory and Social Structure,* 421-36.

6   Nils Christie, Johannes Andenæs and Sigurd Skirbekk, "A Study in Self-reported Crime." In *Scandinavian Studies in Criminology.* Oslo: Scandinavian University Books, 1965, 86-116.

7   Odd Ramsøy, *Social Groups as System and Subsystem.* Oslo: Universitetsforlaget, 1962.

8   Frank Cancian, *Economics and Prestige in a Maya Community.* Stanford, California: Stanford University Press, 1965. Henning Siverts, *Oxhujk.* Oslo: Universitetsforlaget, 1965.

9   On social fission and fusion see E. E. Evans-Pritchard, *The Nuer.* Oxford: Clarendon Press, 1940.

10 Durkheim made the distinction between mechanical and organic solidarity. The division of labor and complementarity furnish the basis of organic solidarity. Emile Durkheim, *The Division of Labor in Society.* New York: The Macmillan Company, 1933.

11 Kaare Svalastoga, "Homicide and Social Contact in Denmark." *The American Journal of Sociology,* 62 (1956), 37-41.

12 Torgny T. Segerstedt, "Tekniskt bistånd och social struktur" ("Technical Assistance and Social Structure"). *Uppsala Universitets Årsskrift,* 1962.

13 Talcott Parsons, Robert F. Bales and Edward A. Shils, *Working Papers in the Theory of Action.* Glencoe, Illinois: The Free Press, 1953, 100. The notion is criticized in George C. Homans, *Social Behavior: Its Elementary Forms,* 113-14.

14 Vilhelm Aubert, *The Hidden Society,* 112-15.

15 George C. Homans, "Elliott Jaques, Equitable Payment." *American Sociological Review,* 27 (1962), 270.

16 Ralf Dahrendorf, *Class and Class Conflict in Modern Industrial Society.* Stanford, California: Stanford University Press, 1959, 157 ff., and "Out of Utopia: Towards a Reorientation of Sociological Analysis." *The American Journal of Sociology,* 64 (1958), 115-27.

17 Torgny T. Sergerstedt, "Utbildning och samhälle" ("Education and Society"). *Uppsala Universitets Årsskrift,* 1957.

18 Jamaica seems to represent such an exception; a very high proportion of its children are born out of wedlock. Judith Blake, *Family Structure in Jamaica.* Glencoe, Illinois: The Free Press, 1961. William J. Goode, "Illegitimacy in the Caribbean Social Structure." *American Sociological Review,* 25 (1960), 21-30.

19 Fred Davis, "The Cabdriver and His Fare: Facets of a Fleeting Relationship." *The American Journal of Sociology,* 65 (1959), 158-65.

20 Gabriel A. Almond and James S. Coleman (eds.), *The Politics of the Developing Areas.* Princeton: Princeton University Press, 1961.

21 Vilhelm Aubert, *The Hidden Society,* 283-84.

22 Sverre Lysgaard, *Arbeiderkollektivet* ("The Workers' Collectivity"). Oslo: Universitetsforlaget, 1961, 72-93.

CHAPTER V

1 The term "prestige," as it occurs in sociological literature, usually refers to the differential evaluation of positions or roles (statuses), whereas "esteem" is reserved for the differential evaluation of how adequately the particular person fulfills the obligations attaching to the role. However, in this chapter, we deal with both types of evaluations, and it did not seem necessary to emphasize the distinction. Thus, the two concepts are not kept clearly apart.

2 Max Weber (ed. Talcott Parsons), *The Theory of Social and Economic Organization.* London: Hodge, 1947, 139.

3 Svalastoga, *Ibid.,* 2, 133.

4 *Ibid.,* 280.

5 *Ibid.,* 12-13, 80-109.

6 Alex Inkeles and Peter H. Rossi, "National Comparisons of Occupational Prestige." *The American Journal of Sociology,* 61 (1956), 329-39.

7 Kingsley Davis and Wilbert E. Moore, "Some Principles of Stratification." *American Sociological Review,* 10 (1945), 242-49. See also

Wilbert E. Moore, "But Some Are More Equal than Others," and Melvin Tumin, "On Inequality." *American Sociological Review,* 28 (1963), 13-27.

8 Fredrik Barth (ed.), *The Role of the Entrepreneur in Social Change in North-Norway.* Bergen: Bergens Universitets Årbok, 1964.

9 Elliott Jaques, *Equitable Payment: A General Theory of Work, Differential Payment, and Individual Progress.* New York: John Wiley & Sons, Inc., 1961.

10 Ralf Dahrendorf, "Dichotomie und Hierarchie. Das Gesellschaftsbild der Unterschicht." ("Dichotomy and Hierarchy. The Image of Society among the Lower Classes"). In *Gesellschaft und Freiheit* ("Society and Freedom"). München: R. Piper & Co. Verlag, 1962, 163-75.

11 Kaare Svalastoga, *Prestige, Class and Mobility.* Copenhagen: Scandinavian University Books, Gyldendal, 1959, 285-305, Gøsta Carlsson, *Social Mobility and Class Structure.* Lund: C. W. K. Glerup, 1958. Seymour M. Lipset and Reinhard Bendix, *Social Mobility in Industrial Society.* Berkeley: University of California Press, 1960. David V. Glass, *Social Mobility in Britain.* London: Routledge, 1954. Pitirim Sorokin, *Social Mobility.* New York: Harper, 1927.

12 J. Jean Hecht, *The Domestic Servant Class in Eighteenth-Century England.* London: Routledge, 1956, 192. David Lockwood, *The Black-Coated Worker.* London: G. Allen & Unwin, 1958, 19-35.

13 Bernard Barber, *Social Stratification.* New York: Harcourt Brace, Inc., 1957, 73-76.

14 Edvard Bull, *Arbeidermiljø under det industrielle gjennombrudd.* ("Workers' Environment During the Industrial Breakthrough"). Oslo: Universitetsforlaget, 1958, 114, 270 ff. and 361 ff.

15 See Ralf Dahrendorf, *Class and Class Conflict in Industrial Society,* 8-35, where references are made to those parts of Marx's work which deal with social class.

16 Karl Renner, *The Institutions of Private Law and Their Social Functions.* London: Routledge, 1948.

17 Eilert Sundt, *Om giftermaal i Norge* ("On Marriage in Norway"). Christiania: P. L. Malling, 1855, 184.

18 Sverre Steen, *Det gamle samfunn* ("The Old Society"). Oslo: Cappelen, 1957.

19 Vilhelm Aubert, "The Professions in Norwegian Social Structure." *Transactions of the Fifth World Congress of Sociology* (1962), Vol. 3, 243-258.

20 W. L. Guttsman, *The British Political Elite*. London: MacGibbon, 1963. See, also "The Parliamentary Profession." *International Social Science Journal*, Vol. 13, No. 4, Paris: Unesco, 1961.

CHAPTER VI

1 Georg Simmel, "Der Streit" (The Strife). In *Soziologie*. Berlin-München: Duncker und Humbolt, 1958. Lewis Coser, *The Functions of Social Conflict*. London: Routledge, 1956. Ralf Dahrendorf, "Die Funktionen sozialer Konflikte" ("The Functions of Social Conflicts"). *In Gesellschaft und Freiheit* ("Society and Freedom"), 112-31.

2 R. Duncan Luce and Howard Raiffa, *Games and Decisions*. New York: John Wiley & Sons, Inc., 1957, 118.

3 *Ibid*, 71-72.

4 Robert Merton characterizes innovations as deviance in "Social Structure and Anomie." *Social Theory and Social Structure*, 141-49. The term "creativity" has recently gained wide currency as applied to positive deviance. Cf. Morris I. Stein and Shirley J. Heinze (eds.), *Creativity and the Individual*. Glencoe, Illinois: The Free Press, 1960. Calvin W. Taylor and Frank Barron (eds.), *Scientific Creativity: Its Recognition and Development*. New York: John Wiley & Sons, Inc., 1963.

5 Wilbert E. Moore, *Social Change*. Englewood Cliffs, New Jersey: Prentice-Hall, Inc., 1963.

6 Vilhelm Aubert and Sheldon L. Messinger, "The Criminal and the Sick." In Vilhelm Aubert, *The Hidden Society*, 25 ff.

7 Cesare Lombroso, *L'uomo delinquente* ("Delinquent Man"). Milan: Rechiedi, 1876.

8 Alf Ross, *On Law and Justice*, 151-155.

9 Kaare Svalastoga, *Prestige, Class and Mobility*, 80. Bernard Barber, *Social Stratification*, 102.

CHAPTER VII

1 Robert K. Merton, "Manifest and Latent Functions." In *Social Theory and Social Structure*, gives a good introduction to the conceptual problems of functional analysis. It should be noted that Merton defines "function" somewhat differently from the present text: *"Functions are those observed consequences which make for the adaptation or adjustment of a given system." Ibid., 51.*

2 The following presentation is to a large extent based upon Sverre Lysgaard, *Arbeiderkollektivet* ("The Workers' Collectivity").

3   *Ibid.*, 147 ff.

4   *Ibid.*, 31 ff.

5   *Ibid.*, 72 ff.

6   *Ibid.*, 41 ff.

7   *Ibid.*, 79 ff.

8   Based to a large extent upon Vilhelm Aubert and Oddvar Arner, "On the Social Structure of the Ship." In Vilhelm Aubert, *The Hidden Society*, 259 ff.

9   Erving Goffman, "On the Characteristics of Total Institutions." In *Asylums*. Garden City, New York: Anchor Books, Doubleday & Company, 1961, 1-124.

10 Vilhelm Aubert, *The Hidden Society*, 243.

11 Per Olav Tiller, *Father Absence and Personality Development of Children in Sailor Families*. Oslo: Nordisk Psykologi, Monograph Series, No. 9, 1958.

12 The following presentation is to a large extent based upon Yngvar Løchen, *Idealer og realiteter i et psykiatrisk sykehus* ("Ideals and Realities in a Mental Hospital"). Oslo: Universitetsforlaget, 1965.

13 Maxwell Jones, *The Therapeutic Community*. New York: Basic Books, 1953.

14 Erving Goffman, "The Moral Career of the Mental Patient." *Asylums,* especially 148 ff.

15 Løchen, *Ibid.*, 163.

16 Kai T. Erikson, "Patient Role and Social Uncertainty—a Dilemma of the Mentally Ill." *Psychiatry*, 20 (1958), 263-74.

17 Ørnulv Ødegård, "The Incidence of Psychoses in Various Occupations." *The International Journal of Social Psychiatry*, 2 (1955), No. 2, 19.

18 Løchen, *Ibid.*, and Goffman, *Ibid.*

19 Maxwell Jones, *Ibid.*

20 The following presentation is to a large extent based upon Johan Galtung, *Fengselssamfunnet* ("The Prison Society"). Oslo: Universitetsforlaget, 1958 and "Prison: The Organization of Dilemma." In Donald R. Cressey (ed.), *The Prison—Studies in Institutional Organization and Change*. New York: Holt, Rinehart and Winston, 1961, 107-45. Thomas Mathiesen, *The Defences of the Weak. A Sociological Study of a Norwegian Correctional Institution*. London: Tavistock Publications, 1965.

21 Johannes Andenæs, *The General Part of the Criminal Law of Norway*. New Jersey: Fred B. Rothman & Company, 1965, 9.

22 Vilhelm Aubert, *The Hidden Society,* 28-30.

23 Mathiesen, *Ibid.* Gresham Sykes, *The Society of Captives*. Princeton: Princeton University Press, 1958, 50-51.

24 Svalastoga, *Ibid.,* 284.

25 Galtung, *Ibid.,* 132.

26 *Ibid.,* 120.

27 Emile Durkheim, *The Division of Labor in Society*.
George Herbert Mead, "The Psychology of Punitive Justice." *The American Journal of Sociology,* 23, 1917-18.

28 Galtung, *Ibid.,* 207 ff.

29 *Ibid.,* 66, 115.

30 Based upon unpublished reports by Francesco Kjellberg, Per Mathiesen and Vilhelm Aubert.

31 Robert Paine, "Entrepreneurial Activity Without Its Profits." In Barth, *Ibid.,* 33-55.

32 The distinction between these two models of justice is due to unpublished work of Torstein Eckhoff.

INDEX

241

244

246